Contemporary general equilibrium theory is characteristically short-run, separated from monetary aspects of the economy, and as such does not deal with long-run problems such as capital accumulation, innovation, and the historical movement of the economy. These phenomena are discussed by growth theory, which assumes a given or shifting production function, and in turn cannot therefore deal with the fundamental problem of growth, for example, how the production period is determined. Moreover traditional theories have a common weakness in that they divorce real economic growth from the activities of the financial sector.

The book provides a much-needed synthesis of growth theory and monetary theory. The problem of the determination of the production period was examined by von Böhm-Bawerk, Wicksell, Hayek and others, but was ignored by post-war general equilibrium theorists. Reconstructing their theories in terms of von Neumann's framework, Professor Morishima examines real growth theory in order to establish the existence of a sequence of temporary equilibria. Economic growth along the line of this sequence is only feasible if sufficient funds are made available by financial markets, preventing involuntary unemployment. Professor Morishima thus draws on the work of Schumpeter, Keynes and the pre-war neoclassical economists to formulate a capital-theoretic general equilibrium theory.

Capital and credit

Capital and credit

A new formulation of general equilibrium theory

Michio Morishima

CAMBRIDGE
UNIVERSITY PRESS

CAMBRIDGE UNIVERSITY PRESS
Cambridge, New York, Melbourne, Madrid, Cape Town, Singapore,
São Paulo, Delhi, Dubai, Tokyo, Mexico City

Cambridge University Press
The Edinburgh Building, Cambridge CB2 8RU, UK

Published in the United States of America by Cambridge University Press, New York

www.cambridge.org
Information on this title: www.cambridge.org/9780521418409

First published 1992
First paperback edition 1992

A catalogue record for this publication is available from the British Library

Library of Congress Cataloguing in Publication Data

Morishima, Michio, 1923-
    Capital and credit: a new formulation of general equilibrium
theory / Michio Morishima.
      p.   cm.
    Includes index.
    ISBN 0 521 41840 2
    1. Capital. 2. Monetary policy. 3. Economic development.
    4. Equilibrium (Economics) I. Title.
    HB501.M7217 1992
    339.5 - dc20 91-34566

ISBN 978-0-521-41840-9 Hardback
ISBN 978-0-521-46638-7 Paperback

Contents

Preface   *page* ix

1   Introduction   1

2   Capitalist production   25

3   Production possibility set   52

4   Temporary equilibrium   83

5   Stability and motion   115

6   Innovations and financing   141

7   Monetary disequilibrium   169

8   Perspectives into the future   194

Appendix I   Existence of temporary equilibrium   204

Appendix II   Increasing returns   208

Index   210

Preface

Economic theory has developed greatly in the post-war period in the field of general equilibrium theory. Existence of equilibrium and its stability and optimality have been discussed carefully by experts in the field. In the purifying process, however, they have lost various ingredients which played essential roles in the pre-war theory. When I was taught the principles of economics, a first year undergraduate course, by Professor Takata in 1942, stars were E. von Böhm-Bawerk, K. Wicksell and F. A. von Hayek. All these names are not frequently mentioned in post-war general equilibrium theory.

I began my study of economics by reading Hicks' *Value and Capital*. As Hicks was a Paretian on the value theory and an Austrian on the capital theory, he was a key figure in connecting the post-war to the pre-war theory. In this volume I will try and formulate the type of general equilibrium theory which such economists as Böhm-Bawerk, Wicksell and Hayek were concerned with. I shall also try and extend their type of capital theory so as to make it compatible with Schumpeter's theory of money and credit. I will try to synthesize these authors' works with the spirit of clearness and rigorousness with which we worked throughout the post-war period. Of course post-war yields in the field have been taken into account in the synthesis.

Another big name is obviously J. M. Keynes who identified the existence of involuntary unemployment with the refusal of Say's law. By assuming full employment the general equilibrium theory is taken, from his point of view, as a theory based on Say's law, so that it is inappropriate for the economy in which the firm's investment is severely constrained financially. Evidently Schumpeter presumes an anti-Say's law; thus our model according to him enables us to discuss the problem of unemployment.

It is acknowledged that parts of my book *Dogakuteki Keizai Riron*, Kobundo, 1950, and my essay, 'General Equilibrium Theory in the Twenty-First Century', *The Economic Journal*, vol. 101, January 1991, have been contained in this volume with some changes. An acknowledgement is also due to the editors of *The Economic Journal* and *The Times Higher Education Supplement* for their permission to use my essays published in their journals.

Finally, I would like to dedicate this volume to the late Sir John Hicks. Although I criticized some aspects of his work in this volume, his influence upon my academic work had always been conspicuous through my life. May I reproduce here in this place my essay 'Michio Morishima chooses *Value and Capital* by Sir John Hicks', *The Times Higher Education Supplement*, 1 April 1983, p. 12, in memory of him and to record my intellectual indebtedness to him.

*   *   *

Sir John Hicks' *Value and Capital* (1939) had a decisive influence upon me, and had I not read the book at the end of my impressionable teenage years I doubt whether I should have come to spend the latter half of my life in this country.

It was in 1942 that I first began to read it in a pirated edition photocopied without permission of the original publisher. The Pacific War had begun only the year before, but a situation of war readiness had prevailed throughout my childhood. Thought control had become stricter every year, and when I was a student at high school even the rooms in my lodging house were sometimes searched by the police.

The newspapers adopted an opportunistic attitude, and many university professors allowed themselves to become the instruments of the military. Marxists were arrested and many *tenkōsha*, 'converts', became fanatical exponents of ultranationalism. The study of political economy along Nazi lines became popular; Nazi-type *Geopolitik* were used to justify Japan's invasion of Asian countries.

Amidst such total national hysteria the reading of a work on economics by an Anglo-Saxon was a kind of passive resistance. There was almost no positive opposition towards the military. The most they could achieve was the passive resistance of continuing pure research into the social science and philosophy of their Anglo-American enemies.

As a university student I belonged to this kind of 'passive resistance' group – the membership was not strictly defined, but the members clearly constituted a single group. I hoped if I survived the war to become a social science teacher at a high school. I therefore visited Professor H. Aoyama, whom I most respected within the group and asked him what sort of book I should read to study economics. His reply was, 'Read Hicks. *Value and Capital* is a book you should read straight away.' I then asked, 'Is it something which a first year student could read?' Professor Aoyama answered, 'You must understand that Hicks' economics is in effect an algebra concerning society. You will be all right if you tackle the book step by step, in exactly the same way as you solved algebra problems at middle school.' At middle school I had been weak not just in algebra but in mathematics as a whole, but under the guidance of Aoyama I acquired the mathematics necessary to read Hicks' work.

Hicks' book introduced me to a refreshing intellectual world far removed from the dismal reality. At the time of my graduation high schools in Japan were excessively specialised, and those students who planned to specialise later in philosophy and sociology, usually took German as their first foreign language. During my high school years, therefore, I had read the works of writers such as Goethe, Heine and Schopenhauer and had happily collected such books as G. Simmel's *Soziologie*, despite my inability to read them. I was consequently quite ignorant of Cartesian clarity. For this reason the influence of Hicks' penetrating logic was all the greater. Furthermore, at a time of international conflict, to study universal principles transcending nations provided considerable 'spiritual' relief.

The group was very small but was a surprisingly advanced one in the field of mathematical economics. The mathematician, Masazo Sono, was known to specialists worldwide for his work on the Dedekind ring; Sono was at this time interested in Hicks' demand theory. His treaties on 'separable goods' published in Japanese in 1943 was the world's first paper in the field which Western academics now term the theory of separable utilities. It was from Sono that I learnt the rudiments of mathematical economics.

At the end of 1943, however, all students studying the arts or social sciences were conscripted into the armed forces and I was forced to leave off for a time (or for ever) my reading of *Value and Capital*. When I was able, with a considerable sense of nostalgia, to take up the book again the war was over and there was no longer any need to worry about the 'thought police'.

I decided to make the mathematisation of the *Value and Capital* system the subject of my postgraduate research. I had already received a thoroughly 'Hicksian' training and was able to complete the study far earlier than I had anticipated. In 1950, to my great satisfaction, my first book in Japanese was published. Nevertheless, I soon felt a keen sense of frustration and isolation that the results of my research had not been recorded in an 'international' language. As I was well aware that my English was appalling, and knew full well that I was not the type of person who could behave with aplomb in Western society, I turned down the chance of studying abroad on several occasions. In 1956, however, I received financial support from an American foundation to study abroad for a year, and chose to study in Oxford, where Hicks was.

I exploited to the utmost the advantages of the Hicksian paradigm. I not only refined and generalised Hicks' work mathematically; in writing my papers I used almost the same conceptual approach as Hicks himself. The publication of my papers in British and American journals might have contributed something to the internationalisation of the Japanese academic world, but my initially wholehearted delight at the publication of several papers gradually became compounded with a realisation that I had ceased to be content with a life repairing mathematical models.

The Chinese, and the Japanese too, are very faithful to the old classics, very bookish, but I perceived now that I had to follow the opposite course, to extricate myself from the Hicksian paradigm and create my own model which fits reality better. In this way I have gradually become aware that post-war mathematical economists have lapsed into the conservatism of not adapting their theories to reality, but tending to accommodate the reality to the theory. Like Procrustes, they have ruthlessly excised any element of reality which fails to conform to their models.

MICHIO MORISHIMA

1 Introduction: a new general equilibrium theory

1 In October 1942, I began my undergraduate study of economics. Following the suggestion of my teacher, Professor Hideo Aoyama at the University of Kyoto, I started to read Hicks' *Value and Capital*.[1] With no substantial knowledge of economics, I could read its Part I with no serious problem, but then realized that I could have understood it much more deeply if I had read a more elementary theory book. I started to read Wicksell's *Lectures on Political Economy* and the study of Hicks was interrupted. The study of Wicksell was also soon interrupted. I was conscripted to the Imperial Navy of Japan, December 1943, when the second year of my university life had just begun. It was only after the war ceased in 1945, that I could return to Hicks. I finished my B.Econ. studies in 1946 and was appointed a Scholarship Graduate Student and was supervised by Aoyama who assigned to me the subject of mathematization of the *Value and Capital* system. The work was completed in 1948 and the thesis, entitled *Dogakuteki Keizai Riron* (Dynamic Economic Theory, referred to as *DKR* below),[2] a relevant part of which will be presented in this volume, was published in 1950.

With this encounter with General Equilibrium Theory (GET) at the very early stage of my academic life my fate was almost decided. It is no exaggeration to say that I confined myself throughout my life in the narrow realm of GET. I do not regret, however, that this has happened, because I regarded and still regard GET as the kernel of economics or even social science. This does not mean, nevertheless, that I was consistently confident with GET through this long period. After having published my first book in English in 1964,[3] I started to query the basic assumptions and structure of the *Value and Capital* regime. I had the same queries concerning the main line models developed after Hicks, such as those discussed by Arrow,

[1] J. R. Hicks, *Value and Capital: An Inquiry into Some Fundamental Principles of Economic Theory*, Clarendon Press, Oxford, 1939.
[2] M. Morishima, *Dogakuteki Keizai Riron*, Kobundo, Tokyo, 1950.
[3] M. Morishima, *Equilibrium, Stability and Growth*, Clarendon Press, Oxford, 1964.

Debreu, Hahn, Malinvaud, Patinkin and others.[4] All these belong to the same regime. Consequently, after 1964, I groped for a more satisfactory model of general equilibrium. At the same time I learned from great masters of the classical period, Ricardo, Marx and Walras, how to construct a dynamic model.[5] In line with these, I published experimental works at various levels.[6] I departed more and more from the main line group.

In this volume I complete this process and present the model which I finally reached and which, I hope, may serve as the analytical base for multi-disciplinary extentions of the general equilibrium theory on which economists must work in the future.[7] This, I consider, may at least temporarily be regarded as the terminus of my long journey. Technically speaking, it may not be so complete (or sophisticated) as those works belonging to the existing regime. To supply views or visions of our modern production society is more important than to polish up given models mathematically, especially, in this field of the general equilibrium theory. I believe it is now time to inject new elements into the subject to stop mathematical inbreeding and to let it move off into a completely different direction.

Let me begin by explaining why I have become dissatisfied with the orthodox way of formulating the theory of general equilibrium. The most basic assumption which is valid through all contemporary GET models is that production possibility sets are granted to and owned by a certain number of select people. They are allowed to use the possibility sets for production, so that the potential number of firms is fixed, though the actual number may be flexible downwards, because those who find their own sets to be unprofitable will not engage in business. Or we may alternatively interpret the economy assumed by GET in the following way. There are a number of firms which were all established in the past, no new firms can be formed in the current period. The heads of these firms are merely managers or administrators of everyday business; they are not entrepreneurs; they do

[4] K. J. Arrow and G. Debreu, 'Existence of an Equilibrium for a Competitive Economy', *Econometrica*, vol. 22, 1954, pp. 265–90; G. Debreu, *Theory of Value*, John Wiley, New York, 1954; K. J. Arrow and F. H. Hahn, *General Competitive Analysis*, North-Holland, Amsterdam, 1971; E. Malinvaud, *Lectures on Microeconomic Theory*, North-Holland, Amsterdam, 1972; D. Patinkin, *Money, Interest and Prices*, Row, Peterson and Company, Evanston, 1956.

[5] M. Morishima, *Marx's Economics*, 1973, *Walras' Economics*, 1977, *Ricardo's Economics*, 1989, all Cambridge University Press.

[6] M. Morishima, *Theory of Economic Growth*, Clarendon Press, Oxford, 1969; *The Economic Theory of Modern Society*, Cambridge University Press, 1976; *The Economics of Industrial Society*, Cambridge University Press, 1984.

[7] M. Morishima, 'General Equilibrium Theory in the Twenty-First Century' (*The Economic Journal*, Special Issue in January 1991), included in this volume as chapter 8 below.

not organize new ambitious projects for producing new production possibility sets at all.

Thus, in the traditional GET economy, there is no entrepreneur in the true sense, so that it cannot be considered as a full model describing the free enterprise system. In an actual modern economy, production possibility sets are not given but produced by entrepreneurs. Also the existing sets are expandable, or may be partly or entirely closed down. Once they are closed down, it is rather difficult to re-open them. To do so, entrepreneurs would have to make almost as much effort as is required for establishing a new firm. In order for somebody (an entrepreneur) to be able to form a new business he should be someone having unusual talents; initiative, authority and foresight, as Schumpeter points out,[8] are all required, but they are embodied in only a small fraction of the population. Moreover, the entrepreneur needs financiers or bankers who give him purchasing power to get necessary things; otherwise he cannot furnish his firm with machines, materials and a working force. In case of an entrepreneur being unsuccessful in finding financial support, he is abortive as entrepreneur. Orthodox GET implicitly assumes that there is no financial constraint on a firm's behaviour. This results in the grave consequence that the Slutsky equation of the firm has no income effect; firms never play the role of destabilizer in the orthodox theory of stability, because, as is well known and as has been discussed by many writers, an equilibrium is always stable, in the orthodox view, if income effects are negligible. Stability has to be examined in a model where the economy is affected by financial constraints.

2 Economics is evidently concerned with various kinds of economic behaviour by human beings, employment, production, exchange, consumption and others. These occur in the actual world through time; each of them is described as an event which happens or happened at a certain, particular point in time. An event at time t, E_t, occurs in relation to other events at a different point of time, $F_{t'}$, $G_{t''}$, etc.; thus economic theory is inevitably concerned with intertemporal relationships. Strictly speaking, economics is intrinsically dynamic in this sense; there is no room, or a very limited room, for static analysis.

However, to specify the point in time at which a certain economic action took place, economists usually do not use a continuous measure of time, but date events or actions in terms of the periods during which they occurred. They ignore, for the sake of simplicity, the order of events in that

---

[8] J. A. Schumpeter, *The Theory of Economic Development*, Harvard University Press, 1951, p. 75.

period and treat them as if they happened simultaneously. In this way, they get discrete time; continuous time is obtained in the limiting case of the length of the period tending to zero. Conversely, where it tends to infinity, all economic actions and phenomena are covered by a single period, and everything is reckoned to be simultaneous. Static analysis obtains its legitimacy as a limiting case of this kind.

Nevertheless, usually GET commences its analysis with an extreme assumption of very long period, so that it is static. In this elementary form, the production period or time lag does not appear; accordingly, no particular consideration is given to the process of constructing production possibility sets. These are treated as if available to the entrepreneurs as soon as they make a decision on production. In addition to this, outputs are produced at the same time as inputs are made, and with this assumption the bad habit of ignoring the problem of how to finance production is justified and becomes very popular among the GET economists. As the proceeds from outputs are available when inputs are made, inputs are paid for from a part of the proceeds, the rest being distributed as profits. Where profits are negative, no production is made. In this way the problem of financing production, together with the one of constructing production possibility sets, makes no appearance in static analysis. Production is completely dichotomized from finance; the theory of the firm has been developed in the form of 'real' theory containing no monetary element.

This is a serious feature of GET, especially in its *static* form. The theory allows for profits from production which are distributed among individuals. But, among what sort of individuals? Under the abstract assumption of no time lag, firms do not need capital; in such a world, there would be neither capitalist nor shareholder, so that entrepreneurs are only candidates who could monopolize the residue, profits.[9] Moreover, they could take that position, not because of their personal abilities of introducing innovations, etc., but simply because of the production possibility sets being allocated to them before the play started. This is a serious problem, indeed. Able students who are taught static GET of this sort at the very beginning of the first year course will lose any trust in economics. Even though they have been taught the existence of GE, its Pareto optimality, the efficiency of the free enterprise system and so on, they will simply laugh at their teacher.

Therefore, we must remove the assumption of very long time period from GET and divide continuous time into a number of periods of short or

---

[9] Of course, in those papers which mainly concern themselves with capital, time lags are introduced. A notable example is Malinvaud's classic article, 'Capital Accumulation and Efficient Allocation of Resources', *Econometrica*, April, 1953, pp. 233–68. But this paper too does not examine how production lags are determined and how they react to a stimulus given by a change in the interest rate. He regards them as given and constant.

medium length, as Hicks actually did in Parts III and IV of his *Value and Capital*. In this form of analysis all variables, output, input, consumption, etc., are dated and expressed as x_t, y_t, c_t, etc., respectively. It is then assumed that each producer is concerned with decision-making over several periods or over infinitely many periods covering 'the very long period'; similarly, for consumers. However, the 'hereditary' assumption that production possibility sets are given to a given number of persons still continues to hold, and each entrepreneur is assumed to be provided with a production function of the form:

$$F_i(x_0, x_1, \ldots, x_t, \ldots : y_0, y_1, \ldots, y_t, \ldots) = 0. \tag{1.1}$$

Accordingly, the problem of constructing the possibility set is avoided. Besides, (1.1) is a 'well behaved' function, that is to say, for any t and t', substitution is always possible between y_t and $y_{t'}$ to the following effect.

Suppose now $(x_0, 0, 0, \ldots; y_0, 0, 0, \ldots)$ is a feasible production plan such that $F_i(x_0, 0, 0, \ldots; y_0, 0, 0, \ldots) = 0$. As substitution between y_0 and y_t is feasible, where all x's and other y's are kept constant, we have after a complete substitution between y_0 and y_t: $F_i(x_0, 0, 0, \ldots; 0, \ldots, y_t, 0, \ldots) = 0$. This implies that a positive output x_0 is produced without making instantaneous input, provided that enough input is made in the future. Obviously this sort of perversity should be got rid of, but orthodox GET's 'dynamic' approach does not take into account that difficulty. This means that not only has proper consideration not yet been paid to the problem of production lags, but also the feasibility of production cannot be well specified by a simple function like (1.1).

Furthermore, Arrow, Debreu and Hahn are concerned with an extension of GET such that there are different markets for commodities at different times, spot markets for commodities delivered in the present period and futures markets for all commodities for each period in the future. With this setup GET, like the previous static one, does not require any capital for collecting the necessary factors and other means of production. Even though outputs are not yet produced in the current period, the entrepreneur can sell them on the futures markets and buy factors and other means of production with the money (or purchasing power) acquired from the futures markets. They can produce the current output by means of inputs bought by the money obtained in this way. The firms do not require any capital. General equilibrium theory books of this sort could be entitled 'Value and no Capital'.

In order for an entrepreneur to produce a new production possibility set, he must have a clear and confident perspective about the future of the new business which is viable enough to convince financiers. To form such a perspective he must have the relevant technological knowledge and administrative skills, but more importantly he must not be 'short-sighted', but have a long-term view. Where people are simply greedy for money, no great innovations are made. A new business is a new mission. Entrepreneurs are even characterized by a passionate fire; therefore, each single innovation is individualistic and may often seem to usual eyes even irrational. It is then clear that innovative activities are not described by the terms of marginal productivity and marginal substitution. It is also impossible to express a change in the production possibility set caused by an innovation within a firm in terms of a systematic shift in the firm's production function, such as the one according to the learning-by-doing hypothesis. The existing tools for the analysis of production which orthodox GET employs are either useless or at least inappropriate for examining the effects of innovations; we must take a distinctly different approach.

3 To carry out an innovation an entrepreneur perhaps has to begin with building a factory, or a production possibility set, for which a substantial construction period is needed. Once it has been built, it lasts for several decades, or several years at least, during which it is used for production. The lifetime of the facility, as well as its construction period, is not a constant fixed naturally or exogenously but can be chosen from among those which are all technically feasible. The lengths of these periods are decided by the entrepreneur who would choose a shorter one if he considers the innovation as being short-lived but would construct a permanent facility if he is confident of his venture.

The problem of determination of the construction period and lifetime of production facilities has been discussed by such economists as E. von Böhm-Bawerk, K. Wicksell, G. Åkerman, F. A. Hayek, and by John Hicks more recently.[10] For this purpose Hicks integrates various firms vertically into one and develops a macroeconomic analysis. This type of macroeconomic approach, however, does not enable us to deal with the problem of the repercussions of an innovation, which is made in one industry, upon other industries. Once silicon chips were made available at reasonable prices, then they induced drastic changes in the types of products, as well as in the methods of production, in the electronics and other industries. A number of other technical changes follow on from the original major innovation. This

[10] E. von Böhm-Bawerk, *Positive Theorie des Kapitales*, Gustav Fischer Verlag, Jena, 1888; K. Wicksell, *Über Wert, Kapital und Rente*, Gustav Fischer Verlag, Jena, 1893; G. Åkerman, *Realkapital und Kapitalzins*, as is reviewed in K. Wicksell, *Lectures on Political Economy*, vol. I, George Routledge, 1935; J. Hicks, *Capital and Time*, Clarendon Press, Oxford, 1973; F. A. von Hayek, *Prices and Production*, G. Routledge, 1931 and *Pure Theory of Capital*, Routledge and Kegan Paul, 1941.

is the trigger effect phenomenon originally discussed by H. Simon as a comparative statics problem and later examined dynamically by myself.[11]

Therefore, when I was asked by Hicks to check the mathematics (on Laplace transformation) that he later used in *Capital and Time*, I made this point to him and pointed out that his problem could alternatively be dealt with in the framework of a von Neumann-like multi-sectoral model. But Hicks did not accept this suggestion and wrote instead:

> Very much better is the *Method of von Neumann*. This is to admit a regular (and high) degree of disintegration. The production process in each 'firm', last just one period. All of the firm's inputs are acquired at the beginning of the period, and at the end it sells – all it has. There is then a regular markets in capital goods (or producers' goods) at all stages of production (in the technical sense); a system of prices is set up, which reflects the state of the general process, at every stage.[12]

This is only an indication of his response to my comment. (I found later that E. Burmeister had a similar view to mine in considering that Hicks' neo-Austrian model could be regarded as a special case of the von Neumann model.[13])

But we should not take it for granted, as Hicks claims, that corresponding to each supply–demand inequality of the von Neumann model, there is a market, so that all prices in the system are market prices. Columns of von Neumann input and output matrices may merely represent the firms' processes at intermediate stages of production, whose outputs, intermediate products, have no market prices; they are transformed into products at later stages within the same firms in the next step of production. For these goods in the production process, internal prices are set within the firms for the purpose of efficient administration and management. Similarly, to what is left of used fixed capital at the end of the period, internal or efficiency prices are set. The von Neumann price vector includes all these internal prices, as well as the market prices, as its components. Intermediate products and used capital may be transferred, not via markets but directly, to the next stage of production within the same firm; from this point of view the internal efficient organization of firms is as important as the market mechanism. In this volume, by developing a von Neumann-like model I will investigate the Böhm-Bawerk–Wicksell–Åkerman problems from an angle which is somewhat different from the one Hicks took in his *Capital and Time*.

[11] H. A. Simon, 'Effects of Technological Change in a Leontief Model', in T, C. Koopmans (ed.), *Activity Analysis of Production and Allocation*, Wiley, New York, 1951. M. Morishima, *Equilibrium, Stability and Growth*, Clarendon Press, Oxford, 1964, pp. 117–22.

[12] J. Hicks, *Capital and Time*, pp. 5–6.

[13] E. Burmeister, 'Synthesizing the neo-Austrian and Alternative Approaches to Capital Theory: A Survey', *Journal of Economic Literature*, June 1974, pp. 413–56.

Production is stoppable and may be interrupted at any point in time. This obvious fact has not received enough attention in traditional theory in terms of the production function. Once the necessary factors of production are inputted, outputs are obtained instantaneously or in due course of time. Where production is stoppable, truncated production is possible, that is described by a truncated production function. The original entire production function may be taken as being composed of a number of truncated production functions producing parts and the final production function as assembling parts. The firm can of course delegate some or all of these parts-production activities to independent firms. In this way, it can externalize the problem of internal efficiency by producing markets between the main firm and its subsidiaries. Where the market is judged to be a better instrument for efficiency, the production activity of one big factory tends to be decentralized among a number of small factories. Thus the delegation of branches or subsections of the total production process to subsidiaries presupposes that the total production function is internally separable,[14] that is to say, it can be described in terms of a technological genealogy.

As for production lags, the following three may clearly be distinguished. First, a certain length of time is required for a firm to be formed and equipped with production facilities. Secondly, a lapse of time is needed to establish the production pipeline. Thirdly, in order to produce the complete product by processing the intermediate product at the end of the pipeline a certain length of time is additionally needed. These are called the construction period, the pipe-filling period and the final stage production period, respectively. Each of them is flexible, and alternative ways of production with different production lags are possible. The entrepreneur decides on the lengths of the three periods such that production is smoothly and efficiently carried out in his firm. The problem of decision-making of this sort, as well as the problem of determining the length of the lifetime of the machines and production facilities, has to be discussed under the assumption that production is separable, stoppable and truncateable. Such an approach will be presented in this volume.

Suppose now the pipe-filling period consists of three elementary periods, while the final stage of production is just one elementary period. Suppose the construction of the production facilities has been completed in the past, and the firm starts to fill the pipeline at the beginning of period 0. Then at the end of period 2 the firm has the intermediate product at the final stage of production at the end of the pipeline; it becomes a complete product at the

---

[14] W. W. Leontief, 'Introduction to a Theory of the Internal Structure of Functional Relationships', *Econometrica*, vol. 15, 1947, pp. 361–73.

end of period 3, that is the commencement of period 4. In period 1, the firm starts production for period 5; this operation produces the intermediate product at the final stage at the beginning of period 4. The operation started in period 2 produces the second-stage intermediate product in period 4 which becomes complete product at the beginning of period 6. In addition, in period 4 the firm has the first-stage intermediate product produced by the activity started in period 3. Thus in period 4 the pipeline is filled up with intermediate products at every stage. We have also complete products, while a new operation for period 8 commences in the same period.

This vertical structure of production implies horizontal coexistence of all three elementary stages and the final elementary stage for completing production. This is true not only for period 4 but also period 5 and afterwards. This synchronized horizontal structure may be described in terms of simultaneous equations or inequalities as was done, for example, by von Neumann. It is also clear that it reflects the vertical structure that was investigated by Hicks.

Construction of production facilities, on the other hand, is not regularly repeated, unlike the production of ordinary commodities. If the construction period is 3, the first stage of construction is carried out in period -3, the second only in period -2 and the third only in -1. The facilities are available for the use at the beginning of period 0. Except for the case of the same type of production facilities being produced repeatedly and consecutively, so that the facilities are newly made available at the beginning of each coming period (this would be the case only in very unlikely circumstances in the case of construction of facilities) the construction activities at different stages are not carried simultaneously in one period.

4 As has already been said, production possibility sets are neither endowments that entrepreneurs inherited from their parents nor manna from heaven. They are produced by the entrepreneurs themselves in collaboration with bankers and other financiers. Of course, there are special cases where entrepreneurs have enough money required for the production of the sets, but in all other cases necessary money has to be raised from wealthy men directly or indirectly through bankers or other financial institutions.

We may then classify production activities into three categories. First let X be the vector of levels of activities, for which it takes one elementary period to carry out and be completed. Secondly, Y is the vector of levels of activities of instantaneous production. X is further divided into subvectors, X_I and X_{II}. The former is financed by outside financiers and fixed at X_I^0 which is determined by the amounts that the financiers agree to lend, while the latter is decided solely by the entrepreneurs because it is financed by the money that the firms own. There is no problem of finance for Y, as I have already seen that instantaneous production activities are self-financed since the firms can use a part or the whole of proceeds to purchase the necessary factors of production; if the cost exceeds the proceeds, the firms never carry out Y.

These activities are not independent but decided interdependently. There are repercussions from X_I^0 to X_{II} and Y, and also between the last two. In the case of such economists as Ricardo and Walras who accept Say's law, it is assumed that no financial constraint is imposed on production activities, so that the set of anti-Say's law sectors, I, is empty. Therefore, repercussions are confined between X_{II} and Y. On the other hand, Keynes concentrates his attention on the economy under depression. Neglecting the pipeline-filling activities he examines the repercussion of an increase in X_I^0 upon Y. One may follow him in assuming that production of consumption goods is instantaneous. His consumpton multiplier process, that is instantaneous, is concerned with the effect of an increase in X_I^0, representing the investment sector, upon Y, representing the consumption goods sector. Thus there is no analysis of repercussions involving production lags, or any other lag, in Keynes. Schumpeter, on the other hand, discusses, in the trade cycle theory, full repercussion effects of an increase in X_I^0 due to innovations upon X_{II} and further upon Y. This book will follow Schumpeter's line.

In this volume the sequence of temporary equilibria is stated in terms of (X_t, Y_t), $t = 0, 1, 2, \ldots$, and (P_t, W_t, r_t), $t = 0, 1, \ldots$, where the latter are the price and wage vectors and the rate of profits in association with (X_t, Y_t); t represents the period in which the relevant variables, X_t, Y_t, P_t, W_t, and r_t, are realized. In this model activities X and Y are assumed to regulate the demand and supply of commodities, but prices, wages and profit rate, P, W and r, are not influenced by them. This type of economy is called the fixprice economy and compared with the traditional, flexprice economy, whose temporary equilibrium is designated by (P_t, W_t, r_t), activity vectors (X_t, Y_t) cannot change independently and are mere reflections, or mirror images, of (P_t, W_t, r_t). The so-called general equilibrium theories, formulated by various contemporary writers such as Hicks, Arrow, Debreu, Hahn, Malinvaud and others, are all of the flexprice economy type, to which the model treated in this book contrasts in various points. It is a model which may be characterized as a mixed flexprice–fixprice model, some of the markets of which are of flexprice type and others of fixprice type. It would be distinguished from those which have been discussed so far by various writers, because they are either a pure flexprice or a pure fixprice economy, rather than some mixture of these two.

We shall give, in the next section, a more detailed explanation of the key concepts, flexprice and fixprice. Prior to the characterization of the two, we note that whilst our model, especially in the specification of production activities, is very similar to von Neumann's growth model,[15] we cannot follow him in some other respects. First, unlike von Neumann, we do not impose the condition that the equilibrium should be a state of balanced growth. Ignoring the division of X into anti-Say's law and Say's law, sectors I and II, and also assuming the absence of instantaneous activities, we may say that the von Neumann balanced growth equilibrium X is not an efficient short-run equilibrium unless $B\bar{X} = BX$, where $\bar{X}$ is the activity vector carried out in the preceding period and B the von Neumann output matrix. To show this we assume that all commodities are available at the beginning of the current period, i.e. $B\bar{X} > 0$. Then without loss of generality we may adjust the level of X such that $B\bar{X} \geqq BX$. Let g be the von Neumann rate of balanced growth. We can then show that $(1 + g)X$ is inefficient, provided that $B\bar{X} \geqq BX$ holds with a strict inequality for at least one non-free commodity.[16] Therefore, the von Neumann equilibrium should not be regarded as a short-run state of affairs but an equilibrium which might be established in the long run. In the exceptional case of $X = \bar{X}$, the equilibrium has already been established in the current period. Otherwise we have to examine whether the economy starting with historically given $\bar{X}$ converges to the von Neumann equilibrium X or not. He has not discussed this.

The second unsatisfactory feature of the von Neumann model is that the primary factors of production are provided from outside of economy, say, by immigration of workers from abroad, as much as required. Von Neumann has made this assumption because otherwise balanced growth would become impossible as soon as the economy is short of some primary factors of production. To avoid this exogenousness of factors one might alternatively interpret the model so that it accommodates a sector where labour is produced with goods consumed by households, these inputs being assumed to be of fixed proportions per labouring activity. Then the two rules which apply to pricing and production in the von Neumann economy are valid for labour and the labour producing sector too. Accordingly, by the rule of free goods for labour, the price of labour, the wage rate, is zero if there is unemployment, and by the rule of profitability, there is no

[15] J. von Neumann, 'A Model of General Economic Equilibrium', *Review of Economic Studies*, 1945–6, pp. 1–9.

[16] Let A be von Neumann's input matrix. The balanced growth equilibrium requires $BX \geqq (1 + g)AX$. In view of $B\bar{X} \geqq BX$, we have $B\bar{X} \geqq (1 + g)AX$, which holds with strict inequality for some non-free goods. Thus there are non-free goods which are in excess supply; this obviously means inefficiency.

production of labour and, therefore, the workers' lives are terminated if they are found to be less profitable than the production of other commodities. Both of these are immoral and unrealistic.

This means that reproduction of labour and other primary factors of production should be treated differently from the production of ordinary commodities. The vector of availability of the primary factors, $\bar{N}$, develops from period to period according to the law of population and the law of reproduction of land and other factors. Some of them develop at considerable speed, while others may be constant or increase at a very slow rate. Because of this a balanced growth of productive activities X becomes impossible. In any case, the economy is subject to two constraints, one by $\bar{X}$ and the other by $\bar{N}$. The von Neumann model has to be revised such that it explicitly supplies a proper place to the factors of production.

Thirdly, a number of assumptions are made so as to keep the model linear. Among them, the following two are most serious. First, the input and output coefficients of each production process are assumed to be constant. This obviously rules out the increasing returns due to economies of the scale. Secondly, in von Neumann's own model the consumption coefficients of workers are constant, while capitalists save and invest their entire income, their consumption being neglected completely. This implies that workers' wages are held at the subsistence level, so that they cannot choose consumption goods. Capitalists are even worse than workers; they are not allowed to make any consumption. Several economists have, therefore, attempted to revise the model such that it becomes compatible with the Slutsky–Hicks type theory of consumers' behaviour for capitalists as well as workers. This has been one of the topics of my previous books,[17] so that in this book I will concentrate our attention on the subject of increasing returns.[18]

5 The concepts of 'flexprice' and 'fixprice' were introduced for the first time by J. Hicks, as the words characterizing the methods of analysis.[19] The flexprice method is the method which is based on the hypothesis that prices adjust themselves according to the demand–supply conditions in the

[17] See M. Morishima, *Equilibrium, Stability and Growth*, Clarendon Press, Oxford, 1964, chapter 5 and *Theory of Economic Growth*, Clarendon Press, 1969, chapters 6 and 7. E. Malinvaud has also been concerned with introducing final demand into von Neumann's model, but his consumption function is linear and independent of prices and inconsistent with the Slutsky–Hicks properties. E. Malinvaud, 'Programmes d'Expansion et Taux d'Intérêt', *Econometrica*, vol. 27, pp. 215–27.

[18] On this subject my work in this volume is greatly benefited from discussion with P. A. Valiasindi of the University of Pisa.

[19] J. Hicks, *Capital and Growth*, Clarendon Press, 1965, chapter 7 and *Methods of Dynamic Economics*, Clarendon Press, 1985, chapter 8.

markets. On the other hand, the fixprice method takes prices as given or assumes that they are determined exogenously. In fact, Hicks says:[20]

> If prices are fixed exogenously, one will naturally begin by assuming them to be constant. The model becomes a Fixprice model. Fixity of prices is in fact the characteristic feature of the models ... it will be convenient to use it as a name for the method. (The Temporary Equilibrium method can then be referred to, by contrast, as a Flexprice method.)

Hicks notes that the flexprice method is more suitable than the fixprice, in the case of a market economy where traded commodities are all non-storable (e.g. fish, strawberries, etc.). He also points out that the storability of commodities is greatly related to the rigidity of their prices. Nevertheless, at this stage of the development of his idea, flexprice and fixprice models are assumptions of convenience that we may equally make for any type of national economy. In particular, the word 'fixprice' is taken by many economists to mean that prices do not change.

Malinvaud has then recognized the fact that prices are more sticky downwards than upwards.[21] He is concerned with a one-commodity, one-factor economy which has two markets, one for the product and the other for labour. There are four possible cases according as whether these markets are in excess supply or excess demand. Case I, in which, Malinvaud considers, Keynesian unemployment prevails, is characterized as a state with both markets being in excess supply. Then free competition, if it works, would tend to decline the price of the product and the wage rate. However, applying the assumption of downwards stickiness of prices, Malinvaud considers that the decline of the price and wage rate is very mild or nil in case I and, consequently, the fixprice method is more suitable than the flexprice method. In case II an excess supply prevails in the labour market while an excess demand (hence, a shortage of the product) prevails in the commodity market. This is called by Malinvaud the case of classical unemployment, which applies to so-called Marxian unemployment caused by a shortage of machines with which workers are equipped. It also applies to unemployment caused by too high wages. In any case, where this happens, the price will be increased and the wage rate remains unchanged. The real wage, therefore, declines and more machines are produced, so that unemployment will be mitigated.

Case III is rather paradoxical as there is an excess demand for labour whereas there is an excess supply of the product. In Malinvaud's own model this is an empty possibility. Finally in case IV, where an excess demand

---

[20] Hicks, *Capital and Growth*, p. 78.
[21] E. Malinvaud, *The Theory of Unemployment Reconsidered*, Basil Blackwell, Oxford, 1977, p. 11.

prevails in both markets, for the product and labour, the price and wage rate explicitly increase in parallel, or otherwise repressed inflation will progress.

As the markets are in excess demand or supply depending on the price p and the wage rate w, the p-w plane is divided into three mutually exclusive domains corresponding to cases I, II, and IV. Then we may conceive a comprehensive theory which uses the fixprice, flexprice and mixed fixprice–flexprice methods accordingly as p and w are set so as to result in case I, IV or II, respectively. Thus these methods have regional appropriateness. The economist must choose a proper method which suits the given case. This is an interesting method, from the use of which we may expect fruitful outcomes. But this is not the way we pursue in this book. Although we too use both methods, we mix them in an entirely different way.

It has already been mentioned above that fishing is a flexprice sector, while it is generally observed that manufacturing is representative of fixprice industries. Besides fishing there are other flexprice industries, such as agriculture, forestry and mining. As for the fixprice sector, on the other hand, the prices of the products are decided by the full-cost principle in the sector of wholesale–retail trade as well as in the manufacturing sector. In addition to these, there are sectors where the marginal-cost principle works, such as gas, electricity and water, transport and communication, storage, and finance, insurance and business services. Prices are decided there by expanding the marginal cost to be charged by some reasonable mark-up ratios, so that these prices are independent of excess demand or supply of the respective commodities. In the remaining two broad sectors, prices are determined by tender in the construction sector including ship-building, while administrative prices prevail in the sector of public administration, etc. In view of the industrial structure of the economies of the developed countries, the weight of the flexprice sectors is at most as high as 20%, and that of the fixprice sectors reaches 70%–80%.

Reflecting on this structure of the national economy, I classify the sectors of the economy according to the principles of price determination which prevail there. The sectors where prices are determined by the flexprice method are called flexprice sectors, while those, which determine prices according to the full-cost or marginal-cost principle, fixprice sectors. In this volume, therefore, the description that a sector belongs to the fixprice group does not imply that prices are never to be allowed to change but may change in a different manner, in different circumstances. They do not necessarily change wherever there is demand–supply disequilibrium, but will change whenever an alteration in prices is justified from the point of view of price–cost relationships, whereas the law of demand and supply is always valid in flexprice sectors.

When Hicks finally describes the fixprice market as a market where 'there is a force which makes for stabilization [of prices], operated . . . by the producer himself',[22] his view becomes very close to mine. The concepts he has introduced are no longer for classifying the methods of analysis the economists adopt but for characterizing the workings of the sectors. The national economy is then grasped as a mixed economy consisting of sectors working according to different principles of price determination. In addition, we assume that it takes some substantial production period to produce flexprice commodities, as is true of agriculture, forestry and other flexprice sectors. It implies that instantaneous production processes are all of the fixprice type because all of them are the final processes of manufacturing sectors. This means that some of X depend on prices, while the rest and all Y are independent of P. In any case, in contrast with Malinvaud's regional appropriateness of the two concepts, we formulate the national economy as a system within which the two methods are sectorally appropriate.

From this point of view, the words flexprice and fixprice may not be considered to be perfectly adequate. The two kinds of sectors might be better named the price-taking behaviour sectors and the full-cost (or marginal-cost) principle sectors, respectively. Nevertheless I have decided to maintain the Hicksian terms in this book. This is because Hicks himself, as I have said, has made it clear that prices may change under the fixprice principle and has realized that, once prices are determined in the full-cost principle sectors, they tend to remain fixed until the producers are justified and convinced to make a change.

Furthermore it should be pointed out that our taxonomy looks to be somewhat paradoxical. To obtain equilibrium prices, the fixprice, full-cost principle, sectors, like the flexprice industries, must adjust prices such that they are increased (or decreased) whenever there is an excess demand for (or supply of) the respective commodities. Such adjustments, however, are only made in the process of finding the right prices. Where Say's law holds true, the economy, as will be seen in chapter 5 below, will obtain these prices, while where it does not hold, prices are not determined in the same way and kept fixed even though demand and supply are not equated to each other.

6 It is the basic assumption of GET that for each commodity there is one and only one market where the price of commodity is determined.

[22] J. Hicks, *A Market Theory of Money*, Clarendon Press, Oxford, 1989, p. 25. The model of his book, a mixed economy of the two kinds of sectors according to this classification of the pricing principles, is similar to the economy which I discussed in my *Economics of Industrial Society*, Cambridge University Press, 1985. Reference should also be made to P. Wiles, *Price, Cost and Output*, Basil Blackwell, 1961, and A. Okun, *Prices and Quantities*, Basil Blackwell, Oxford, 1981.

However, there are exceptional commodities: fixed capital goods and consumer durables, each of which has two related but separate markets, one for the services which the commodity provides and the other for the commodity itself. They determine the service price (or rental) and the commodity price, respectively. These two, however, are not completely independent of each other; the service price of a commodity, after allowing for depreciation, must be equal, in equilibrium, to the rate of interest times the price of the commodity (i.e., Keynes' proposition that the marginal efficiencies of capital goods are equal to the rate of interest must hold).

This relationship between service and commodity prices of capital goods may be confirmed in the following way. A person who has an amount of money £P has two options: one is to buy bonds from which he gets interest at the rate r', and the other is to buy a capital good, its price being £P. If he takes the second option, he will get, at the beginning of the next period, £q by selling capital services from it *plus* the capital good used for one period, in kind. Let this be estimated at £ψ. Where there is an equilibrium between the two options, we should have the equality: $(1+r')P = q+\psi$, from which we get $q/P = r'+\delta$, where δ stands for the rate of depreciation, $(P-\psi)/P$. This establishes Keynes' law, as q/P may be referred to the marginal efficiency of this capital good.

Now we have $q = (r'+\delta)P$, so that q depends on P and cannot play the role of an independent variable, besides P. Where the rate of interest is determined elsewhere, the two markets, the market for a capital good i and the market for capital services i, have only one price as a variable regulating demand and supply in the two markets. Moreover this price is determined by the equation of the full cost principle, because i is produced by a fixprice industry. It is true that the production activity of the commodity i may be adjusted in such a way that an equilibrium is established in the market for capital services i. But there must be an additional variable in order to clear the market for the capital good i too. Otherwise, at least one of the two markets is left uncleared. As soon as the system includes either capital goods or consumer durables, the existence of GE is not generally warranted.

This is the place where Say's law is introduced into GET. In his model of capital formation, Walras regarded the investment (i.e., the demand for the durable commodity) as a variable. This means that there is no *ex ante* investment function and the demand for capital goods is flexibly created wherever there is a supply of any magnitude. For Walras this is enough for resolving the problem of overdeterminacy, while Keynes has viewed the same problem from a different angle. He has taken a macroeconomic approach and finds that a full employment equilibrium can be established in the case of no *ex ante* schedule of investment, so that investment can adjust itself to any level of savings. This is what I have called Say's law in the sense of Keynes, in my previous books, which should be distinguished from Say's law in the sense of Lange and Patinkin, an idea which is now very familiar among contemporary economists.[23] Needless to say, it is entirely unsatisfactory to use Say's law as a *deus ex machina*, because it is a very unrealistic assumption; once we reject it, as Keynes has done, then the fixprice model has no GE solution unless we assume a very tricky investment function.

Say's law, especially that of Keynes' version, has never been a subject of Hicks. He has not given any attention to the duality between capital services and capital goods markets discussed above. Therefore, even if capital goods are present in the economy, he treats them in the same manner as we deal with usual commodities; he assumes that each of them has a single market that is regulated by its price. No problem of overdetermination is discussed, and, hence, he is not successful in generating involuntary unemployment in a serious way. Although he refers to Keynes in many places, the *Value and Capital* economics is an economics of full employment.

Contemporary GE theorists followed in his footsteps and, as a consequence, they have not seen the problem of the non-existence of general equilibrium; thus GET remains an economics of the full employment equilibrium. In an economy, on the other hand, where the amount of purchasing power which entrepreneurs can use for carrying out activities X_I^0 is decided by banks, the industrial investment for each capital good is not a free variable as Say's law assumes, so that an anti-Say's law prevails. Activities X_I^0 and X_{II} are, respectively, called anti-Say's law and Say's law activities, because the rigidity of X_I^0 is responsible for the ruling of the former law in the market, while flexible activities X_{II} have no responsibility for it. Thus the structure of the GET dramatically changes once durable commodities, machines and consumer durables, are permitted. Walras is the nearest person to realize this, because he formulated his model of capital formation very appropriately but entirely differently from the model of production, but he has failed to discuss the problem of Say's law, because he has treated the demands for capital goods as free variables. Unfortunately all contemporary GE theorists do not distinguish the GET of capital formation from that of production. Their formulation of the former is a simple extension of the latter without any essential modification.

Other elements which cause unemployment are factor prices. Factor

[23] *Walras' Economics*, pp. 185–94 and *Ricardo' Economics*, pp. 164–7. Other formulations of the law are possible because it is a vague proposition with many aspects and implications, so that various interpretations can be made. But I only deal with Keynes' version in this volume as I am interested in generating involuntary unemployment in the framework of GET.

markets are very different from commodity markets as sociological elements, in addition to market factors, have significant effects upon the determination of factor prices.[24] First, so as not to be blamed for being unfair, the entrepreneurs have to pay wages which are at least as good as those paid by their competitors. Secondly, by the same reason of fairness, the system of wages must satisfy the relativity conditions. The relativities which have been established in the past tend to be recognized as 'fair'. These social attitudes contribute to preventing the wages from adjusting themselves freely and flexibly to the demand–supply situations in the labour market, and causing unemployment of the Keynesian type due to downwards rigidity of wages.

Moreover, it must be added that social power would be preserved. The people's sense of fairness, as has just been said, depends on the reputation of the jobs in the past, and the relative wages are determined such that they are consistent with the sense of fairness prevailing in the society. A new system of reputation would be formed by taking into account the current relative wages thus determined. In the next period, wages will be determined to be fair according to the new sense of reputation, which is based on the current wages being, in turn, based on the reputation in the past. In this way, the feeling of reputation and fairness is preserved among people for a long period, though we of course observe many occasions when the demand–supply conditions in the market affect the relativity.

Similarly, in the land market an important role is played by sociological elements including those of legacies from feudal days. Especially, where negotiation is made face-to-face between a landowner and a tenant, their personalities, social positions, respect and contempt influence the rent; it is not a simple matter of demand and supply. It is often seen in many countries that feudalistic social attitudes place hurdles on the road to efficient utilization of land. In chapter 4 below, we first examine the problem of existence of temporary equilibrium without paying any consideration to sociological elements in the factor markets, as a first approximation of reality. We shall then see how the established equilibrium is affected where the sociological elements are allowed to work. From these we are enabled to conclude that the factor markets are not flexprice, neoclassical markets. They are not impersonal but personal, not mechanical but human, and even not clear-cut but subtle.

[24] J. Hicks, *A Market Theory of Money*, Clarendon Press, 1989, pp. 27–37. R. M. Solow, *The Labour Market as a Social Institution*, 1990. In his many books, Professor Yasuma Takata wrote in Japanese in 1920–50, he explained how sociological elements would influence wages. He also argued that because of the repercussions from wages to prices these too would deviate from purely economic equilibrium prices. See, for example, Y. Takata, *Seiryoku-setsu Ronshu* (Essays in Power Theory of Economics), Nihon Hyoron Sha, Tokyo, 1941.

Finally, I would like to make two remarks. First, in spite of the existence of involuntary unemployment, I describe the state obtained at the end of a period as an equilibrium, rather than a disequilibrium state. This is because conditions are realized in the economy at the end of a period, under which entrepreneurs have no incentive to change their scale of operations and workers do not propose an alteration of wages; hence there is no change in employment. We are still in a position far from proposing a pure theory of disequilibrium states; it is almost an impossible task, at least at the present state of development of economics.

The second remark is on Hicks' methodology. As we have already seen above, the concepts of flexprice and fixprice were introduced by him as the words signifying the methods of analysis. In his last book, however, he observed that various markets, corn, fish, manufactures and labour markets, work entirely differently. Although he did not connect these with each other to form a national economy, the book strongly suggests that he would have no objection to formulating it as a mixed economy consisting of flexprice industries (agriculture, forestry, etc.) and fixprice industries (manufacturing, transportation, etc.) as we shall do below. I have said that I started economics with Hicks' *Value and Capital* and wandered out from its paradigm. It seems, however, that I return to the place where Hicks was going to.[25]

7 Let us now put subscript t to X and Y in order for X_t and Y_t to signify that they are activities carried out in period t. Where anti-Say's law activities are absent, and sociological frictions in the factor markets are ignored, temporary full-employment equilibrium is established in each period at X_t and Y_t taking on equilibrium values X_t^e and Y_t^e respectively. The sequence $\{X_t^e, Y_t^e\}$, $t = 0, 1, \ldots$ is constrained at the beginning of period 0 by the stock of commodities then available, $B\bar{X}$, which is the legacy of the activities in the previous period, $\bar{X} = X_{t-1}^e$. It traces out the path of production through time and is in association with the path of equilibrium prices, wages and rate of profits $\{P_t^e, W_t^e, r_t^e\}$.

The so-called stability theory has been concerned with investigating whether the temporary equilibrium *point* (P_t^e, W_t^e, r_t^e) of each period t is stable or not, but never deals with the stability problem concerning the equilibrium *motion* or *path* $\{P_t^e, W_t^e, r_t^e\}$, $t = 0, 1, 2, \ldots$ It is true that the theory of economic growth has been concerned with whether the physical path of economic development $\{X_t^e, Y_t^e\}$, $t = 0, 1, \ldots$ is stable or not. In this case too, however, the stability analysis has been developed in the form of

[25] The course of development of my own idea may be depicted by connecting the following books: *DKR* (Dynamic Economics), 1950; *Equilibrium, Stability and Growth*, 1964. These books are followed by those listed in footnote 6 above.

stability of point, which examines whether the path converges to a particular point that is the long-run equilibrium point or the growth equilibrium. In fact, Ricardo concerned himself with the long-run equilibrium, a stationary state. It is also true that whereas, on the very surface, the stability of growth equilibrium may look like a stability of motion, it is, in fact, essentially a stability of point (or a relative stability as Solow and Samuelson have called it[26]), because it discusses whether the path converges to a fixed point of relative outputs. As a number of stringent conditions are needed for the existence of a long-run equilibrium or a balanced growth equilibrium, we do not assume it. We rather follow Walras in this respect; his GE of capital formation and credit is not a long-run equilibrium but shifts from period to period in spite of a number of economists insisting that it is a long-run equilibrium. This idea of economic motion without a terminus has been succeeded by La Volpe and Hicks, but none of them has developed the stability theory as the theory of stability of motion which I want to offer in chapter 5 below.

Where sociological forces work in the factor markets, the full employment of factors is not necessarily realized and the economic path that is effective in this actual world will deviate from the neoclassical sequence of temporary equilibria $\{X_t^e, Y_t^e\}$. This would occur even though anti-Say's law processes X_I^0 are absent. In the actual world, however, it is impossible to carry out X_1 at the equilibrium level X_1^e unless the entrepreneurs are granted financial help by banks and other financial agents as much as they want. Schumpeter has examined the circumstances where bankers set X_{1t}^0, $t = 0, 1,$ ... higher than their equilibrium values, so that the path $\{X_t, Y_t\}$ generated from them is associated with the price path $\{P_t, W_t, r_t\}$ which is inflationary. He is in contrast with Keynes who sets X_{1t}^0 $t = 0, 1, \ldots$ lower than the equilibrium, so that the path $\{X_t, Y_t\}$ with involuntary unemployment of some of the primary factors results. Thus the vision that the financial sectors play a crucial role in the economy is common between Schumpeter and Keynes.

It then follows that the path the economy will trace out depends on the attitudes of the financial organizations. It is obvious that the capital goods accumulated when they support, say, the electronics industry would be completely different from those accumulated when they support the ship-building industry. In the long run the economy will turn out to be of a greatly different kind according to which of these options is taken. This means that the motion of the economy $\{X_t, Y_t\}$ is *unstable* with respect to

[26]   R. M. Solow and P. A. Samuelson, 'Balanced Growth under Constant Returns to Scale', *Econometrica*, vol. 21, 1953, pp. 412–24.

anti-Say's law processes X_{It}^0; and the fate of the national economy crucially depends on the choice of X_{It}^0, which is made by the entrepreneurs in collaboration with bankers.

Schumpeter's theory of innovation has been developed in close relation to the entrepreneurs' choice X_I^0 and the bankers' backing up of their decisions. However, there is no idea of anti-Say's law processes in the traditional general equilibrium theory of the Hicks, Arrow–Debreu, Arrow–Hahn line. Consequently, there is no problem of the choice of X_{It}^0 and hence no instability. It is then no wonder that general equilibrium theory is grounded and cannot fly in the actual world.

There are several sources of purchasing power which enables the firms to make investments. The first is the amortization fund in which the firms' depreciation allowances are accumulated; the second the reserved profits; the third the money obtained by issuing equities (stocks and shares) or bonds; the fourth money borrowed from banks. (The lending is of course made by either releasing the money banks have or creating credits.) These means are simultaneously available to the firms which make a choice from among them such that the financial position of each firm is to be optimum. In *DKR* it is assumed that the firms borrow money from banks or other agents and issue securities to the lenders as certificates of their borrowing; it is also assumed that all lendings and borrowings are of one period (or week). In chapter 2 below, however, we are concerned with the case where the firms can raise money only by issuing equities, while we return in chapter 6 to a more general economy which has a lending–borrowing market of the *DKR* type, in addition to the equity market.

They are the chapters that discuss how the firms of the model of this book are financed. Of course it is true that the way of financing investment by borrowing money from banks, rather than issuing equities, is not dominant in the Anglo-American world. But, besides the fact that Schumpeter assumed this type of financial market when he discussed the innovation,[27] there is an additional reason for me (as a Japanese economist) to stick to this assumption. That is, it is the most prevalent way of financing firms in post-war Japan. With the help of banks Japanese industries carried out various innovations and succeeded in developing fast in this period. Chapters 5 and 6 enable us to see how important collaboration between firms and banks is in achieving economic progress. Japanese experiences show that firms can be giants even though the proportion of their own capital is small.

Whereas both Schumpeter and Keynes emphasized the importance of

---

[27] Schumpeter, *The Theory of Economic Development.*

anti-Say's law processes X_I^0,[28] there is a big difference between them. Notwithstanding that *ex ante* collaboration between entrepreneurs and bankers is essential in Schumpeter's theory of innovation, Keynes observes that any investment carried out by entrepreneurs is *ex post facto* covered by savings generated, regardless of whether there is the *ex ante* support of bankers or not, when entrepreneurs decide on the investment decisions. Suppose now an investment plan is implemented without any borrowing from banks. Then instantaneous activities Y are expanded according to the multiplier theory and, therefore, workers' and entrepreneurs' incomes are increased. (Keynes neglects, as I have stated before, repercussions from X_I^0 to X_{II}.) This also means that the firms' reserved profits and depreciation are expanded, on the one hand, and the households' savings increase, on the other.

Savings are made in the form of either lending or an increase in the cash balance or deposits. The latter improves the position of city or commercial banks, whose loanable funds are thus increased. In this way, households' and banks' lending will be increased. These increases are enough to fill the gap between the investment and the firms' savings.[29] The equality between savings and investment is established in the *ex post* sense.

This is one of the most important differences between Schumpeter and Keynes. In the former, the entrepreneurs cannot make innovations without the help of bankers; and thus the theory of the firm is completely integrated with the theory of money and banking. On the other hand, in the latter the entrepreneurs can make their own decisions on investment independently of bankers. Production and investment made by the firms may still be independent from bankers' behaviour. Like Keynes' government investment, the private investment in his economy too can be carried out without *ex ante* financial arrangements. It is of course true, as the above multiplier process shows, that the aggregate savings are *ex post facto* formed in the amount that is equal to the aggregate investment. But this equality is realized only on the aggregate level, so that there may be firms whose investment remains unfinanced, because bankers and other lenders do not like their investment. They will go bankrupt; and bankruptcy may easily spread from one firm to another. Keynes ignored this possibility, by assuming that investment projects are realized in the order of their profitability, so that the marginal efficiencies are equalized through all projects that are carried out. But even though *ex ante* marginal efficiencies

[28] M. Morishima and G. Catephores, 'Anti-Say's Law versus Say's Law: A Change in Paradigm', in H. Hanusch (ed.), *Evolutionary Economics: Applications of Schumpeter's Ideas*, Cambridge University Press, 1988, pp. 23–53.
[29] This mechanism can easily be traced and confirmed by consulting the 'table of economic linkages' of my *The Economics of Industrial Society*, p. 141.

are expected, corresponding *ex post* efficiencies may be different from each other. *Ex post* savers will not like their savings to be poured into those projects whose *ex post* efficiencies are bad; they will remain unfinanced. This possibility is minimized in Schumpeter's economy because of the *ex ante* financial arrangements being made between entrepreneurs and bankers. We shall follow him in this book.[30]

The economic system is composed of the two subsystems, 'real' and 'monetary'. Conventional general equilibrium theory is only or mainly concerned with the former. In this volume too, chapters 3–5 discuss the existence and stability of the 'real economic' equilibrium, without being deeply involved in investigating the monetary aspects of the economy. The complete isolation of the real subsystem from the monetary one is possible only where Say's law holds true. Where it is not validated, investment activities depend on finance; there are repercussions from financial to real sectors. On the other hand, regardless of Say's law being true or not, there are converse repercussions from real to financial, because financial activities are carried out in order to support and accomplish investment projects. Thus the real and monetary subeconomies are conjugate and influenced by each other under anti-Say's law. Then how are they consolidated in a complete whole system? This is the subject of chapter 6.

In chapter 7, the monetary economy is examined in order to see how it works. This is the problem Wicksell was concerned with. We shall generalize his theory by removing unsatisfactory assumptions he made in deriving his conclusion. First of all, the assumption of full employment is got rid of. Secondly, the assumption of the real equilibrium being stationary is also unnecessary. We shall show that the cumulative process as he observed it will be seen to be generated even though the real economy is changing. It may occur during the time when the economy grows.

We may therefore conclude that the economy is likely to be monetarily unstable; it is always subject to a danger of inflation or deflation. Besides, it is shown that the real economy too will be unstable with respect to entrepreneurs' choice of investment projects. It is obvious that their decisions on investment will be abortive unless they are approved and

---

[30] It is well known that motives for holding cash are analysed into income, business, precautionary and speculative motives by Keynes. These, however, do not include the investment motive for holding cash to bridge the interval between the accumulation of the firms' own funds for investment and their disbursement. See J. M. Keynes, *The General Theory of Employment, Interest and Money*, Macmillan, 1936, pp. 195–6.

Although money does not appear explicitly as a means of exchange in the following chapters, it is easy to take the demand for money for transaction motives into our system in the same way as I have derived it in my 'Optimal Transaction Demand for Money', M. Morishima *et al.*, *Theory of Demand: Real and Monetary*, Clarendon Press, Oxford, 1973, pp. 271–84.

supported by bankers, so that the economy will perform better if they work in collaboration with each other.[31]

Finally, this book deals with an economy where no futures market is open. International trade is also ruled out. Chapter 8 puts GET in the perspective of the twenty-first century.

---

[31] It may be very natural that R. Hilferding, the author of *Das Finanzkapital, Eine Studie über die jüngste Entwicklung des Kapitalismus*, 1910, which had been concerned with the linkage between industry and banks, later advocated the idea of organized capitalism.

2   Capitalist production

1 It would be convenient to start our visit to general equilibrium theory from its section on the theory of the firm. According to its advanced formulation, it is constructed in a highly rigorous manner which uses the axiomatic method. It seems logically perfect, and recent books on general equilibrium, or microeconomics text books, repeat more or less essentially the same prototype theory of the firm due to Hicks' *Value and Capital*, though one may notice some technical developments in analysis and exposition.

This conventional theory, however, is only concerned with that part of the firm's behaviour which belongs to its everyday decision-making, or its routine work of production. It establishes the propositions of marginal productivity and examines their implications, leaving out the important financial aspects of the firm's activities, such as how to raise the initial capital of the firm for building up its production possibility set, how to increase its capital for development, or, more generally, how to finance production – all of these are completely ignored. It is obvious, however, that unless a firm has some amount of purchasing power at its beginning, it can do nothing. Its activity entirely depends on the amount of money the entrepreneur can use for his business. The conventional theory lacks such a perspective and, therefore, the budget constraint has no relevance to the theory of the firm. This is a serious misspecification of the model of the firm and it, in the end, has led us to an erroneous observation that the Slutsky equation of the firm has no term of income effect.

The consequence of this error is far-reaching. First, as the gross substitution matrix is symmetric as far as the firms are concerned, because of the absence of income effects upon them, it can be asymmetric only because individual households' behaviour is constrained by the budget equations. As Hicks, Samuelson, Arrow and others have all confirmed,[1] general equilibrium may be unstable only if income effects are not

[1] See, for example, F. H. Hahn, 'Stability', in K. J. Arrow and M. D. Intriligator (eds.), *Handbook of Mathematical Economics*, vol. II, North-Holland, Amsterdam, 1982.

negligible. Therefore, the conventional theorists have to conclude that only individuals could be blamed for destabilizing the equilibrium, while the firms are all regarded as innocent.

Secondly, as will be discussed in this chapter and, especially, chapter 3 below, it is very important to see that the production possibility sets, which the conventional theorists have considered as given, are not, in fact, given but can totally or partially be made flexible, or expandable, by the will and ability of the entrepreneurs, i.e., their ability to construct, change or expand the firms' technological possibilities, depending on the purchasing power they can command and use to buy land, labour and capital equipment. Thus technological possibility sets are left undetermined and, therefore, unexplained unless the firms' financial positions are specified; technology thus depends on money. This important, but obvious, fact has been ignored by most eminent conventional theorists. Even Grandmont's excellent survey of general equilibrium theory has not noticed this point.[2]

To investigate all this, let us first examine the standard, static theory of production, mainly according to Hicks' *Value and Capital*. All other contemporary GE theorists follow Hicks, and it seems that there is no significant difference between them in the points discussed below. The theory assumes that there are a given, finite number of (potential or actual) firms, each of which is provided with a production function, or a number of production functions. Technology determines these functions, but there are other elements which constrain the extent of production possibilities. Hicks says: 'For short period problems, the fixed equipment or plant of the firm, which has been built up in the past, and is likely to be to some extent unique, fits the case fairly well. For long-period problems, we have only the ultimate control, exercised by the entrepreneur himself.'[3] Hicks is concerned with long-run equilibrium in static equilibrium theory, while he leaves open the problem of short-run equilibrium to the dynamic part of the book dealing with temporary equilibrium.

In static theory, the production function which is available to an entrepreneur i is written, in terms of his output and input vectors, x^i and y^i respectively as $f^i(x^i, y^i) = 0$. It is assumed that production is instantaneous; there is no time lag between the point of input and the point of output. (Or alternatively we may say that the static theory does not ask when the factors are employed and when the products are made available. It deals with a very long period, in which inputs of factors are made in order to obtain outputs; since the long period is very long, the timing of inputs and outputs is considered, from its point of view, to be insignificant and immaterial so that

[2] Jean-Michel Grandmont, 'Temporary General Equilibrium Theory', in K. J. Arrow and M. D. Intriligator (eds.), *Handbook of Mathematical Economics*, vol. II, North-Holland, Amsterdam, 1982. Jean-Michel Grandmont (ed.), *Temporary Equilibrium Theory: Selected Readings*, Academic Press, New York, 1988.   [3] J. R. Hicks, *Value and Capital*.

they are treated as if they are simultaneous.) Moreover, all outputs are assumed to be sold and all inputs to be bought in the markets. Stocks of commodities (products and factors of production) of the firm, therefore, remain unchanged, because an excess of output of a commodity over its supply and an excess of demand for a factor over its input, either of which creates an expansion of the stock of the respective commodities or factors held by the firm, are assumed to be zero. Thus the problem of accumulation of capital goods or inventories is naturally or intrinsically ruled out in the static theory.

Hicks assumes that each (potential or active) entrepreneur possesses some amount of entrepreneurial resources which cannot be disposed of on the market but can be used, in combination with other factors of production, to produce products. Thus an entrepreneur's own production function depends on both his own entrepreneurial resources and the technology available. Unless the resources are large in quantity and high in quality, the entrepreneur cannot control a large enterprise efficiently; thus he must be content with a firm of an appropriate size. This implies that the production function $f^i(\ldots)$ is not homogeneous of degree zero in outputs x^i and inputs y^i. Where the scale of production of the firm i is too large, the entrepreneur's management will become inefficient, so that outputs cannot be expanded proportionately in spite of a proportional increase in inputs. Making this fact explicit, one may write the individual production function above in the following form:

$$f^i(x^i, y^i, er^i) = 0, \tag{2.1}$$

where er^i stands for the entrepreneurial resources available to the firm i.

With given price vectors p and q for outputs and inputs respectively, the firm i maximizes its profits subject to (2.1). If its maximum profits are positive the production is carried out, whereas if they are not positive, the firm remains to be merely a potential one, no production being made.

Where one formulates the theory of production in this Hicksian manner, no problem of financing production can be raised in his framework. As production is instant, x and y are simultaneous quantities, so that the entrepreneur can use the proceeds of his outputs, px^i, to buy necessary inputs, y^i. He has always a sufficient amount as means of payment because $px^i > qy^i$ is at the point of maximum profits. No advanced provision of capital is needed for production; consequently the firm is not subject to any capitalist or other master. In an economy consisting of only such firms it is needless to say that no capitalist class will emerge. Like Marx's 'simple commodity production economy'[4] it is a system which can hardly be called

[4] M. Morishima, *Marx's Economics*, Cambridge University Press, 1973, p. 28 and pp. 42–5. M. Morishima and G. Catephores, *Value, Exploitation and Growth*, McGraw-Hill (UK), 1978, pp. 182–91.

a capitalist regime. All the static models of general equilibrium which neoclassical theorists have developed[5] are nothing more than mathematical elaborations of this prototype due to Hicks' *Value and Capital*, Part II, which, as he himself admits, abstracts from capital and interest, as well as from savings and investment. These economists never seriously ask what is capital, or what is a capitalist.[6]

Provided with some additional, but reasonable, assumptions, it can be shown that the instant production economy is reduced to Marx's simple commodity production economy. First of all it is assumed that all necessary factors of production can be obtained from the markets, and all production possibilities are open to every entrepreneur. Also, it is assumed that entrepreneurs are all homogeneous and achieve the same performance if they are engaged in the same kind of business. Moreover, the entrepreneur himself may work within his firm as a worker or a middle-class manager, or in any other capacity, and would, therefore, maximize his total income (including his wage or salary income), rather than just the profit part of the total. The perfect mobility of entrepreneurs through all available spheres of production, together with the assumed homogeneity of entrepreneurs, would establish the equality of the entrepreneur's total income per man-hour throughout the society. This is exactly a 'pre-capitalistic' state of equilibrium existing in those societies which Marx calls simple commodity production economies, distinguishing them from economies where the capitalist mode of production prevails. He, in fact, observes and emphasizes that equilibrium prices are equal to labour values in the former, while equilibrium production prices deviate from the values in the latter.

Finally, we make a remark on increasing, diminishing or constant returns to scale which play an important role in later chapters. It has already been stated that, for each producer i, the individual production function (2.1) does not necessarily yield returns which are constant per scale; they may be increasing or decreasing. At the point of maximum profits, however, marginal profits are revealed to be diminishing; this is so because if the scale of production is expanded further at the point of maximum profits, total profits of course decrease while the scale expands; therefore, the profits or returns per scale inevitably have to decrease. Nevertheless, under the law of variable returns yielding non-negative profits for individual firms, a general

[5] See, for example, G. Debreu, *Theory of Value*, John Wiley, 1959. J. Quirk and R. Saposnik, *Introduction to General Equilibrium Theory and Welfare Economics*, McGraw-Hill, 1968. K. J. Arrow and F. H. Hahn, *General Competitive Analysis*, North-Holland, 1971. E. Malinvaud, *Lectures on Microeconomic Theory*, North-Holland, 1972. H. R. Varian, *Microeconomic Analysis*, W. W. Norton, 1978.
[6] Capitalists may be defined in this place as individuals who have financial means or stocks of commodities that are provided with firms for production. As neither financial means nor initial stocks of factors are needed in the static formulation, it cannot be a theory for discussing the problem of capital.

equilibrium will be established at a point where profits are zero for each firm, if entrepreneurial resources (of equal quality) are not scarce. This can be seen in the following way. Under the assumption that each firm is provided with the same amount of entrepreneurial resources of equal quality, the performance made by firm i with entrepreneur i can be reproduced by firm j with entrepreneur j. There is no obstacle, under this assumption, to duplicate what firm i has been doing before by building another firm j exactly like firm i. Each of i and j produces the same amount of outputs and the economy produces twice the outputs. This replication procedure assures constant returns to scale for the economy as far as the primary factors of production are available. The factor prices will start to increase and profits will decrease when the supply of the factors ceases to be elastic. This process will only stop at the point where profits are all zero, and this would happen only in the case of entrepreneurial resources being available infinitely. Then the static theory would tend to attribute positive profits, not to capital, but to the scarcity of entrepreneurial resources.

2 We have already acknowledged that there is no concept of capital in the case of production being timeless. Accordingly, for those economists who are interested in investigating the workings of the capitalist economy, it is essential to recognize the fact that it takes some time to obtain x^i from y^i. We must replace the long-period, static production function (2.1) by the following (2.1*) below, which is appropriate for a short-period, dynamic economy, by taking the fixed equipment and intermediate products of the firm, which have been built up in the past, into account explicitly. That is to say, we are concerned here with extending the previous model of instantaneous production into a model which takes minimum consideration for production time lags. We assume that outputs x^i are obtained in period t if inputs y^i are made in period $t-1$ as is described by the production function:

$$f^i(x_t^i, y_{t-1}^i) = 0. \tag{2.1*}$$

It is noted that some elements of the vector y_{t-1}^i designate inputs of the ultimate means of production, land and labour, while others are themselves results of production activities by some firms in the past. To obtain these amounts of commodities which are required for inputs to be made in $t-1$, production has to be made in the previous period $t-2$, for which y_{t-2}^i is needed. This further requires production in period $t-3$. Going backwards in this way we get a historical chain of production $(x_t, y_{t-1}), (x_{t-1}, y_{t-2}), (x_{t-2}, y_{t-3}) \ldots$, where x and y are the total output and input vectors of the economy, that is $x = \sum_i x^i$ and $y = \sum_i y^i$. This chain of capitalist production can be ended by assuming that at some point of time, say $t=0$, the economy is provided with certain amounts of stock of commodities, $\bar{x}$, which have been saved and accumulated by people in the society in the age of the capitalist mode of production having not yet prevailed.

Using this stock, $\bar{x}$, referred to as primitive accumulation by Marx, as capital for further production, the capitalist mode of production may commence in period 0. Thus the explanation of capitalist production cannot be self-contained. It must first assume the existence of primitive non-capitalistic accumulation in an age long past. Secondly the movement of the availability of the ultimate factors of production through periods is mainly autonomous, although, to some of them, we may give an endogenous explanation to their dynamics, as Ricardo and other classical economists have done to labour. Then the analysis is divided into two parts: the first is concerned with the problem of how the capitalist mode of production can emerge from a non-capitalist (say, medieval) world, while the second with the problem of reproducibility of the capitalist way of production after the capitalist system has been established.

Before being involved in the discussion of these problems, let me make a few remarks on how I regard them. As I have already stated, capitalists are individuals who have financial means or real stocks of commodities. Among these the latter, that is, the capitalists who own $\bar{x}$ in period 0, are essential for the emergence of capitalist production. In fact, no production can be made if $\bar{x} = 0$. On the other hand, the capitalists of the first type, i.e., those having financial means only, may be dispensable; and moreover, the capitalist regime does not come out from them if $\bar{x} = 0$. We show their dispensability by discussing below how the capitalist production can be carried out in a moneyless economy with $\bar{x} \neq 0$. Secondly, though I have called the pre-capitalist stage 'medieval', I have no intention to use the following argument in order to explain the process of historical transformation of the medieval economy to the capitalist one. It is, of course, impossible that at one particular period $t = 0$ firms suddenly become profit maximizers, consumers utility maximizers and fully developed competitive markets formed, as is being assumed in the following. The actual historical process was always gradual and can be explained by making appropriate modifications to the analysis below. But it provides a theoretical base on which we show that the capitalist production can start if $\bar{x} > 0$ at the end of the pre-capitalist stage.

Let us now begin with the first problem. We may first ask how the initial stock of commodities $\bar{x}$ at $t = 0$ enables entrepreneurs to buy commodities which are useful as inputs for production. As has been said, the stock $\bar{x}$ is distributed among a number of individuals (capitalists). A capitalist k evaluates the stock of commodities he owns in terms of market price p_0 and contributes the amount being equal to $p_0 \bar{x}^k$ to a firm or a number of firms.

In proportion to the amount being contributed, capitalists issue to each firm tickets assuring that their holders may, in exchange for them, obtain the equivalent amount of $\bar{x}$ from capitalists (such a device seems necessary, because we are concerned with a moneyless, real economy). On the other hand, as a counterpresentation, each firm issues to the capitalist k a number of certificates assuring that the holder of the certificates will receive, at the commencement of each subsequent period, a certain amount of dividends in proportion to the number of certificates he holds. The certificate issued by the firm i is called its shares or equities, and the total amount of shares of the firm i held by the capitalist k is denoted by s^{ki}. Thus, an individual capitalist k having the stock of commodities $\bar{x}^k$ will get the shares s^{ki} from various firms i amounting to $p_0\bar{x}^k$ in total; so we obtain:

$$\sum_i s^{ki} = p_0\bar{x}^k \text{ for each } k. \tag{2.2}$$

On the other hand, by issuing the shares, an individual firm i acquires the purchasing power (or tickets) of the amount $\sum_k s^{ki}$ which is paid out for obtaining the factors of production in order to make input y_0^i in period 0. Denoting the vector of input prices in period 0 as f_0, we get:

$$\sum_k s^{ki} = q_0 y_0^i \text{ for each } i. \tag{2.3}$$

Therefore:

$$p_0\bar{x} = q_0 y_0 \tag{2.4}$$

because $\bar{x} = \sum_k \bar{x}^k$ and $y_0 = \sum_i y_0^i$. Capitalists determine s^{ki} so as to maximize their income obtained from their shareholding, $\sum_i s^{ki}$, while firms determine y_0^i, so as to maximize their profits. In the following we denote the value of s^{ki} in period 0 by s_0^{ki}.

Let us first be concerned with profit maximization. We put the production function (2.1) in the following form:

$$f^i(\xi_1^i, y_0^i, er^i) = 0, \tag{2.1'}$$

where the date of outputs being produced and the date of inputs being made are explicitly designated by subscripts, 1 and 0, attached to the symbols representing output and input vectors, respectively. That is to say, outputs ξ are available in period 1, while inputs y are made in period 0. Also, it is noted that expected outputs are distinguished from actual outputs by using

ξ for the former and x for the latter. Subject to (2.1'), firm i maximizes expected profits:

$$\pi_0 \xi_1^i - q_0 y_0^i \qquad (2.5)$$

where π_0 represents the expected prices, at date 0, of the outputs ξ, to be made available at date 1. Note that π_0 and ξ_1 are vectors (row and column vectors, respectively) because joint production is allowed for. Furthermore, it is noted that, since expectations are not always correct, expected price π_0 may be different from the actual market price p_1 to be established on date 1. π_0 is formed subjectively on the basis of the information concerning current prices p_0, so that it depends on p_0 but may differ among the firms. Where p_0 and q_0 are given, so are π_0 and q_0 in the profit function (2.5), and solutions to the maximization problem can be written as:

$$\xi_1^i = \xi_1^i(p_0, q_0) \text{ and } y_0^i = y_0^i(p_0, q_0).$$

We may then calculate the expected rate of profit per unit of the value of capital invested, that is, $(\pi_0 \xi_1^i - q_0 y_0^i)/q_0 y_0^i$, for each firm i.

Comparing these rates among all possible firms, capitalists are only interested in those firms whose rates are the greatest. These may be referred to as top firms. To non-top firms, that is, those which would yield profits at a rate less than the greatest, capitalists do not supply any amount of the purchasing power they hold. Thus, for non-top firms we have $s^{ki} = 0$ for all k, while $s^{ki} \geqslant 0$ for top firms. Thus only top firms are realized and issue shares so as for (2.3) to be fulfilled. Top shares held by capitalists satisfy the distribution condition (2.2).

Next, we classify outputs into two categories, the first being the group of consumer goods and the second that of producer goods. Denoting outputs of the two groups by x' and x'' respectively, we have $x^T = (x'^T, x''^T)$, where T applied to a vector signifies its transpose, a row vector. For the initial stock of commodities in particular, we have:

$$\bar{x}^k = \begin{bmatrix} \bar{x}'^k \\ \bar{x}''^k \end{bmatrix}.$$

Similarly input vector y^i may be partitioned in the form:

$$y^i = \begin{bmatrix} y'^i \\ y''^i \end{bmatrix},$$

where y'^i is the vector of inputs of land and labour and y''^i the input vector of produced goods (i.e., various kinds of material, tools and machines). Household j can supply either land or labour or both.

Let $\bar{z}'^j$ be the initial endowments of land and labour of household j. It may withhold a part of the endowments which is denoted by z'^j. Then the total value of household j's supply of land and labour amounts to $q_0'(\bar{z}'^j - z'^j)$ which is spent on buying consumer goods. Obviously q_0' is the vector of prices of services of land and labour which is a subvector of q_0. We then have the budget constraint:

$$p_0'x'^j = q_0'(\bar{z}'^j - z'^j), \tag{2.6}$$

where x'^j stands for the demand for consumer goods of the household and p_0', a subvector of p_0, is the price vector of consumer goods. x'^j and z'^j are determined such that they maximize the utility $U^j(x'^j, z'^j)$ subject to the budget equation (2.6). We then obtain demand and reservation demand functions:

$$x_0^j = x_0^j(p_0', q_0') \text{ and } z_0^j = z_0^j(p_0', q_0')$$

respectively.

We shall now have three sets of market equilibrium conditions, the first establishing the equality between demand and supply for consumer goods, while the second and third are the conditions for producer goods, materials, tools, etc., and those for land and labour, respectively. They are written as:

$$\sum_k \bar{x}'^k = \sum_j x_0^j(p_0', q_0') \qquad \text{for consumer goods,} \tag{2.7}$$

$$\sum_k \bar{x}''^k = \sum_i y_0''^i(p_0, q_0) \qquad \text{for material, tools and machines,} \tag{2.8}$$

$$\sum_i y_0'^i(p_0, q_0) = \sum_j (\bar{z}'^j - z'^j(p_0', q_0')), \text{ for land and labour.} \tag{2.9}$$

Note that $p_0 = (p_0', p_0'')$ and $q_0 = (q_0', q_0'')$, where p_0'' denote the output prices of material, tools and machines, while q_0'' the input prices of them. We have $p_0'' = q_0''$ for material, but $p_0'' \neq q_0''$ for durable (repeatedly usable) capital goods (tools and machines). Throughout this chapter, for the sake of simplicity, durable capital goods are assumed to be entirely absent, so that $p_0'' = q_0''$ and, therefore, $q_0 = (q_0', p_0'')$. One of the prices, p_0 and q_0, is fixed at unity by normalization, so that the number of equations of (2.7), (2.8) and (2.9) exceeds the number of variables contained in them by 1. One of the equilibrium conditions, however, may be shown to follow from the rest because equations (2.4) and (2.6) are satisfied. It has been proved by such mathematical economists as Debreu, Arrow–Hahn, McKenzie, Nikaido and others that the system of equilibrium conditions, (2.7), (2.8) and (2.9), supplemented with (2.4) and (2.6), has a set of solutions.[7]

This procedure of eliminating one equation corresponds to the following circulation of goods and services between the firms and the individuals. First the firms use the purchasing power tickets which are obtained from the capitalists in exchange for the shares the firms issue, and buy, with them, the means of production and the services of land and labour in order to start production. The stock of means of production which capitalists hold are transferred to the firms (as equation (2.8) implies). In exchange for the services workers and landowners offer the firms pay them an equivalent amount of purchasing power (or tickets) as wages and rent (see (2.4), (2.8) and (2.9)). Being provided with this amount of purchasing power, workers and landowners are able to buy all of the existing amounts of consumer goods held by the capitalists (because of equations (2.6) and (2.7)). All the tickets issued by capitalists return to their pockets in this way; tickets are then abolished.

Thus the entire stock of capital $\bar{x}$ is transferred from the capitalists to the firms. The latter combine $\bar{x}$ with land and labour and carry out production. Outputs ξ_1 are expected to be produced, but actual outputs turn out to be as large as x_1. Without any stochastic disturbances ξ_1 equals x_1, of course, but they may differ from each other because we may always be provided with windfalls or suffer from unexpected sabotages. Capitalists have no longer any stock of commodities, all of which have been sold to the firms or the individuals. They instead have shares, while the firms own their outputs x_1 which they can sell. In period 1, capitalists, the owners of commodities in period 0, become shareholders and the firms, the original buyers of the physical means of production in period 0, turn out to be either their suppliers (the capital goods industry), or the producers and hence the suppliers of consumption goods forming the consumption goods industry.

3 Let us now be concerned with the second problem of how the capitalist economy established in period 0 in the way described above will work and

[7] See the books referred to in footnote 5 above. Especially see Arrow and Hahn, *General Competitive Analysis*, pp. 25–9. Also, M. Morishima, *The Economic Theory of Modern Society*, Cambridge University Press, 1976, chapter 6, may be useful for beginners.

It has been assumed in the text that the accumulation $\bar{x}$ from the past is entirely invested for future production. In the actual world, however, capitalists may sell only a part of $\bar{x}$ to firms, the rest being consumed by themselves in period 0. It is not difficult to extend our analysis to this more realistic case, as we may modify the capitalist k's budget equation to include, on its income side, the value of the part of the primitive accumulation $\bar{x}^k$ retained for consumption and remove the corresponding part from (2.4). Then what has been said in the above, *mutatis mutandis*, holds true; the obtained revised version of the system (2.7)–(2.9) determines price.

reproduce itself in later periods, 1, 2, . . . At the beginning of period 1 capitalist k has no longer the stock of commodities $\bar{x}^k$ which has all been sold to the firms or to the individuals. He has instead the shares s^{ki} of various firms i (which have been carried over from period 0) and is paid dividends upon them. If we may assume that the total amount of profits is entirely distributed among the shareholders, the expected rates of dividends may be considered to be equal for all shares because the expected rates of profits are equal through all firms. Expectations, however, are not always correct concerning prices as well as quantities produced. Thus we may have $p_1 \neq \pi_0$ and $x_1^i \neq \xi_1^i$; therefore $p_1 x_1^i - q_0 y_0^i \neq \pi_0 \xi_1^i - q_0 y_0^i$, which implies that the actual rate of dividends may be different from one share to another, in spite of the fact that the expected rates of profits are equalized.

Let r_1^i be the actual rate of dividend of the shares issued by the firm i. Since r_1^i depends on p_1 by virtue of the definition of the rate of dividend, r_1^i and p_1 are simultaneously determined at date 1. Capitalist k's dividend income amounts to $\sum_i r_1^i s_0^{ki}$ and he can sell his shares s_0^{ki} and buy shares from other shareholders in the market. His budget equation may be written:

$$p_1' x_1'^k + \sum_i \sum_h v_1^i s_1^{khi} = \sum_i v_1^i s_0^{ki} + \sum_i r_1^i s_0^{ki}, \qquad (2.10)$$

where $x_1'^k$ is the vector of capitalist k's demands for consumption goods, p_1' the vector of their prices, v_1^i the price of share i, and s_1^{khi} the amount of share i which k wants to buy from h. All of these are the quantities and prices at date 1. In (2.10) we implicitly assume that k does not buy any capital goods.

Let v_1 be the vector of current prices of shares and r_1 the vector of current rates of dividends, while v_1 and ρ_1 are the vectors of expected share prices and expected rates of dividends at date 1, respectively. Both $x_1'^k$ and s_1^{khi} depend on p_1', v_1, v_1, r_1, and ρ_1. Taking v_1 and ρ_1, as depending upon their respective current values, v_1 and r_1, and bearing in mind the fact that r_1^i depends on p_1, we may finally write:

$$x_1'^k = x_1'^k(p_1, v_1, s_0^k),$$
$$s_1^{khi} = s_1^{khi}(p_1, v_1, s_0^k),$$

where s_0^k represents the shareholding of k in period 0, that is his initial shareholding in period 1. Clearly in period 1 the firm i can sell its outputs.

Subtracting $q_0 y_0^i$ from the proceeds $p_1 x_1^i$, we obtain profits, $p_1 x_1^i - q_0 y_0^i$, which is distributed among shareholders, while the retained part, $q_0 y_0^i$, of the proceeds is used for buying inputs for reproduction and determines the level of the production activity in period 1. As the firm i keeps the same purchasing power $q_0 y_0$ as it had in the previous period, its budget equation may be written as:

$$q_0 y_0^i = q_1 y_1^i.$$

Maximizing its expected profits subject to the production function and the budget equation, the firm i determines its inputs and expected outputs in a similar way as described in the last section; we have:

$$\xi_2^i = \xi_2^i(p_1, q_1) \text{ and } y_1^i = y_1^i(p_1, q_1).$$

The firm i buys material, tools and machines, $y_1^{mi} = y_1^{mi}(p_1, q_1)$, from other firms, and services of land and labour, $y_1^{ti} = y_1^{ti}(p_1, q_1)$, from landowners and workers. It is needless to say that these output and input functions are subject to income effects as well as to substitution effects, because of maximization being constrained by the budget equation, or the financial constraint.

In this way, landowners and workers are supplied with purchasing power, which is, in total, equal to the amount that the firms have decided to spend on land and labour. In exchange for this, they must, of course, supply to the firms services of land and labour of the amounts $\sum_j (\bar{z}^{tj} - z_1^{tj}(p_1, q_1))$ which are equivalent in value to the total amount of the purchasing power they have received from the firms. They use their income to buy consumption goods and also can use it to buy shares. The budget equation of individual j (landowner or worker) may be written as:

$$p_1' x_1^{tj} + \sum_i v_1^i (\sum_k s_1^{jki}) = q_1'(\bar{z}^{tj} - z_1^{tj}) \qquad \text{for all } j, \qquad (2.11)$$

where x_1^{tj} is the vector of the individual j's demands for consumption goods and s^{jki} is the amount of shares of the firm i which j buys from capitalist k. Each individual j, as usual, maximizes his utility subject to this budget equation; we then have:

$$x_1^{tj} = x_1^{tj}(p_1', q_1', v_1), \quad z_1^{tj} = z_1^{tj}(p_1', q_1', v_1), \quad s_1^{jki} = s_1^{jki}(p_1', q_1', v_1).$$

In this way workers and landowners become shareholders. All shareholders are, of course, capitalists, and *vice versa*. Here is completed a transformation of capitalists as investors of the real capital $\bar{x}$ to capitalists as shareholders.

Equilibrium between supply and demand is described in terms of the following equations:

$$x_1' = \sum_k x_1^{tk}(p_1, v_1, s_0^k) + \sum_j x_1^{tj}(p_1', q_1', v_1) \qquad \text{for consumer goods} \quad (2.12)$$

$$x_1'' = \sum_i y_1''^i(p_1,q_1) \qquad \text{for material, tools and machines,} \quad (2.13)$$

$$\sum_i y_1'^i(p_1,q_1) = \sum_j (\bar{z}'^j - z_1'^j(p_1',q_1'v_1)) \qquad \text{for land and labour,} \quad (2.14)$$

$$\sum_k s_0^{ki} = \sum_k \sum_h s_1^{khi}(p_1, v_1, s_0^k) + \sum_j \sum_k s_1^{jki}(p_1',q_1',v_1) \qquad \begin{array}{l} \text{for shares of} \quad (2.15) \\ \text{each firm } i. \end{array}$$

On the left-hand side of each of the first two equations, outputs x_1' and x_1'' are yields from the production activities in period 0 and are, therefore, fixed in period 1. Similarly, in period 1, all s_0^k are constant since they are distributions of the shares in period 0. Remembering the assumption implicitly made, that is, that there are no durable capital goods, we have $p_1'' = q_1''$, that is to say, output prices are equal to input prices for all kinds of commodities used as material and non-durable tools. Prices p_1,q_1,v_1 are then all determined by equations (2.12)–(2.15). One of the prices may be fixed at 1, in order to normalize prices. It is evident that the existence of a set of equilibrium prices can be proved in the usual way by using the familiar method developed by Debreu, Arrow–Hahn and others.

The economy works in a similar way in period 2. But period 2 differs from period 1 in the following two points. First, those who will receive dividends at the beginning of period 2 are not those capitalists who have originally provided the firms with some amount of the purchasing power, but those workers and landowners who have bought shares in period 1 or the capitalists who still keep some increased or decreased amount of shares. This is because shares are the certificates which promise the holders of the shares that profits of the firms will be distributed among them at the beginning of each period, as long as they hold the shares. Secondly, they may sell the shares to someone else in period 2, if they want to do so. In this way, the shareholding is dispersed among individuals, and correspondingly the concept of capitalist is altered so as to mean shareholder. The analysis of the firms' profit-maximization behaviour and that of the individuals' utility-maximization behaviour, as has been made for period 1, would *mutatis mutandis* hold for period 2; we then get four equilibrum equations, similar to (2.12)–(2.15) with appropriate alterations, which determine equilibrium prices in period 2.

The position and role of shareholders are entirely obscure in Hicks' original model. As far as his mathematical formulation is concerned, nothing is stated explicitly about shareholders; it is even hinted that his firms are more or less like family businesses. In Debreu's book as well as the original paper by Arrow and Debreu, there are shares apparently but they are unfortunately assumed untradable; throughout the process of establishing equilibrium prices, the distribution of shares is assumed to remain unchanged among individuals.[8]

It is Arrow and Hahn who first discuss the problem of shares in the framework of general equilibrium in a serious way, but their analysis too is unfortunately still far from being satisfactory.[9] It is true that in their model of temporary equilibrium, the households' holding of shares is regarded as variable during the process of price formation. But in their model it is only the prices of the commodities (consumer and producer goods) plus bonds, but not the share prices, which can influence equilibrium being established. The model is constructed such that the final share allocation after the transactions does not affect the household budget constraint. The amount paid for obtaining some units of shares is recovered by the capitalized value of the stream of dividends which the acquired shares bring forth. This means that the individuals' budget equations are independent of transactions of shares; hence the demand for and supply of commodities and bonds are not influenced by the redistribution of shares.

This very restrictive form of the budget constraint is obtained because Arrow and Hahn have made the four assumptions stated below. First, in their model of temporary equilibrium, it is assumed that each individual j appraises each firm i in terms of its total value of profits. The activities of the firm in the future are evaluated in terms of expected prices and the expected profits in the future are discounted back to their current value by using the price of bonds as the discounting factor.[10] The total discounted value of profits of a particular firm i may differ from one individual to another, because individuals' expectations of prices are not uniform but may be diversified. Arrow and Hahn assume that shares are transacted such that they are held only by those individuals who appraise most highly the firm's performance over current and future periods (this is their second assumption). They also assume that dividends are paid, not for the shares held initially, but for those held finally after the transactions have been completed (their third assumption). Finally they assume that the initial endowment of bonds held by a household is precisely its anticipated volume of receipts in the future (the fourth assumption). All these together imply that the price of a share is equal to the capitalized value (or the discounted

[8] It would be worth mentioning in this place that G. La Volpe, before Hicks, has constructed a dynamic general equilibrium model in order to develop a temporary equilibrium theory. It is true that he, unlike Hicks, has explicitly taken account of the fact that profits are distributed among shareholders. But, unfortunately, his treatment is exactly the same as Arrow's and Debreu's. That is to say, shares exist but are untradable. See Guilio La Volpe, *Studi sulla teoria dell'equilibrio economico dinamico generale*, Napoli, 1936, p. 43.

[9] Arrow and Hahn, *General Competitive Analysis*, pp. 136–51.

[10] Note that Arrow and Hahn are concerned with a two-period world with current and one-future periods in perspective.

sum) of the stream of dividends per unit of a share and because of this the household budget constraints are made independent of the respective final share allocation. Obviously, this independence makes the analysis simple because it enables Arrow and Hahn to apply the previous Arrow–Debreu method of establishing static equilibrium, which assumes no change in the allocation of shares, to the problem of the existence of temporary equilibrium. It is indeed a formulation which is convenient from the point of view of analysis.

However, it must be noted that the above equality between the share price and dividends – though it is not explicitly stated by Arrow and Hahn, it must be derived from the assumptions they make – may be considered to hold in the long-run equilibrium but should not be regarded as a condition for temporary equilibrium as it is done by them. In the short run, the price of a share usually fluctuates by a large margin according to whether the demand for the share exceeds or falls short of its supply. It may deviate greatly from the capitalized value of the dividend stream in the same way as the market price of a (flexprice) commodity does not settle, in the short run, at its natural or production-cost price. In the analysis of temporary equilibrium the condition of equality between the share price and the capitalized value of dividends has to be removed and replaced by the equality between the demand for and supply of shares, which is absent in the Arrow–Hahn economy.

Demand and supply functions are then derived as functions of the prices of shares and their expectations; and the prices will be determined in the share market at a point where the demand and supply are equated. Thus for each share an equation corresponding to our (2.15) above is obtained. This is very natural, because the share market is a typical example of perfect competition, to which the demand–supply analysis of the Walrasian type is perfectly applicable. The fact that the excess demand functions of shares has no place in the Arrow–Hahn model should be taken as revealing its peculiarity, though they give a logical justification for the absence by presenting the four assumptions above.

Also it is noticed that the model's prospects extend to only two periods, present and future. Each period is uniform; no change is observed within any period. Accordingly, the distribution of shares may change only once at the end of the present period, while it is kept constant throughout the future. This implies the impossibility of the model to discuss the effects upon the present prices of commodities and bonds of transactions of shares or other commodities to be carried out in a future period. The number of periods the model deals with should, therefore, be at least as large as three, as we see in the model presented in the final section of this chapter, the length of the planning period v of the economic agent being at least two, since week 0 denotes the current period, and weeks 1, 2, . . . v the future periods, so that $v \geqq 2$ means that the model is concerned with at least three weeks.

Finally, it is added that whilst transactions of existing (old) shares between individuals have no direct effect upon the financial position of the firm which had issued the shares, they may have significant indirect effects on it because shareholders can cast votes in proportion to the numbers of shares they hold, in the firm's annual general meeting of the shareholders. Where either a shareholder himself has more than 50% of the shares, or he forms a coalition with other major shareholders, he may be able to put the firm under his control; he may even be able to replace the president and executives of the firm by those he wants to appoint. This is a matter of acquisition and merger, and transactions in the actual share market evidently include those which are made with the intention of taking over a firm. In this book we are not concerned with this problem at all.

4 Unfortunately I have to point out one more aspect of the model which is also found to be unsatisfactory. It is, however, not an aspect peculiar to Arrow's and Hahn's model; our model developed in the earlier part of the last section too may be criticized in a similar way. In these models it is, in fact, assumed that only those shares which have been issued in the past are traded in the current period. This means that no firm can be newly established and no existing firm can make any increase in shares. This would be a serious shortcoming because it would imply that no new equity-financing investment is made in the current period. Where there is no new firm, or where no firm issues new shares, the problem of innovations would be left undiscussed, and the theory of the firm would only be concerned with the routine aspects of production. Then the producer would not be an entrepreneur; in the worst case, a manager or even a foreman may be sufficient as the head of the firm. The analysis is not dynamic in Schumpeter's sense, as will be seen later. It cannot discuss creation and financing of new firms, so that the model must be extended so as to accommodate new shares.

It is, of course, true that conventional long-run equilibrium theory does deal with the problem of new firms' entry into the industry. But it is not concerned with the problem of how the firms are provided with the initial purchasing power which is necessary for establishing facilities for production and for employing workers and staff members for the start. The long-run theory simply regards the number of active firms as a variable of the model and concludes that there are n' new entrants into the industry where the equilibrium value of the number exceeds the existing number n by n'. In spite of their discussion of the subject of bankruptcy to which they have devoted so many pages, it is disappointing that Arrow and Hahn do not pay much attention to its counterpart, that is the problem of formation (or birth) of new firms. It is indeed a weak point of neoclassical economists that they have traditionally been holding aloof from the problem of analysing how potential entrepreneurs are enabled to make an actual start in their businesses.

This is the problem which Schumpeter has proposed. While his book *Entwicklung*, originally published in German in 1912 and translated into English in 1934,[11] has put the problem in terms of languages of the Walrasian equilibrium theory, its influence upon the mainline general equilibrium theorists has remained minimal for a long time. Schumpeter's name is not found in the index of Hicks' *Value and Capital* or that of Varian's *Microeconomic Analysis*, while he is referred to twice in Malinvaud's *Microeconomic Theory* and once in Arrow's and Hahn's *General Competitive Analysis*. It is further noted that one of Malinvaud's references and that of Arrow's and Hahn's are not made to Schumpeter's *Entwicklung* but to his *History of Economic Analysis*. Even the remaining, exceptional discussion of Schumpeter by Malinvaud is merely less than half a page long.

On the other hand, it seems that the position of Schumpeter is not correctly appreciated even by the so-called Schumpeterians. They emphasize the concepts of 'entrepreneurs', 'entrepreneurial profits', 'innovations' and 'new combinations' as the key words of his economics. More precisely speaking, however, Schumpeter himself is interested in how innovations are financed and realized, rather than how innovations come into the entrepreneurs' minds. As is well known, during his academic life he had an interlude of political and business life; served, *inter alia*, as minister of finance of the Austrian Republic and as president of an Austrian bank. These services are not entirely unrelated to his fundamental academic view that credit, or the creation of credit, serves industrial development, which has been discussed in detail in his 1912 *Entwicklung*, much earlier than his ministerial appointment in 1919. Since the beginning of his academic career, he was a monetary economist, rather than a specialist of industrial economics. He saw that the entrepreneur needs to get purchasing power 'in order to produce at all, to be able to carry out his new combinations, to become an entrepreneur. He can only become an entrepreneur by previously becoming a debtor.'[12] Thus *Entwicklung* is an investigation of the functions of bankers in the formation of new enterprises, not just an advocacy of a new vision which emphasizes the importance of innovations in economic development. In fact, he developed a *monetary* theory of the

[11] J. A. Schumpeter, *Theorie der Wirtschaftlichen Entwicklung*, 1912; 2nd rev. edn., 1926; English trans., *The Theory of Economic Development*, Harvard University Press, 1934.

[12] Schumpeter, *The Theory*, p. 102.

firm in contrast with the conventional *technological* theory of production. Neo-classical economists base their theory on the technical premise of the production function, while 'Schumpeterians' see innovations as caused by technical progress brought about by science, or technical improvements in marketing or management. Schumpeter himself concentrated his interest on the investigation of the bankers' midwife role in giving birth to enterprises.[13]

In order to start his business, the new entrepreneur needs to be given a certain amount of purchasing power. Otherwise he cannot get and combine the services of land and labour and the other means of production in his own way. In order for them to be legally transferred to his new firm from previous employments, he needs purchasing power. As has been discussed in section 2 above, society must have some amount of primitively accumulated stock of the means of production when it makes a new start in capitalist production; but once it has got going, new enterprises can legally poach them from other firms by making proper payments to them.

How can they obtain the purchasing power? There is no unique answer to this question, except saying that it depends. The answer for one country may vary from another because the financial market may be organized differently between countries. While Schumpeter naturally assumes the German/Austrian banking system, we shall examine in this section below, by assuming the British financial system, how a firm may acquire purchasing power by issuing new shares. Let us now suppose that in period $t = 2$ a firm called m is to be newly established. Its production function is written, as before, in the form:

$$f^m(\xi_3^m, y_2^m, er^m) = 0,$$

subject to which the firm's profits, $\pi_2 \, \xi_3^m - q_2 y_2^m$, is maximized, where π_2 stands for the expected prices at date 2 of the outputs ξ_3^m which will be produced and sold at date 3; π_2 is assumed to be a function of the current prices p_2 at date 2. It is then obvious that the maximization yields:

$$\xi_3^m = \xi_3^m(p_2, q_2) \text{ and } y_2^m = y_2^m(p_2, q_2).$$

Then the firm m needs the purchasing power of the amount, $q_2 y_2^m$, which is raised from among individuals; we denote the firm m's share issued to individual j by s^{jm}, so that:

$$\sum_j s^{jm} = q_2 y_2^m(p_2, q_2). \tag{2.16}$$

In order to make this contribution, individual j must reduce his expenditure by the same amount. Therefore, his demand for other shares, as well as his

---

[13] Ibid.

demand for consumer goods, will diminish; his supply of the services of land and labour may also be affected, though the increase in the supply thus created may be supposed to be negligible. In the factor markets, on the other hand, the appearance of the firm m will give rise to an increase in the demand for factors. This will have repercussions on consumer goods; the newly employed workers of the firm m and the landowners who lend land to it appear in the market to buy consumer goods. This increase in demand for consumer goods will offset a decrease in the demand of those individuals who become shareholders in the new firm m, to a considerable degree. On the whole, there would be no significant net decrease in the demand for consumer goods; it would even be highly probable that it will in fact be increased. On the other hand, there will be an increase in demand in factor markets, with a decrease in share markets.

Consequently we may say that the prices q_2 of the factors of production will be increased, while the prices v_2 of shares will be reduced. As for the prices p_2 of consumer goods it is possible that they, or some of them, will be reduced, but the reduction, if any at all, is probably insignificant, while there may be other prices which are raised. Thus an inflation of prices, especially those of the factors of production, inevitably follows whenever a new firm enters into the economy. It is not surprising to see this because the new firm carries out production by outbidding old producers and drawing the necessary means of production from them. It must also be noted that the contribution equation (2.16) for the new firm m does hold only where the expected rate of dividend of m is higher than the corresponding rates of the old existing firms. Otherwise no individual wants to acquire the shares of the new firm by giving up old shares or consumer goods; hence $s^{jm} = 0$ for all j. Moreover, expectations are subjective; it may be possible that only a few individuals expect a sufficiently high rate of dividend for the firm m while all others do not. Then the firm has to start its business with a very small amount of the capital contributed. In this case, it has to restrict its activities within a severe budget constraint; still it will start its business if the entrepreneur himself believes that the activity at the reduced scale which meets the budget condition will yield profits at a rate more than the rates of the existing firms.

Finally, some comments on Schumpeter and Schumpeterians. First, on him it may be pointed out that the idea which is usually ascribed to Schumpeter has already been advocated by some economists before him. Ricardo, for example, wrote:

He, indeed, who made the discovery of the machine, or who first usefully applied it, would enjoy an additional advantage, by making great profits for a time; but, in proportion as the machine came into general use, the price of the commodity produce, would, from the effects of competition, sink to its cost of production, when the capitalist would get the same money profits as before . . .[14]

This is compared with the following passages from Schumpeter's *Entwicklung*; it will be also found that the latter is nothing else but an expounding or an elaboration of the former.

If anyone in an economic system in which the textile industry produces only with hand labour sees the possibility of founding a business which uses power-looms . . . If a worker with such a loom is now in a position to produce six times as much as a hand-worker in a day, it is obvious that . . . the business must yield a surplus over costs . . . [Then] new businesses are continually arising under the impulse of the alluring profit. A complete reorganisation of the industry occurs, with its increases in production, its competitive struggle, its supersession of obsolete businesses, its possible dismissal of workers, and so forth. . . . [T]he final result must be a new equilibrium position, in which, with new data, the law of cost again rules . . . Consequently, the surplus of the entrepreneur in question and of his immediate followers disappears.[15]

On the other hand, on the provision of purchasing power to the new firm Walras wrote:

The diversion of productive services from enterprises that are losing money to profitable enterprises take place in various ways, the most important being through credit operations . . .[16]

It is seen, however, that Schumpeter too wrote to exactly the same effect:

the problem of detaching productive means (already employed somewhere) from the circular flow and allotting them to new combinations. This is done by credit . . .[17]

We may now conclude from these as follows. Not only can the same analysis as Schumpeter made of the effects of imitation of innovations be found clearly in Ricardo but also Walras distinguished 'technical progress' from 'economic progress'; while the latter is obtained where factors of production are substituted with no change in the production function, the former may be interpreted as including Schumpeter's innovation.[18] Moreover, the significance of the role of credit in realizing innovation, which is stressed by Schumpeter, had already been pointed out by Walras. Consequently we may say that to ascribe the theory of innovations and economic development entirely to Schumpeter, as is usually made by Schumpeterians, might be rather unfair to his predecessors from whom he might have got ideas. There was indeed a continuous, smooth flow of

[14] D. Ricardo, *The Principles of Political Economy and Taxation*, Cambridge University Press, 1953, p. 387.   [15] Schumpeter, *The Theory*, pp. 129–32.
[16] Leon Walras, *Elements of Pure Economics*, Richard D. Irwin, 1954, p. 380.
[17] Schumpeter, *The Theory*, p. 71.   [18] Walras, *Elements*, p. 386.

thought from them to him, though we must acknowledge that it is Schumpeter who compiled the theory with materials from scattered sources, in a comprehensive way.

Secondly, it is said that during recent years there has been a revival of Schumpeterianism, or a Schumpeterian renaissance. An academic society named after him has been established, and many writers have been concerned with explaining the rise and decline of industries and nations from the point of view of the technical inventions adopted, or innovations. For example, Dasgupta and Stiglitz have explored the factors that influence the relative growth or decline of industries and pointed to new inventions as the most important explanatory factors.[19] They have observed the fact that innovations involve costs but have ignored the problem of how entrepreneurs finance them. This is merely an example. Most recent theoretical works on innovations are of a similar nature: they discuss the economic impact of technological changes without asking how these are materialized in spite of the high costs for introducing new methods of production. In ignoring this crucial problem of financing innovations, the neoclassical theory of innovations by contemporary economists may be said to be non-Schumpeterian. Of course it is true that there are papers which have been concerned with the monetary aspects of technological development.[20] Although these provide important information on economic theory, they themselves are not analytical, so that general equilibrium theory cannot accommodate them as instruments, at least in their present forms.

5 So far I have assumed that it is impossible for new firms to acquire purchasing power, except when they issue shares. As I have stated before, however, there are alternative ways of securing the power, in order to buy the necessary means of production. First of all, the firms may be owners of the means of production themselves; secondly, they may have money or, thirdly, they may borrow money by issuing or selling the bonds. The implications of these ways of financing innovations have to be made clear. There is another aspect of the production model in this chapter which is worth re-examination. That is the implicit assumption that the factors of production which are bought in the current period are automatically put

[19] P. Dasgupta and J. Stiglitz, 'Entry, Innovation, Exit', *European Economic Review*, vol. 15, 1981, pp. 137–58. Also see G. Eliasson, 'Schumpeterian Innovation, Market Structure, and the Stability of Industrial Development', in H. Hanusch (ed.), *Evolutionary Economics: Applications of Schumpeter's Ideas*, Cambridge University Press, 1988, and the papers referred to by him.
[20] See, for example, E. Santarelli, 'Financial and Technological Innovations during the Phases of Capitalist Development', in M.Di Matteo, R. M. Goodwin and A. Vercelli (eds.), *Technological and Social Factors in Long Term Fluctuations*, Lecture Notes in Economics and Mathematical Systems, Springer-Verlag, 1989.

into the process of production without delay, while the current outputs are sold as soon as they are produced. Thus the conditions of input = demand and output = supply hold for factors of production and commodities produced, respectively. There is no doubt that these are stringent and unnecessary conditions. For the study of capital accumulation of firms it is necessary to discuss how a firm's input–output plan and its demand–supply plan may diverge from each other; it is, in fact, seen that the difference between these two plans will give the plan of accumulation of stocks of capital goods and inventories of products and materials.

I worked on these points a long time ago. In my *Dogakuteki Keizai Riron* (*DKR* in the following) I have been concerned with an economy, in which money and securities (of loan of one period) are present but no shares can be issued. Secondly, although the book (which is my first work) is written along the lines of Hicks' *Value and Capital* and discusses the dynamic movement of temporary general equilibrium, I try and develop, in the part where the firm's behaviour is discussed, a theory which distinguishes the firm's input–output plan from its demand–supply plan, so as to make its accumulation plan explicit. Nevertheless, it may still be considered to be very Hicksian, because, as will become clear soon, I have used the same production function as he used in his short-period, dynamic model. Although it is commonly used by many contemporary writers, I now regard it as unsatisfactory. Removal of such a neo-classical production function is one of the main undertakings of this book, and in order to enhance the understanding of the characteristics of the main model of the present volume a relevant section on *DKR* is reproduced as follows:[21]

Firm's planning

It must first be noted that firms, unlike households, have two sets of planning; demand and supply planning and production planning. Firms will supply their products, consumption goods or capital goods, and demand producers' goods, primary factors of production or capital goods. They will issue securities and redeem them. Let firm A's supply of good i in week ι be denoted by $y_{i\iota}$ and its demand for good j by $x_{j\iota}$. Regarding supply as negative demand and putting $y_{i\iota} = -x_{i\iota}$, then A's demand and supply plan will be described in terms of x's. However, firm A will not necessarily produce the same amount as supply $y_{i\iota}$ in week ι, and put in production the same amount as demand $x_{j\iota}$ in week ι. Denoting output of good i and input of good j in week ι by $x'_{i\iota}$ and $y'_{j\iota}$ respectively and regarding input as negative

[21] M. Morishima, *Dogakuteki Keizai Riron*, pp. 21–30 of the original Japanese version.

output so that $y'_{j_t} = -x'_{j_t}$ there may be a discrepancy between A's production plan (described in x'_{i_t}) and its demand and supply plan (in x_{i_t}). An excess of output over supply gives an increment in the stock of that product and an excess of demand over input gives an increment of the stock of the producer's goods. Writing the stock of good i in week ι as x''_{i_t} we have:

(a) $\qquad x'_{i_t} - y_{i_t} \equiv x''_{i_t} - x''_{i_t-1}$

for product i and:

(b) $\qquad x_{j_t} - y'_{j_t} \equiv x''_{j_t} - x''_{j_t-1}$

for the producer's good j. Considering the definition $y = -x$ both (a) and (b) can be put in the same form:

(c) $\qquad x_{i_t} + x'_{i_t} \equiv x''_{i_t} - x''_{i_t-1} \qquad (i = 2, \ldots, n)$.

This gives relationships connecting the demand and supply planning and the production plan. As A's initial stocks for week 0, $x''_{i,-1} \equiv \bar{x}_{i0}$, are given, we can derive a stock plan from its demand and supply plan and its production plan. These three plans are not independent; one of them is derived from the others.

In determining the values of the items of plans for demand, supply and production, firm A takes into account the following conditions. The first condition is the relationship (c) mentioned above and the second is the condition of technical limitations on production. If all inputs of producers' goods and all outputs except the output of good i in week ι, x'_{i_t}, are specified, then the maximum value which is technically feasible for this remaining output, x'_{i_t}, will be technically determined. Conversely, if all outputs for every week are given and all inputs except the one for good j in week ι, i.e., y'_{j_t}, are given then the minimum value of this remaining input y'_{j_t} which is required will be technically determined. These technical limitations may be mathematically translated into the language of implicit functions. We assume that there exists an implicit function of the sort:

(d) $\qquad f(x'_{20'}, x'_{30'} \ldots, x'_{n0}, x'_{21}, \ldots, x'_{nv}) = 0,$

which is called the production function or production technique function.

We have thus assumed that the technical limitations on production can be expressed by a single production function but in reality technical conditions are so complicated that they can hardly be described by a single function, e.g., it may be conceivable that, for each ι, outputs in week ι are independent of those in the subsequent weeks $\iota + 1, \iota + 2, \ldots$ and depend on inputs in some preceding weeks only. Generally speaking technical limitations can only be described by a number of implicit functions but not

by any single one. However as a first approximation to reality we have
accepted our present assumption which would enable us to put our analysis
of the firm in a simple and clear form.

Next we must explain the concept of profit which we use in the following
analysis. After retaining some amount of money, say k_ι from firm A's
proceeds in week ι the rest will be distributed among the firm's shareholders
and executives as dividends or bonuses. This may be called the profit or the
net income of the firm. The amount k_ι will be spent by A on producers'
goods, etc. in week ι and may be called the cost which A incurs in week ι.
Representing the profit in week ι by R_ι we have the definitional relationship:

(e) $R_\iota = -\sum p_{i\iota} x_{i\iota} - k_\iota,$

where the summation, $\sum$, is taken only over all products which A supplies,
excluding producers' goods which A demands. Discounting R_ι $(\iota = 1, 2, \ldots, v)$
by the ratio:

$$\beta_\iota = \frac{1}{(1+r_0)(1+r_1)\ldots(1+r_{\iota-1})},$$

respectively, and summing up, we obtain:

(f) $V = \sum_0^v \beta_\iota R_\iota,$

which is, following Hicks, called the capitalized value of the stream of
profits.

In week ι firm A has purchasing power amounting to:

$$x_{0,\iota-1} + (1+r_{\iota-1})x_{1,\iota-1} + k_\iota,$$

where $x_{0,\iota-1}$ and $x_{1,\iota-1}$ are the amounts of cash and securities, respectively,
which A holds in week $\iota - 1$. With that sum A buys some amounts of factors
of production in the market and carries forward cash of the amount $x_{0\iota}$ to
the following week. If it remains a positive residual then the firm will make
loans $(x_{1\iota} > 0)$; otherwise it will borrow the necessary amount (i.e., $x_{1\iota} < 0$).
Therefore A's plan must satisfy the following $v + 1$ budget equations:

(g) $x_{0,\iota-1} + (1+r_{\iota-1})x_{1,\iota-1} + k_\iota = x_{0\iota} + x_{1\iota} + \sum p_{i\iota} x_{i\iota}$ $\iota = 0, 1 \ldots, v,$

where the summation $\sum$ is taken only over all producers' goods which A
demands, excluding products which it supplies. It is clear that k_ι has a
character of working capital. The budget equations are the third
constraints which are imposed on A.

Finally, we explain what I call the liquidity function. As was pointed out
by Keynes, we can receive potential conveniences or safeties if we hold some
amounts of assets and maintain the right of disposing of them at our own

will. For example, an unexpected difficulty may occur in carrying out some trade; in that case, the greater the cash balances or the quantity of securities we hold, the more easily we can evade the difficulty. Firms which have big stocks of producers' goods can continue their production relatively easily and smoothly even if the supply of these producers' goods diminishes. The adaptability of firms to unforeseen accidents is closely related to their cash balances, holding of securities and inventories. It is also related to prices, interest rates and their expected values; in fact it is obvious that cash of £1,000 at price level 1 and the same amount of cash at price level 100 give different adaptabilities to firms. Therefore, we may assume that the adaptability of a firm to unforeseen events depends on:

$$X = (x_{00}, x_{10}, x_{01}, \ldots, x_{1v}, x''_{20}, \ldots x'_{nv}, p_{20}, \ldots, p_{nv}, r_0, \ldots, r_{v-1}).$$

We assume that firm A can compare any two X's in the adaptabilities these X's provide to A, and determine indices Φ so that:
  (i) $\Phi(X^0) < \Phi(X^1)$, if X^0 gives less adaptability than X^1,
 (ii) $\Phi(X^0) = \Phi(X^1)$, if they give the same adaptability,
(iii) $\Phi(X^0) > \Phi(X^1)$, if X^0 gives more adaptability then X^1.
The function $\Phi(X)$ is called A's liquidity function. As is seen below, A will keep Φ at a certain fixed level, Φ^0, so that:

(h) $\phi^0 = \phi(X)$.

In determining demand and supply plans and production plans over $v + 1$ weeks from week 0 to week v, firm A maximizes profits over the production plan period rather than profits in a particular week. In other words, A will maximize the capitalized value of the stream of profits (f). A will, at the same time, take its liquidity position into account. It should not be left in a position of no adaptability to unforeseen events; it should keep some degree of adaptability which is determined by the type of entrepreneur. It is a principle of the firm's planning to maximize the capitalized value of the stream of profits subject to the condition that the value of the liquidity function be as large as a given level, Φ^0. Thus, in maximizing their profits, firms always pay consideration to the safety of their business.

   In addition to that liquidity condition (h) A must consider conditions (c), (d), and (g). Then the problem is mathematically one of conditional maximization of the capitalized value of profits.

6 The above is an excerpt from the *DKR*. In this formulation of the theory of the firm, we usually assume a well-behaved production function $f(\ldots) = 0$, or its set-theoretical equivalent. It is assumed that not only contemporary but also intertemporal inputs or outputs are substitutable for each other. We may then substitute inputs y'_τ in a particular week τ in the

future for inputs in all other weeks and similarly outputs x_0' in the current week for all outputs in the future, where y_τ' stands for the input vector in τ and x_0' for the output vector in 0. The feasible input–output plan satisfying (d) may be transformed, by making the substitutions specified above, into output and input streams $(x_0', 0, \ldots, 0)$ and $(0, \ldots, y_\tau', \ldots, 0)$ satisfying:

(d') $f(x_0', 0, \ldots, 0; 0, \ldots, y_\tau', \ldots, 0) = 0$,

as I have already stated in the previous chapter. Evidently, this means a negative production lag; in addition τ may take on any positive number, so that the lag is arbitrary. If this were possible, the firm would postpone inputs as much as possible and input y' would only be made at the end of the production plan, that is $\tau = v$.

In order to assure that this should not happen, the dynamic production function needs further specifications. Especially, (d') ignores the stoppability of production activity; in fact, if this feasible production process is stoppable at the end of each week, then $(x_0';0)$, $(x_0', 0; 0, 0)$ and so on should all be feasible. These sequences evidently contradict the assumption of no land of Cockaigne; especially the first one obviously denies the usual static version of the assumption. This means that substitutions between outputs and those between inputs have to be locally limited within a certain domain; we must precisely define the feasibility region only in which substitutions, temporal or intertemporal, are possible. This is a very difficult and almost impossible task. In the following, therefore, instead of being troubled with this problem, we shall take an entirely different approach, that is the process analysis advocated by von Neumann and Georgescu-Roegen.[22]

Our final comment is on expectations. Evidently, prices for weeks, 1, 2, . . . are not actual prices but merely expected ones; similarly for the rate of interest. As Hicks himself stated clearly and I repeated almost the same argument in *DKR*, the expectations concerning prices, like all other expectations, are neither precise nor definite and are subject to some probability distributions. As for the price of a commodity at a certain specific point of time in the future, individuals or firms expect not a single value but a number of values as possibilities. They will judge one of these values as most probable and other expected values as less probable. It would be generally true, as the theory of portfolio selection developed after *DKR* shows, that not only most probable values of expected prices but also their probability distributions have significance in the individual's or the firm's decision-making. That is to say that even though the most probable

---

[22] N. Georgescu-Roegen, 'Production Process and Dynamic Economics', in M. Baranzini and R. Scazzieri (eds.), *The Economic Theory of Structure and Change*, Cambridge University Press, 1990, pp. 198–226. Also see his other works listed in the reference of the paper above.

expected prices remain unchanged, the decision may be affected if the probability distribution of a certain price is changed. But I shall confine myself to the case of precise expectations throughout the following as I have done in *DKR*. Of course we all know the theory of endogenous formation of expectations, such as rational expectation theory which has been developed after the publication of *DKR*. But I do not want to complicate general equilibrium theory too much by introducing such a theory of expectations into it.

3   Production possibility set

1 The conventional description of a production possibility set or production function is obscure and unsatisfactory, if it is applied to dynamics. Its original function is for static analysis. It cannot precisely describe series of events which happen during the process of production. Production of any commodity may be stopped at any stage of execution. Such a truncated production resulting in intermediate products and more or less worn-out machines and equipment may itself form a complete activity for which an independent firm may be established which aims to produce intermediate products as its final products and sells them to other firms as parts of their products. For example, in the case of motorcar producing companies, the ratio of parts produced by other companies is high (over 70% of the total production of motorcars) in Japan, while considerably lower (40–50%) in the USA. It is rather difficult, though not impossible,[1] to deal with this problem within the conventional framework of production functions or possibility sets.

In relation to the production possibility set there are three time elements. They are the production time of the commodity, the construction time of a production possibility set and the lifetime of capital goods. First the production time consists of the time needed to fill up the pipeline and the time it takes to produce one unit of a commodity after the pipeline to produce that commodity has been entirely filled up. The latter period of

---

[1] Leontief was once concerned with internal structures of production and finds that a production function may be *separable*, so that it may be put in the form: $x = f(g(y, \ldots, y_m), y_{m+1}, \ldots, y_n)$. (See W. W. Leontief, 'Introduction to a Theory of the Internal Structure of Functional Relationships', *Econometrica*, vol. 17, 1950, pp. 361–73.) The subfunction g may be interpreted as producing parts z. We may conceive of two types of economy, one consisting of vertically integrated large firms with production function f only, while the other being separated into main firms and parts firms which have production functions $x = f(z, y_{m+1}, \ldots, y_n)$ and $z = g(y_1, \ldots, y_m)$, respectively. They are not equivalent, especially in the case of the market of the product x being monopolistic and the market of z, if it exists, being competitive. The production of the parts z will, in fact, not be efficient in the vertically integrated economy, because the monopoly affects the production of both x and z, while it is efficient in the horizontally disintegrated economy, because of competition among factories producing z.

time is surprisingly short for a number of commodities, for which the modern conveyor belt system of production is adopted. It takes a matter of seconds, or minutes at most, where the final stage of production of books, TV sets, motorcars, etc., is concerned. Before reaching the final stage of the production pipeline intermediate products must go through process or processes for which it takes considerable time, say, the subediting and type-setting processes in the case of the production of books. Moreover, the period for constructing production facilities is much longer and easily comes up to the order of years. The firm must first buy the site for the new factory and then build buildings for the works. After having carried in machines the firm finally is ready to fill up the pipeline of production. Thus the total production period is the sum of the construction period, the period needed for filling up the pipeline and the final period required for bringing intermediate products at the exit of the pipeline to completed products.[2] We refer to the sum of the last two as the production period as distinguished from the *total* production period which includes the construction period. Where machines are not able to be obtained from the market and have to be produced by the firm, the time which is necessary for their production should be included in the construction period.

There are a number of alternative ways of production, for which the construction periods may differ. Moreover, the other parts of the total production period may depend on the conveyor belt system which is adopted. Furthermore, even though the same belt system is used, it may be entirely possible that the production period is variable, as the level of the movement of the belt is variable, depending on the skill of workers. Thus, both construction and production periods may be flexible; the actual lengths of the periods are decided by the firm's decision on the choice of techniques.

The maximum span of time during which a machine is serviceable depends on its quality and use. Where it is operated roughly or excessively, its lifetime will become shorter. In fact, when it becomes economically inefficient, it will be discarded before its physical lifetime has expired. Thus, the economic life time of a machine may be shorter than its physical lifetime which is the maximum period during which the machine can work at any rate. It is an economic judgement to decide when it will be discarded, so that the economic life time is a variable, but not a datum, of the production plan which the firm makes. It depends not only on economic parameters such as

---

[2] Note that our second period corresponds to Burchardt's die Durchlaufszeit der Zwischenprodukte, that is the time which is needed for intermediate products to pass through all stages of production until they reach the final stage. See Fritz Burchardt, 'Die Schemata des stationären Kreislaufs bei Böhm-Bawerk und Marx, I', *Weltwirtschaftliches Archiv*, 34 Band, Heft 2, 1931, S.561.

prices, wage rates and interest rates as well as their expected values but also on the perspective of technological development. It may even become obsolete unexpectedly when a powerful machine for similar purposes is suddenly made available.

If we truncate the production process at an arbitrary point in time, it will leave at the end of the process used capital goods in addition to goods in process at various stages; all these may be regarded as outcomes of the truncated production activities. Where time is taken as continuous, the analysis will be complicated, because we have to deal with infinitely many kinds of capital goods at various stages of utilization as well as infinitely many kinds of intermediate goods at various stages of production. To avoid the difficulty of handling the infinitude of commodities we may alternatively assume that time is discrete and may divide the whole production process into short elementary periods, in order to grasp it as a succession of such periods. We economists very much owe the analysis of the production process to Karl Marx, who formulates it as a sequence of working-days, his elementary periods. Marx says: 'When we speak of a working-day we mean the length of working time during which the labourer must daily spend his labour-power.'[3] It is well known that Hicks called his elementary period a week. One pitch of the movement of the conveyor belt could be taken as the elementary period; its length is of a magnitude of minutes or even seconds. Where a minute, a day or a week is considered to be too short, a month or a quarter may serve as the elementary period of the analysis. It should not be very short in order to avoid complications in the analysis. It should not be very long in order to make the analysis dynamic; we have to neglect all the short-run phenomena which may happen and be over during the elementary period chosen.

As has already been outlined in chapter 1, time-taking production is carried out in the following manner. At the beginning of the first working-day workers operate on raw and auxiliary materials with the help of machines and at the end of the day produce intermediate products at the first stage. On the second day another group of workers operate on these intermediate products, the outcomes of the first working-day, with the help of materials and machines, in order to obtain intermediate products at the second stage at the end of the day. Proceeding in this way we reach the final n-th working-day, on which workers operate on intermediate products at the final stage $n-1$ with the help of materials and machines again and produce the final outputs. Marx refers to n as the production period which differs from one commodity to another. He mentions that cotton yarn is

---

[3] K. Marx, *Capital*, vol. II, Progress Publishers, Moscow, 1967, p. 234.

turned out daily or weekly, while it takes perhaps three months to produce a locomotive.

After having completed the initial stage of production on the first working-day, it would occur on the second day that two groups of workers work in the factory, one being engaged in processing intermediate goods obtained as the result of the previous working-day in order to produce those at the second stage, and the other in repeating the production of the first stage which eventually ripens into the final products on the day $n+1$. Similarly, on the third day, three groups of workers work on the third, second and first stages of production, respectively, and so on. Finally, on the day n, each and every stage of production is operated by a group of workers, and this simultaneous production enables the firm to produce a stream of outputs commencing on day n. It will have, on day $n+1$, outputs of the production which had started on the second day; similarly, for day $n+2$ and afterwards. Thus we have the synchronization of production, as was discussed in chapter 1 above.

We have, so far, given a description of production, on the assumption that the factory has already been established. Where we have to start from scratch, we must first buy a site and then build a factory on it. These activities are also analysed into a number of elementary periods. On the one end of each period there are inputs of machines, materials and labour, while on the other end there are outputs of intermediate products such as unfinished factory buildings at an appropriate stage of completion. The construction period defined above is the time m which is needed for constructing the factory. It is noted that the activities of construction are not 'synchronized' because, unlike the products of manufacturing industries, the outputs of construction activities, i.e., factories, are not produced in a stream.

Next there are two ways of treating durable capital goods. Suppose a capital good k is usable for ten elementary periods. According to the quantitative conversion method a unit of i-period old capital good k is regarded as equivalent to e_i unit of the brand-new good k, where $e_{i+1} < e_i < 1$ $i = 1, 2, \ldots, 9$. The movement of e_i traces out the time profile of efficiency of good k. e_i takes on a minimum positive value at $i = 9$, and it is zero for all $i \geqslant 10$. Although this method is conventionally adopted by firms for accounting purposes, the most serious weak point of this method is that we do not know the correct values of e_i's. We are often satisfied with assuming that $e_1 = 9/10$, $e_2 = 8/10$, $\ldots$, $e_9 = 1/10$, a very crude assumption.

The second method of qualitative conversion treating capital goods at different stages of wear and tear as qualitatively different and determining their values by solving price-cost equations was introduced, according to

Sraffa, by Torrence and adopted first by Ricardo and then by Malthus and Marx.[4] It is, however, von Neumann who first discussed how to deal with the method of qualitative conversion analytically. According to his method capital goods of different ages are regarded as being qualitatively different, so that a capital good k whose maximum physical life time is 10 periods is accompanied by nine other capital goods $k+1, k+2, \ldots, k+9$ of the same kind. These belong to the family of capital good k, and good $k+i$ represents an i-period old capital good k, $i = 1, \ldots, 9$. Then an elementary process which uses capital good $k+i$ produces not only final or intermediate products but also capital good $k+i+1$. This is because good $k+i$, after the use, still exists in the form of $k+i+1$ and, therefore, we may consider that $k+i$ brings forth $k+i+1$.

Thus elementary processes are usually joint production processes. Outputs in the form of old capital goods stay in the places where they were originally fixed and continue to be used for production, while outputs of intermediate products are used as inputs in those elementary processes which are higher by one stage in the pipeline of production than those where they have been produced. The routes via which materials are finally transformed into products are shown in terms of a 'production tree'.

2 In figure 1 let a dot represent an elementary production process and a straight line connecting two dots stand for a flow of intermediate products from the lower dot to the upper one. A production tree may be explained in terms of the example which has been described in detail by Adam Smith in a famous section on the division of labour in *The Wealth of Nations*. As is at once seen, it perfectly fits modern activity analysis:

But in the way in which this business is now carried out, not only the whole work is a peculiar trade, but it is divided into a number of branches, of which the greater part are likewise peculiar trades. One man draws out the wire, another straightens it, a third cuts it, a fourth points it, a fifth grinds at the top for receiving the head; to make

---

[4] See P. Sraffa, *Production of Commodities by Means of Commodities*, Cambridge University Press, 1960, pp. 94–5. But this assertion by Sraffa should be queried, because Torrence only says: 'Supposing that a tenth of these fixed capitals is annually consumed, then . . . the value of his [the woollen manufacturer's] capital has been reduced by the process of production from £1,500 to £1,350 . . .' Clearly, in this passage he gets the value of used capital (£1,350) from the given rate of depreciation of 1/10; he never obtains it by solving the set of price-determination equations with respect to the used capital good as a joint output. Therefore, the most we can say is, as I actually did in my *Marx's Economics*, that 'Marx *almost came up with this* [method] . . . but he did *not* follow it through. . . . Marx used the neoclassical account' (italics by M. M. this time). One may consider even this a bit overstated. See R. Torrence, *An Essay on the Production of Wealth*, London, 1821, pp. 28–9. M. Morishima, *Marx's Economics*, Cambridge University Press, 1973, p. 164n.

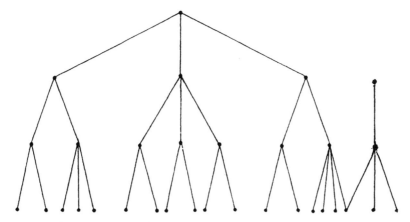

Figure 1 The genealogy of production

the head requires three distinct operations; to put it on is a peculiar business, to whiten the pin is another; it is even a trade by itself to put them into the paper; and the important business of making a pin is, in this manner, divided into about eighteen distinct operations, which, in some manufactories, are all performed by distinct hands.[5]

What Smith calls a 'distinct operation' is the same as what we have called an 'elementary process', that is a process carried out in an elementary period. Passing through the processes vertically arranged, the raw material (metal wire) gradually matures through higher stages of intermediate products and is finally transformed into a certain number of pieces of pin. However, it is rare that the finished product can be arrived at along one of these vertical channels alone. As Smith observed, operations which have been organized into vertical channels take place simultaneously, and at certain stages the fruits of these several operations are combined. Repeating such confluences of the streams and, if necessary, divergences into several branches the final products are at last obtained. As has been pointed out before and also recognized by Smith, a branch or a substream may form an independent trade and may be delegated to a different firm.

These processes are so standardized that it takes one unit of time for the raw material or an intermediate good to go through each of them. Taking explicit account of used machines as joint products of operations, input–output relations of elementary processes may be charted as in the following arrow scheme:

⁵ Adam Smith, *The Wealth of Nations*, vol. I, Everyman's Library, 1910, pp. 4–5. Also see my *Economic Theory of Modern Society*, Cambridge University Press, 1976, pp. 33–5.

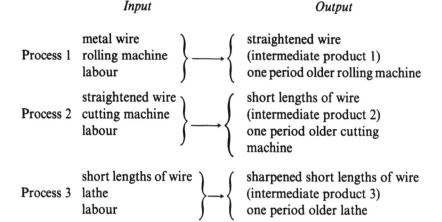

	Input	*Output*
Process 1	metal wire rolling machine labour	straightened wire (intermediate product 1) one period older rolling machine
Process 2	straightened wire cutting machine labour	short lengths of wire (intermediate product 2) one period older cutting machine
Process 3	short lengths of wire lathe labour	sharpened short lengths of wire (intermediate product 3) one period older lathe

and so on for the other fifteen processes. When the whole system of operations is shown diagrammatically it takes the form of a tree.

Where constructing a factory building and equipping it with necessary machines are taken into account, the tree is expanded and complicated but the whole set of elementary processes can be systematized in the same way into the shape of a tree. This systematization may be referred to as the genealogy of production. Thus each firm has one tree. These trees are connected with each other because an elementary process can supply its outputs to several firms through the market.

However, the most convenient representation of the structure of production would be in terms of input and output matrices which are denoted by H and K, respectively. Let there be n_1 elementary processes to be usable for firm 1, and let there be m_1 goods which are involved, either as output or as input, in these processes. Thus both H and K are m_1 by n_1 matrices. If a good is not employed as input by a certain process, the corresponding element of H is zero; similarly elements of K are zero if the corresponding goods are not produced. In addition to these goods, each process employs labour. The labour-input coefficient vector is designated by M which is a row vector. (Throughout the following we rule out land from the list of primary factors of production, for the sake of simplicity of description.)

Of course, elements of H, K and M are all non-negative. In addition to this property we assume for H that each process uses at least one good as input, that is, nothing is produced by labour only. This means that each column of H has one positive element. For K, we assume that any one of the n_1 processes produces some of the m_1 goods, that is to say, each column of K contains at least one positive element. As for M, we assume that firm 1 is not fully automated, so that at least one component of M is positive. We allow, however, for partial automation which implies that some components of M may be zero. The arrow representation of production processes may now be put in terms of matrices in the following form:

Input   *Output*

$$\begin{pmatrix} H \\ M \end{pmatrix} \longrightarrow K$$

Let us next note that the coefficients listed in H, K and M are all normalized. Those processes which have positive labour-input coefficients l_i are normalized such that l_i takes on the value 1 where the processes are operated at the unit level. Those for which l_i is zero have to be normalized in a different way. A machine or a material which is positively used by such a process may be taken as the standard commodity for normalization, so that the unit level of such a process is defined such that the input coefficient of the standard commodity takes on the value 1. As we do not compare activities at their unit levels with each other throughout the rest of the book, the fact that the standard commodity may change from one process to another does not give rise to any difficulty. In any case where the standardization is clearly defined, the activity levels of elementary production processes are also clearly defined, which we designate by x, an n_1 dimensional column vector.

Where durable capital goods are employed, the genealogy of production is inevitably the one of joint production, because used capital goods left over by a process for use in the future are regarded as joint output of the process. Moreover, in such cases, the firm is provided with alternative sets of production processes. In one set only brand-new capital goods are used and all used capital goods are immediately transferred to the second set. The second set may be the one in which only one period old capital goods are used, and the third set uses two period old capital goods, and so on. (Also the set may be a mixed one which uses capital goods of different age groups.) We have such sets until the physical life time of the capital goods is exhausted; we include all these alternative processes of production in H, K and M. Then it must be asked which processes are adopted, or rejected, by the entrepreneur of firm 1 when he makes a production plan. This problem of choice of techniques solves the problem of determining the economic life time of capital goods. In fact, where the process which uses the i period old capital goods is adopted, while the one which uses the $i+1$ period old goods is rejected, then it is obvious that the economic lifetime of the goods is i. After use for i periods, they will be discarded.

Let activity levels in periods t and $t-1$ be denoted by x_t and x_{t-1}, respectively. At the beginning of t, outputs of the amounts Kx_{t-1} are available within firm 1 which needs inputs of the amounts Hx_t to operate the processes at the intensity x_t. If $Kx_{t-1} \geqslant Hx_t$, everything which the firm wants to obtain is available in it, so that it has no demand for any commodity produced by some other firms. On the other hand, where the above inequality does not hold, the part of Hx_t which is not fulfilled by Kx_{t-1} has to be satisfied by buying necessary amounts from other firms. To deal with the problem of trade between firms, we may imagine the whole national economy to be as if it is a giant firm to which n activities are available to produce m goods. Obviously $n \geqslant n_1$, and $m \geqslant m_1$. Let us write input and output coefficient matrices and the labour-input coefficient vector of the whole economy as A, B and L, respectively. It is evident that H and K of firm 1 are submatrices of A and B, respectively. Similarly M is a subvector of L. Where no international trade is permitted,[6] the production of the whole economy is feasible if and only if:

$$BX_{t-1} \geqslant AX_t + D_t \tag{3.1}$$

is fulfilled, where D_t is the vector of the consumption demands for commodities of the workers and other individuals, and X_t and X_{t-1} are activity vectors of the economy at t and $t-1$. x_t of firm 1 is a subvector of X_t, and the same holds true for x_{t-1}. LX_t is the amount of labour required for the processes to be operated at X_t. In order for production to be feasible a sufficient amount of labour, N_t, which is at least as large as LX_t should be available at t, that is:

$$LX_t \leqslant N_t. \tag{3.2}$$

Both (3.1) and (3.2) are the conditions for a feasible production of the national economy. (Note that in (3.1) and (3.2) storage activities are included in A, B and L. We shall discuss the problem of storage in section 7 below.)

In the following we assume that (a) each column of A has some positive elements, (b) each column of B has some positive elements and (c) L is a non-negative and non-zero row vector. The economic implications of these three assumptions have been made clear with regard to individual firm 1's matrices and vector (H,K,M). For the aggregate output matrix B we additionally assume that (d) each row of B has some positive elements. This means that all goods can be produced by some firms within the economy; it is a necessary condition for no international trade.

Let us now return to the problem of determination of the economic lifetime of a capital good. Let i be the i period old capital good of a certain type.

---

[6] Where the economy is open to international trade, matrices A, B and L must be further extended to include firms in foreign countries.

If it is available in the economy at the beginning of period t, then we have $\sum b_{ij} X_{jt-1} > 0$, where X_{jt-1} is the j-th component of X_{t-1}. If the capital goods are not transferable[7] and only usable within the firm where they are fixed, then $a_{ij} = 0$ for all processes j which do not belong to this firm. By assumption, within the firm, there are processes k which use the good i, so that $a_{ik} > 0$ for all such k. However, if these processes are all found to be inefficient, they are not operated in period t; therefore $X_{kt} = 0$ for all such processes k. Then we have:

$$\sum b_{ij} X_{jt-1} > \sum a_{ik} X_{kt} = 0; \tag{3.3}$$

$D_{it} = 0$ for capital goods. Since only those processes which use the i period old capital good can produce the $i+1$ period old capital good, the fact that $X_{kt} = 0$ for all k implies:

$$\sum b_{i+1k} X_{kt} = 0,$$

that is to say, there is no capital good $i+1$ in the economy at the beginning of period $t+1$. It is evident, of course, that if there is no $i+1$ period old capital good in $t+1$, there is also no $i+2$ period old good in $t+2$. Thus (3.3) is the condition which implies that the capital good in question has the economic lifetime of $i-1$ periods. At age i it still exists in the economy but is completely idle. After that it is discarded and entirely disappears from the economy.

We have so far assumed there is only one kind of labour, so that L is a row vector. This is, however, not an essential assumption at all. Where several kinds of heterogeneous labour are used, the above formulation is kept intact except for reinterpreting L as an l by n matrix, where l is the number of the types of labour. Correspondingly, the wage rate w is reinterpreted as an l-dimensional wage rate row vector; wLX stands for the total wage bill.

3 Our list of goods includes commodities for which there are markets and goods for which there is no market. The concept of price is obvious for the former, but for the latter it is only an accounting price or an efficiency price attributed to the good. Market prices change from time to time, and then efficiency prices calculated so as to be amicable with market prices are also induced to change. In the following, however, we are concerned with a state where market and accounting prices are fixed at equilibrium values. P represents the vector of equilibrium market and efficiency prices, an m-dimensional row vector. We assume that the price equilibrium is strongly stable, so that deviations of actual prices from P are all insignificant.

---

[7] In this case capital good i fixed in firm 1 should be regarded as qualitatively different from the same i in other firms.

The existence of an equilibrium price vector P has already been discussed in my *Theory of Economic Growth*.[8] Its arguments will be outlined in chapter 4 below for the convenience of the reader. As far as the present chapter is concerned, we may take the existence of P for granted. The following analysis is particularly fitted to the fixed price economy, whereas it should be supplemented by the analysis of price adjustment in case it should be applied to an economy where prices are flexible.

Let us now take any arbitrary process j; let the j-th columns of A, B and L be denoted by a^j, b^j and l^j respectively. Evaluate input vectors a^j and l^j at current prices P and the current wage rate w^9 and output vector b^j at the vector of prices ψ which is expected to prevail in the next period. Denoting the actual or imputed financial cost per unit of the production cost of process j by q_j, profits of process j per unit activity are given by:

$$\psi b^j - (Pa^j + wl^j)(1 + q_j),$$

so that the rate of profit r_j of process j is defined as:

$$r_j = [\psi b^j - (Pa^j + wl^j)(1 + q_j)]/(Pa^j + wl^j)(1 + q_j) \qquad j = 1, \ldots, n.$$

Comparing these rates of profit with each other and writing the maximum as r, that is $r = \max(r_1, r_2, \ldots, r_n)$, then as $r \geqslant r_j$, we have from the above equations:

$$\psi b^j \leqslant (1 + r)(Pa^j + wl^j)(1 + q_j) \qquad j = 1, \ldots, n, \qquad (3.4)$$

or:

$$\psi B \leqslant (1 + r)(PA + wL)(I + Q), \qquad (3.5)$$

where I is the identity matrix and Q the diagonal matrix with q_j on the diagonal.

Let r' be the rate of interest which the firm has to pay per week, per unit of the amount of money it has borrowed from the bank. If the firm borrowed the entire amount which is necessary for carrying out the operation of process j, then it must pay interest to the amount, $Pa^j + wl^j$, per unit activity. This means that q_j equals r'. On the other hand, if the production of process j is made entirely by using the firm's own revolving fund, q_j is zero. Hence, where these two are only possibilities, the matrix Q may be written as:

$$Q = r'J,$$

with J denoting a diagonal matrix which has, on the diagonal, 1 for the

---

[8] M. Morishima, *Theory of Economic Growth*, Clarendon Press, Oxford, 1969, pp. 133–48.
[9] Note that w is the vector of equilibrium wage rates, which is assumed to prevail in the current period, if there are several kinds of labour.

processes financed by the bank and 0 for the processes using the firm's own money. Of course, as will be seen later, especially in chapter 6, there are several ways of financing. Where the financial markets are perfectly organized such that the Modigliani–Miller irrelevance theorem is to hold, $q_j = r'$ not only for those processes which are financed by the money borrowed from the bank but also for those financed by the firm's own capital obtained by issuing new shares. Otherwise q_j's for the latter may differ from r'; in general, Q depends on how production is financed.

In expression (3.4), if strict inequality ' < ' holds, it is meant that the profit rate of process j is lower than the maximum. Then the firm will not employ process j, so that the level of operation of j will be zero. Thus $X_j = 0$. It then immediately follows that, for those processes which are operated, (3.4) must hold with equality. In short, (3.4) with ' < ' implies $X_j = 0$, while $X_j > 0$ implies (3.4) holding with ' = '.

Thus, processes are chosen according to the principle of maximizing the rate of profit. As far as construction activities are concerned, the choice of processes means the choice of production possibility sets to be established, while for production processes it means the determination of how to produce the products. Although $X_j > 0$ implies (3.4) being an equation, the converse is not necessarily true. There may be a number of construction processes for which (3.4) is an equation but whose X_j is zero. If some of such X_j's become positive, production possibility sets are produced in some places in the economy, while if other X_j's take on positive values, new possibility sets are produced in other places. Similarly, production processes may not be adopted (that is, their $X_j = 0$), even though they satisfy (3.4) with equality.

Let us now reintroduce instantaneous production processes which have been dismissed in chapter 1. It is true that it takes some time, however short, to accomplish the production activity of any process; in the case of producing a TV set, it takes a minute or so for the good in process to pass over the final step of the conveyor belt system. If we divide the whole production process of the entire economy into elementary processes of such a short length of time, our matrices (A, B) or vector (L) would be of an enormous size. To obtain a manageable formulation of production, we have to be satisfied with elementary processes which have a uniform production period that is much longer than a minute or minutes, probably of the order of, say, a week.[10] Then all of the production processes whose duration is substantially shorter than a week are regarded as instantaneous

---

[10] The length of production period will be decided, depending on the aim and application of the analysis. For macroeconomic purposes, it would be convenient to take a rather long period, say, a quarter of a year.

processes in the sense that their production activities are completed within the production period of the standard elementary process.

Let n' be the number of instantaneous processes and A', B' be the matrices of input and output coefficients of these processes and L' the matrix of their labour input coefficients. Of course, either of A' and B' is an m by n' matrix, while L' is an l by n'. It is evident that we have (3.4') below, instead of (3.4), for each of these instantaneous processes:

$$Pb^j \leqslant (1+r)(Pa^j + wl^j) \qquad j=1,\ldots,n'. \qquad (3.4')$$

Note that output prices are not expected but current prices, so that we have P in (3.4') in the place where ψ appears in (3.4). Also note, as will be seen later, the financial cost for operating any instantaneous production process is zero. Hence we obtain:

$$PB' \leqslant (1+r)(PA' + wL'). \qquad (3.5')$$

In these expressions, r is the largest among the various rates of profits of all production processes including non-instantaneous ones. One might perhaps regard (3.5') as a rather strange condition and argue that r would (or could) be zero for instantaneous production processes. Although this might be reasonable in an economy with no non-instantaneous production process, r should appear in (3.5'), where both instantaneous and non-instantaneous processes are operated side by side in the economy. This is because no entrepreneur will use his ability or time, if not the firm's revolving fund, for operating a process that yields profits at a rate less than the maximum rate r of the economy. He would instead use it for operating a non-instantaneous process from which he obtains profits at r.

Let us now call those processes for which (3.4) or (3.4') is an equation the most profitable processes or 'top' processes. In order to determine equilibrium solutions of X_j's or Y_j's for the top processes, we need, in addition to (3.4) and (3.4') or (3.5) and (3.5'), other conditions, which will be discussed in chapter 4 below. Here we are not involved with the problem of determination of X and Y, and only discuss how production activities in period t are financed. For this purpose it is important to note that ψ is the vector of expected prices which will be found in the next period whether it is correct or wrong. What we can say about ψ in the present period is no more than that expectations ψ are formed dependent on current prices P; thus $\psi = f(P)$ but we simply write ψ without mentioning P.

For non-instantaneous processes, firms' receipts in the current period from the sale of outputs $B\bar{X}$ is $PB\bar{X}$, which is compared with their expenditure for production which amounts to $(PA + wL)(I + Q)X$, including interest or financial costs. Where the latter is greater than the former, only a part of the expenditure is covered by current income, the excess:

$$(PA + wL)(I + Q)X - PB\bar{X}, \tag{3.6}$$

being interpreted as follows. First in view of (3.4) or (3.5) and the rule of production discussed previously,[11] that is, that $X_j = 0$ if (3.4) is a strict inequality, we have:

$$\frac{\psi}{1+r} BX = (PA + wL)(I + Q)X. \tag{3.7}$$

Therefore, the above expression (3.6) may be put in the form:

$$\frac{\psi}{1+r} BX - PB\bar{X}, \tag{3.8}$$

where the first term represents the expected value of the stocks of goods of the next period, excluding profits, while the second stands for the value of the stocks of goods in the current period. Thus the difference gives the increase in the stock, that is, the aggregate investment.

To finance production activities X in the current period, the firms are short of purchasing power by the amount equivalent to (3.8). There are several alternative ways for them to acquire the purchasing power. In the case of a newly formed firm, it will issue shares, as has been discussed in the previous chapter. Sometimes, especially when it wants to expand and establish a new branch of its business, it may increase capital by issuing new shares. Conversely, when it reduces its business to a small scale or completely dissolves itself, it partly or wholly redeems its shares. Additionally, it may use its depreciation fund and reserved profits. Furthermore, the firm may borrow money from banks and may issue debentures. Without the support of the purchasing power raised in these ways, it is impossible to realize the investment (3.8). It is noted that, depending on the ways of financing production, actual or imputed financial costs at appropriate rates q_j are charged and included in the production costs.

Suppose that the firms have, by some means, obtained the purchasing power of the amount of (3.8), then they have, together with the purchasing power $PB\bar{X}$ obtained by selling their own stock of goods $B\bar{X}$, the total amount of purchasing power which is $\frac{\psi}{1+r} BX$. This is evidently sufficient for paying the total cost $(PA + wL)(I + Q)X$. As has been said above, (3.8) is partly financed by the firm's own capital, that is, (a) depreciation, (b) voluntary reserve of profits and (c) new issue or increase of shares. To

[11] As I have named in other places, I will call it the rule of profitability throughout the following.

obtain (a) and (b) we may put the price–cost equation of the last period in the form:

$$PB\bar{X} = (P_{-1}A + w_{-1}L)(I + Q_{-1})(I + R)\bar{X},$$

where I is the identity matrix, Q_{-1} the diagonal matrix Q in the last period and R the diagonal matrix with the rate of profits of each process in the previous period on the diagonal. This is an *ex post* relationship, so that P is not necessarily equal to ψ_{-1}, which is the vector of the current prices expected in the previous period and the *ex post* rates of profits are not necessarily the same as the uniform *ex ante* rate and, therefore, diagonal elements of R may be different from each other. The amount, $(P_{-1}A + w_{-1}L)(I + Q_{-1})R\bar{X}$, stands for the total profits, a part of which is distributed to shareholders as dividends, while the rest may be reserved. The latter forms (b) above which is invested in expanding the stocks of goods.

To obtain (a), A and B are divided into $A^\dagger$ and $A^{\dagger\dagger}$, and $B^\dagger$ and $B^{\dagger\dagger}$:

$$A = A^\dagger + A^{\dagger\dagger}; \quad B = B^\dagger + B^{\dagger\dagger},$$

where $A^\dagger$ is the matrix of inputs of materials and intermediate products, and $A^{\dagger\dagger}$ the matrix of inputs of durable capital goods. Similarly, $B^\dagger$ is the matrix of outputs of final and intermediate products, while $B^{\dagger\dagger}$ the matrix of 'outputs' of used capital goods. Equation (3.7) may then be written as:

$$\frac{\psi}{1+r} B^\dagger X = (PA^\dagger + wL)X + [(PA^{\dagger\dagger} - \frac{\psi}{1+r} B^{\dagger\dagger})X] + (PA + wL)QX.$$

$$(3.9)$$

On the right-hand side the first part represents the production cost, the second part in the square brackets the total amount of *ex ante* depreciation of the current period and the third part the financial cost. The total value of *ex post* depreciation of the previous period is defined in the same way as *ex ante* expected depreciation is defined; therefore:

$$(P_{-1}A^{\dagger\dagger} - PB^{\dagger\dagger}(I + R)^{-1})\bar{X}.$$

It is the latter which is the reinvestment referred to as (a) above. As for (c) the explanation of the procedure of issuing shares in the previous chapter *mutatis mutandis* holds.

The rest of the investment is financed by borrowed capital. Where banks have an amount of the loanable fund which is enough for supporting all the investment programmes that seek funds, the full amount of investment (3.8) will be realized. However, where bankers do not or cannot finance some of the firms' investment programmes, the production activities X originally intended to be undertaken are not fully carried out. They must be content with activities at lower levels. Clearly, this forced decrease in X gives rise to a reduction in employment.

On the other hand, for instantaneous production processes there is no problem of finance, because by the rule of profitability applied to (3.5) only the 'top' processes are operated, so that:

$$PB'Y = (1+r)(PA' + wL')Y,$$

where Y is the vector of activity levels of instantaneous processes. The total cost $(PA' + wL')Y$ is at once covered by the proceeds $PB'Y$, and the surplus is either distributed to shareholders as dividends or reserved for investment in the future. In any case, except for instantaneous production processes, the problem of finance is crucial and vital for production. There can be no satisfactory theory of the firm which ignores the problem of how to finance production.

4 Let us consider a man who wants to start a new business. If bankers approve the investment plan proposed by him and lend the necessary amount of money for the plan to him, he can build up a production possibility set on the basis of the loan he has obtained. Otherwise his plan is only a castle in the air. This rejects the view, common among conventional general equilibrium theorists, that each entrepreneur is provided with a production possibility set which he can exploit to obtain a maximum profit. The production possibility sets, save for exceptional cases, are neither endowments inherited from their parents nor manna from heaven. It is, instead, something to be produced by the entrepreneur himself in collaboration with bankers or by using his firm's own capital. Production possibility sets are never given, as fixed sets, to a number of persons individually, but we may only at most assume that the knowledge of producing production possibilities is available for use to all people in the economy. Of course, it would be wrong and simplistic if one concludes from this that anybody is in a position that he is able to put the knowledge to practical use. Many are not so ambitious to be an entrepreneur. They may conceive that they might have inherited only a low level of entrepreneurship from their parents. Or they might be unable to understand technology. There may be many people who, unfortunately, do not find bankers or moneyed men who are willing to support them because their plans are found to be so poor that they fail to convince potential supporters of the profitability of the plans, or because they are simply unlucky.

This link between entrepreneurs and financiers puts an end to the traditional approach of dichotomizing economics into 'real' and 'monetary' subeconomics. According to this approach exchange and production are the subjects of the real economists and prices of commodities are determined in terms of some standard commodity that is called numéraire. This commodity itself is taken from among the commodities belonging to the 'real' economy, and the determination of the money price of the numéraire is the subject of monetary economists. This division of labour between real and monetary economists has been peaceful because an implicit assumption has been made to the effect that they do not disturb the work of each other. The real economic sector does not contain any monetary element, so that the relative prices determined in the real sector are not influenced by the money price of the numéraire determined in the monetary sector. This view obviously justifies the quantity theory of money and is, therefore, not supported by those economists who are critical of the theory. The most eminent name among these is, of course, Keynes. He has very much emphasized the indecomposability of real and monetary phenomena. It is nevertheless true that he accepts the conventional 'real' analysis of the firm as is evidenced by his agreement with the proposition of marginal productivity: the output which the firm wants to produce is determined at a point where the marginal physical productivity of labour is equal to the real wage.[12] It is true that he has clearly observed that investment influences production via the channel of effective demand. But, as will be seen later, he has failed to observe that a number of production activities are not carried out because of a lack of *ex ante* financial support by bankers. In his economy investment is without fail equal to savings but it is only an *ex post* equality. The problem of dichotomy will be revisited and discussed in more detail in chapter 6 below.

The financial position of the firm plays an important role in production. The share of own capital in total (i.e., own and borrowed) capital is dispersed among major economic countries. The figures for all industries for the USA and the UK are high (66.6% and 47.7%, respectively, for 1983), while Japan's figure is the lowest (17.1% for the same year). West Germany, France and Italy are between them. West Germany is nearest to the USA and the UK, whilst France is nearest to Japan. (The figures do not change much from those in the late 1980s.) Where firms tend to be confined to their own capital in financing their investment plans, as they are in the UK, it is very difficult for them to carry out ambitious investment plans because of the deficiency of capital. Thus the amount of *ex post* investment tends to be usually small, although as these firms more or less stay aloof from bankers or other lenders, their financial positions are relatively stable.

On the other hand, at the other extreme case of firms heavily relying on borrowed capital, as the Japanese firms usually do, they are always put

---

[12] J. M. Keynes, *The General Theory of Employment, Interest and Money*, Macmillan, 1936, p. 5.

under the pressure of lenders, and the financial cost tends to be high. In compensation for this disadvantage, however, the finance by means of borrowed capital facilitates the firms' expansion at a high speed. Also, because the investment projects to be supported will tend to be selected by the financiers, rather than the entrepreneurs themselves, the financiers are more or less in a position to be able to determine the course that the economy will take in the future. In making decisions on loans, financiers will not only examine the technological aspects of the proposals but also carefully test personal qualities (trustability, leadership, etc.) of the entrepreneurs, especially in the case of applications from small businesses. Decisions are not entirely economic, but sociological and philosophical too.

What is the cost of capital to a firm when capital can be obtained in various ways? How much of the surplus from production activities should be paid as dividends to shareholders? (Or this second question may be put in different terms as: how much of it should be retained within the firm as an addition to general revolving funds or as capital for some particular investment projects?) Modigliani and Miller have been concerned with these questions, in regard to which they have, respectively, obtained the following irrelevance theorems: First, the cost of capital is equal to the rate of interest on bonds, regardless of whether funds are acquired through debt or through new issues of shares. Secondly, the firm's dividend policy is a matter of indifference to shareholders; they are indifferent even between the following two extreme policies. One distributes the whole earnings to shareholders (so that new investment projects are financed either by issuing new shares or by borrowing from banks), while the other reserves the entire amount of earnings for the sake of financing investment activities. Modigliani and Miller have derived these conclusions under a number of assumptions which they have carefully spelt out. They include, however, such unrealistic assumptions that there is no asymmetry of information between directors and shareholders of the firm regarding its investment policy, that there are no taxes on dividends or capital gain, that there are no transaction costs in buying and selling shares, and so on.[13]

In the actual world it is clear that these assumptions are not fulfilled. Moreover, they have ignored the fact that different ways of raising investment funds have their own merits and demerits, as will be briefly discussed in chapter 8 below. For example, if the borrowing from banks becomes too big, the firm will be put under the control of them, while if the

[13] F. Modigliani and M. H. Miller, 'The Cost of Capital, Corporation Finance and the Theory of Investment', *American Economic Review*, 1958, vol. 48, pp. 261–97. M. H. Miller and F. Modigliani, 'Dividend Policy, Growth, and the Valuation of Shares', *Journal of Business*, 1961, vol. 34, pp. 235–64.

total number of its shares becomes too large, it is possible that the major shareholders' ownership of the firm may be exposed to danger. Consequently, there must be an optimum capital structure from the viewpoint of the firm, and shares of such firms whose capital structures are optimum or near optimum will be sold and bought at a high price in the market. In any case, it is very important to see whether the optimum capital structure of a firm contains more of funds through debt instruments and less of equity funds, or converse.

5 As has been seen before, activity levels of the current period, X and Y, are constrained by the availability of commodities, $B\bar{X}$, and the existing labour force, N, of the same period. We thus have:

$$B\bar{X} + B'Y \geqslant AX + A'Y + D, \tag{3.1'}$$

and:

$$N \geqslant LX + L'Y. \tag{3.2'}$$

Components of the vector X may be grouped into two classes. The first class consists of those X_i's which are directly related to such investment activities as construction of new factories, introduction of new methods of production, improvement of facilities for prevention of industrial pollution, and others, for which entrepreneurs raise capital from financiers or the financial market. Assuming, for the convenience of explanation, that they raise the necessary amount exclusively from bankers, the levels of these activities are determined by the amount of capital which bankers are ready to invest for these purposes. Let us suppose that these X_i's take on the values, X_i^0's.

The second class includes the current production activities, X_i's, which are operated by the firms' revolving funds, so that there is no need to obtain new money from financiers to support them. These X_i's, as well as instantaneous Y_i's, are flexible and adjusted so as to satisfy (3.1') and (3.2'). Let X_i^*'s and Y_i^*'s be the adjusted values of X_i in the second class and that of Y_i, respectively. Then the whole vector X is partitioned into two subvectors, X_{I}^0 and X_{II}^*, representing activity levels of the two classes. The equations (3.11) below define X^{0*}, X^0 and X^*. Then, in view of (3.11) below, (3.1') and (3.2') may be put in the form:

$$B\bar{X} + B'Y^* \geqslant AX^{0*} + A'Y^* + D, \tag{3.1''}$$

$$N \geqslant LX^{0*} + L'Y^*. \tag{3.2''}$$

Note that for any activity j in the second group II the profit inequalities (3.4) hold with $q_j = 0$, since it is financed by the revolving fund of the firm.

It is now evident that X_{II}^* and Y^* are not arbitrary sets of X_{II} and Y, but there are some relations between X_{I}^0 and (X_{II}^*, Y^*) to fulfil (3.1″) and (3.2″), as will be explained in more detail in the next section. In any case, this means that, when X_{I}^0 changes, there will be repercussions from the first class, X_{I}^0, to some of the second-class activities, X_{II}^*, and instantaneous production activities, Y^*, which further give rise to repercussions between the activities X_{II} and Y. Obviously, the pattern of these repercussions is determined by input–output relationships defined by (A, B, L) and (A', B', L'). It then follows that despite no change in the existing stocks of goods, $B\bar{X}$, they are distributed and used in a different way, depending upon the financial support made on investment activities X_{I}. This means that, if the economy is in a state of full utilization of the stocks of commodities and full employment of labour, those factories which become unfavourable by the decision on loans made by bankers will obtain only some less amounts of stocks of goods and labour. They are, in fact, legally 'poached' by those factories which are given by bankers a sufficient amount of purchasing power for their investment schedules.

It should be noted, however, that, even in the case of a significant amount of unemployment being present, the firms newly established will try and poach their key members from other firms. This is simply because a firm which is formed by raking up unemployed workers will only have a feeble working force, so that, in order for it to be successful, it should employ able and talented persons, at least for key positions.

From the above we may say that bankers play the role of traffic controller or helmsman of the economy, who allocate the existing stocks of goods among firms and determine the course which the economy will take in the future. Although it was Keynes who emphasized the importance of investment in the determination of the aggregate amount of effective demand, it was Schumpeter[14] who, before Keynes, developed a theory explaining how finance would affect the total production through input–output relationships. It will be seen in the section below how Schumpeter's analysis of the effects of investment upon the total production differs from Keynes'. Anyhow, we may now conclude this section by saying that the banking sector plays the role of the control tower allocating chances and capabilities to establish production possibility sets among entrepreneurs in the economy.

6 Let V be the aggregate amount of investment. We then have from (3.8):

$$V = \frac{\psi}{1+r} BX - PB\bar{X}. \tag{3.10}$$

[14] J. A. Schumpeter, The Theory.

Partitioning $\bar{X}$ and X into two groups, class I consisting of those X_i's which are supported by the firms' own capital obtained by newly issued shares or by loans from financiers, and class II consisting of those which are financed by their revolving funds, we may write:

$$\bar{X}=\bar{X}^{0*}=\begin{bmatrix}\bar{X}_I^0\\\bar{X}_{II}^*\end{bmatrix},\ \bar{X}^0=\begin{bmatrix}\bar{X}_I^0\\0\end{bmatrix},\ \bar{X}^*=\begin{bmatrix}0\\\bar{X}_{II}^*\end{bmatrix},$$

$$X=X^{0*}=\begin{bmatrix}X_I^0\\X_{II}^*\end{bmatrix},\ X^0=\begin{bmatrix}X_I^0\\0\end{bmatrix},\ X^*=\begin{bmatrix}0\\X_{II}^*\end{bmatrix}.$$

(3.11)

Then (3.10) may be put in the form:

$$V=\left[\frac{\psi}{1+r}BX^0-PB\bar{X}^0\right]+\left[\frac{\psi}{1+r}BX^*-PB\bar{X}^*\right],$$

(3.12)

the parts in the square brackets being simply represented by V_I and V_{II}, respectively, and being referred to as the anti-Say's law part and the Say's law part. The total value of the Say's law part V_{II} is determined, when the entrepreneurs make decisions on the second-class activities, X_{II}^*. There is no financial restrictions on the decisions; as soon as they are made, the money needed for them is immediately available from their own revolving funds. Thus X_{II}^* determines V_{II}, but not vice versa. On the other hand, in the case of the anti-Say's law part, bankers or the financial markets determine the total amount and its allocation of V_I. For this part, therefore, V_I determines X_I^0 but not vice versa.

As BX stands for the supply of commodities, we may say, as far as the Say's law part is concerned, that an increase in supply creates an increase in demand for materials and capital goods AX^* and for labour LX^*, which are equal, in value, to supply:

$$(PA+wL)X^*=\frac{\psi}{1+r}BX^*,$$

by virtue of the rule of profitability and because $q_j=0$ for all Say's law processes. Regarding the anti-Say's law processes X^0, on the other hand, we have an inequality:

$$(PA+wL)X^0<\frac{\psi}{1+r}BX^0$$

because $q_j>0$ for them. For the whole activity set $X=X^{0*}$, the sum of the above two hold: if there is at least one anti-Say's law activity, the sum holds as an inequality, while it is an equation if there is no anti-Say's law activity. We may thus be able to say that, under Say's law, the total supply from activities X equals the total demand from them, as long as the rule of profitability is fulfilled.[15]

Where the set of the first-class activities X_I^0 is empty, the anti-Say's law part disappears in (3.12), we have no financial constraint on investment. In this case Say's law prevails through all sectors of the economy and there is no deficiency in funds, so that production is never hindered for financial reasons. Then, as will be shown in chapter 4 below, a full employment equilibrium exists, provided sociological elements working in the factor markets, as will be discussed later, are all ignored. This was paraphrased by Keynes in the form of a statement that under Say's law there is no obstacle to full employment.[16]

Next, let us be concerned with the case of the set of the first-class activities being not empty. Where the financiers are generally reluctant to support proposed investment plans, activity levels X_I^0 will be restricted to low levels. It then follows that the consumption demands D will also tend to be low, because D depends on the total wages and total profits, either of which depends on activity levels X_I^0, X_{II} and Y. (Of course, D depends on prices and wages, P, w, too; we assume, throughout this volume, that D is homogeneous of degree zero in P and w.) X_I^0 fixed at low levels pushes the level of consumption D downwards. Also, where X_I^0 is low, the demands for materials and capital goods from the first-class activities, too, will be low, so that bigger amounts of these goods will be left unsold. In fact, for example, if a certain construction plan belonging to class I, say X_i^0, is not supported by bankers, then a considerable loss in the demand for bricks will be expected in the future, which will result in a reduction of the current activity level of brick production, X_j^*. Further, if this low level of production of bricks is expected to last several periods, the current production of clay will be discouraged. Thus we have repercussions from X_i^0 to X_j^* and from X_j^* to another X_k^*. It is evident that there are repercussions from X^0 or X^* to instantaneous activities Y^*, too. These decreases in X^* and Y^* give rise to a further decline in consumption D. It is now evident that an excess supply will prevail in the market of each consumption good. Obviously, these unsold commodities are carried forward to the market of the next period, so that the current activity levels of producing consumption goods for the next period will be low, though the activities for storage that will be discussed later are high. Thus, in general X_{II} and Y will be settled at a low level, say X_{II}^* and Y^*.

---

[15] Say's law has been interpreted in various ways. According to Keynes it is a proposition which asserts that 'supply creates its own demand'. Our interpretation is different from his, but we may say that they are similar in important respects.

[16] Keynes, *The General Theory*, p. 26.

In this way, the anti-Say's law part of investment which is fixed at a low level results in activities X_1^0, X_{Π}^* and Y^* at reduced levels. Then an excess supply is obtained in each market; with X^{0*} defined as (3.11), we have:

$$B\bar{X} + B'Y^* > AX^{0*} + A'Y^* + D(P,w,X^{0*},Y^*),$$ (3.13)

$$N > LX^{0*} + L'Y^*.$$ (3.14)

This shows that the economy is driven into a state of depression, where financial means are insufficient. Conversely, it is evident that when financiers are positive in supporting the investment programmes proposed, X_1^0 is high, which results in high X_{Π}^* and Y^*. An excess demand prevails in every market, including the labour market. The sense of inequality will be reversed in both (3.13) and (3.14), and production is not feasible when this type of inequality is seen. To restrict the demand for goods and labour such that it does not exceed their respective supply, prices and wages must be altered, then activity levels decrease or become zero for less profitable processes, and finally the feasibility conditions will be fulfilled, after the adjustments of prices and wages.

As has been mentioned briefly, it is clear from the above that the process of adjustment of X and Y to the low level X^{0*} and Y^* is different from the principle of effective demand emphasized by Keynes. The latter is obtained only in a special case. To show this, we begin, in the following, by investigating the case where the set of consumption goods and the set of materials, intermediate products and new and old capital goods are distinct. The first m^* goods are consumption goods and the last $m - m^*$ goods are materials, intermediate products or capital goods. Moreover, we assume that the consumption goods are produced instantly and are not used for production, whereas it takes time to produce any other goods. Then the elements of the first m^* rows of B, A, and A' are all zero, while the elements of the last $m - m^*$ rows of B' are also all zero. Deleting these respective rows from B, A and A' and from B' we designate the matrices of reduced sizes as B^*, A^*, $A^{*'}$ and $B^{*'}$. Corresponding to this, the dimensions of X, $\bar{X}$ and Y are reduced appropriately. Then under these assumptions, we may rewrite (3.1'), (3.2') and (3.12) as:

$$B^{*'}Y \gtreqqless D^*(P, w, X, Y),$$ (3.15)

$$B^*\bar{X} \geqslant A^*X + A^{*'}Y,$$ (3.16)

$$N \geqslant LX + L'Y,$$ (3.17)

$$V = \frac{\psi}{1+r}B^*X - PB^*\bar{X},$$ (3.18)

where D^* stands for the m^* dimensional vector of the demands for consumption goods, namely, the vector obtained by eliminating the last $m - m^*$ components of D which are all zero.

Next, let us assume that the set of class II activities is empty, so that there is no Say's law part of investment. Thus $V_{II} = 0$; therefore, $V = V_I$ and $X = X_I$. This case is diagonally opposite to the case of no anti-Say's law part which has been discussed previously. It is at once understood that all activities in the vector X are financially constrained and their levels are determined by the amount of loans which entrepreneurs can obtain from financiers. Let X thus determined be X^0 and assume it is low. Then in (3.15), the D^* which corresponds to this low X^0 will be low, so that the Y on the left-hand side of (3.15) will also be low. It then follows that the income (wages and profits) from the consumption goods industries will be small. This gives rise to a decline in D^*, so that there will be a further reduction in Y. There are mutual influences of D^* upon Y and of Y upon D^*. Finally Y will be settled at a low level which satisfies (3.15). As both X^0 and Y are fixed low, they will satisfy (3.16) and (3.17) too, without difficulty.

The above process of determination of Y by (3.15) has been put forward as the theory of consumption multiplier by Keynes. It is important to point out in this place that there is no interindustrial relationship between time-requiring and instantaneous production activities X^0 and Y, as long as X^0 is set at a low level. It is true of course that for a high level X^0, the existing stocks of commodities, $B^* \bar{X}$, may be insufficient for providing enough amounts of materials, intermediate products or capital goods for consumption goods industries, because those consumed by processes Y, i.e., $A' Y$, are too big. Accordingly, the level of Y has to be restrained. However, while X^0 is low and hence Y is also low, (3.16) is not a binding condition; Y is fully realized as it is determined by the multiplier theory (3.15). Moreover, because the production of consumption goods, Y, is assumed to be instantaneous, the low output, $B^* X^0$, resulting from a low X^0 in the next period, even though it is expected to be so, does not affect the current production Y at all. This is the economy which Keynes is concerned with. The assumptions of the absence of the Say's law part of investment and of the instantaneous production of consumption goods allow Keynes to construct his theory on the basis of the multiplier theory (3.15) and the investment function (3.18) only, in complete disregard of the input–output relations (3.16).

We have now seen that there are three cases: (1) there is no anti-Say's law activity, that is, class I of activities $= \emptyset$ and class II $\neq \emptyset$, where $\emptyset$ signifies that the relevant set is empty; (2) both Say's law and anti-Say's law activities exist, i.e., class I $\neq \emptyset$ and class II $\neq \emptyset$; (3) there is no Say's law activity, i.e., class I $\neq \emptyset$ and class II $= \emptyset$. Cases (1) and (3) are the cases with which the classical economists and Keynes are concerned respectively, while case (2) is more general than either of them. In case (1), it will be shown in the next chapter that there exists an equilibrium with stocks of commodities and labour being fully employed. What are working in the general case (2) are both Keynes' principle of effective demand and input–output repercussions from X_I to X_{II} and Y. In fact, in this case (3.15) is put in the form:

$$B^{*\prime}Y \geqslant D^*(P, w, X_I, X_{II}, Y),$$

where X_I is set at X_I^0, Y is determined so as to fulfil the above expression of the consumption multiplier; the Y thus determined depends on X_{II} which we regard as though it is given. Hence we have $Y = Y(X_{II})$. Substituting this into (3.16), we obtain:

$$B^*\bar{X} \geqslant A_I^* X_I^0 + A_{II}^* X_{II} + A^{*\prime} Y(X_{II}),$$

which determines repercussions from X_I^0 to X_{II}. This shows that both the principle of effective demand (the consumption multiplier) and the input–output repercussions work in the general case of (2). In Keynes' world (3), however, there is no effect of X_I upon X_{II}, simply because of the assumption that the set of class II activities is empty. It is noted that, even in this case, the input–output relations may be effective if the other assumption that consumption goods and other commodities (materials, intermediate goods and capital goods) are distinct is invalid, so that commodities produced by Y are used for the production of other commodities.

7 We have so far tacitly assumed that production coefficients of each process are all constant. Such economies with linear production processes are often referred to, in the case of no joint production, as Leontief economies which are further extended by Arrow–Hahn to an L-economy, which assumes, among other things, (a) constant returns to scale, (b) no joint production, (c) no durable capital goods, and (d) only one non-produced input (labour).[17] It is Georgescu-Roegen, Arrow, Koopmans and Samuelson who were first concerned with this type of economy to give an interpretation to the Leontief system and established the so-called substitution or non-substitution theorem.[18] The economy may permit a number of alternative processes for each industry and the theorem asserts

---

[17] Arrow–Hahn, *General Competitive Analysis*, pp. 40–1. We should also note the name of N. Georgescu-Roegen; he made a most careful study of the production function and process. See his *Analytical Economics*, Harvard University Press, 1966 and *Energy and Economic Myths*, Pergamon, 1976.

[18] All their works on this subject are included in T. C. Koopmans (ed.), *Activity Analysis of Production and Allocation*, John Wiley, 1951.

that a change in the final demand does not give rise to any change in the set of production processes chosen by the entrepreneurs. It not only assures that Leontief's assumption of constant production coefficients may be consistent with the existence of alternative processes but also enables us to proceed with the input–output analysis by regarding coefficients obtained from the input–output table as the equilibrium values of the production coefficients chosen by entrepreneurs which are not affected by a change in the final demand. Among those assumptions which the theorem is alleged to require, most harmless is the assumption (d) of only one non-produced input, which may safely be replaced by a more general assumption of many non-produced inputs. As long as the relative prices of these inputs remain unchanged, they can be lumped together into one commodity 'labour', so that the theorem can easily be extended to the case of multiple primary factors, with the additional proviso concerning their relative prices.[19]

On the other hand, the most serious assumption is assumption (c), because of which no profits accrue in the L-economy of the above mentioned scholars. They have obtained a most uninteresting economy in which production prices are proportional to the labour values. Even Ricardo and Marx who are considered as advocates of the labour theory of value did not believe that relative prices are equal or proportional to labour values.[20] My version of the non-substitution theorem is concerned with an economy where durable capital goods are used for production, and Samuelson himself later extended his original theorem so as to include heterogeneous capital goods.[21] However, how to treat these goods is not a crucial point of the present argument. The point is: can we construct an L-economy model which accommodates processes yielding increasing returns to scale?

Our economy which I have discussed in the previous sections of this chapter is an extended or generalized L-economy in the sense that it allows for joint production, durable capital goods and multiple primary factors of production. It cannot, however, yet get rid of the assumption of constant returns to scale, as long as the production coefficients of each process are

[19] M. Morishima, Sangyo Renkanron Nyumon (An Introduction to Input–Output Analysis) (in Japanese), Sobunsha, 1956, pp. 173–4.

[20] M. Morishima, 'The Good and Bad Uses of Mathematics', in P. Wiles and G. Routh (eds.), Economics in Disarray, Basil Blackwell, 1984, pp. 60–3. It is known that the substitution theorem can be proved in several different ways. This paper compares my proof with Samuelson's. As for the former, see M. Morishima, Equilibrium, Stability and Growth, Oxford, 1964, pp. 56–69, and my book in Japanese cited above. Also F. H. Hahn adopts a similar line in his article, 'The Neo-Ricardians', in his Equilibrium and Macroeconomics, Basil Blackwell, 1984, pp. 363ff.

[21] See M. Morishima, Equilibrium, Stability and Growth, pp. 56–69, and P. A. Samuelson, 'Equalization by Trade of the Interest Rate Along with the Real Wage', in The Collected Scientific Papers of Paul A. Samuelson, vol. II, MIT Press, 1966, pp. 919ff.

constant. In the following, beginning with clarifying the conditions under which the production coefficients can be constant, we try and extend the model to a more general one, in which elements of variable returns are permissible.

It is first noted that a particular production activity, say, of j at the level X_j is expressed in terms of production vectors, i.e., output vector $b^j(X_j)$, physical input vector $a^j(X_j)$ and labour input vector $l^j(X_j)$ as:

$$(a^j(X_j), \, l^j(X_j)) \longrightarrow b_j(X_j).$$

For X_j^u taken as the unit of activity, i.e., $X_j^u = 1$, if:

$$a^j(X_j) = ta^j(X_j^u), \; l^j(X_j) = tl^j(X_j^u), \; b^j(X_j) = tb^j(X_j^u) \qquad (3.19)$$

hold for X_j such that $X_j = tX_j^u$ for all $t \geqslant 1$, we say that activity j satisfied the *multiplicity* conditions, or production coefficients are proportional to X_j, because (3.19) implies:

$$a^j(X_j) = a^j X_j, \; l^j(X_j) = l^j X_j, \; b^j(X_j) = b^j X_j \text{ for } X_j \geqslant X_j^u, \qquad (3.19')$$

where $a^j = a^j(1)$, $l^j = l^j(1)$, $b^j = b^j(1)$. It is assumed, in the following, that conditions (3.19) or (3.19') are all satisfied, because the firm can always duplicate itself by establishing another firm of exactly the same size by its side; as was seen in chapter 2, all firms can thus exhibit at least constant returns to scale. Strictly speaking, it is true that by the replication procedure we can verify the validity of (3.19), only for those X_j with t being an integer, and should obtain, for non-integer $X_j > X_j^u$, the formulas similar to (3.20) and (3.21) below, but we assume, in the following, for the sake of the argument's simplicity, that it holds for all t's which are real numbers not being less than 1. (This assumption that regards some non-sensical values of t as if being feasible is very common in orthodox mathematical economic analysis, so that it should not be criticized too harshly in this particular case of replicating a large-scale plant. For example, the consumer theory assumes that the quantity of a commodity to be bought may take on any positive value, but actually a purchase of pairs of glasses of a quantity such as 3.3 pieces is not feasible and meaningless.)

In the opposite case of t being less than 1, the production activity j is divided into, say, halves if $t = 0.5$. However, the capital good (machine) i used by the unit activity j is useless if it is cut into halves. The firm has to use the whole machine i even where the intensity of activity j, X_j, becomes less than $X_j^u = 1$, so that the capital input coefficient per activity level should take on a value a_{ij}/X_j, for $X_j < 1$. Input of materials, intermediate products and labour, on the other hand, will decrease in proportion to the activity level, so that these input coefficients per activity level remain constant. On the output side, ordinary outputs (finished or intermediate) will decrease in proportion to X_j, while used capital good i, as joint product, will be produced at the rate b_{ij}/X_j per activity level. Thus, due to the indivisibility of capital goods, the production activity is written, for X_j, such that $X_j < X_j^u$, as:

$$(a^j(X_j), l^j) \longrightarrow b^j(X_j),$$

where the i-th component, $a_i^j(X_j)$, of $a^j(X_j)$ and that, $b_i^j(X_j)$, of $b^j(X_j)$ are, respectively, defined as:

$$a_i^j(X_j) = \begin{cases} a_{ij} & \text{where } i \text{ is a material or an intermediate product} \\ a_{ij}/X_j & \text{where } i \text{ is a brand-new or old capital good,} \end{cases} \quad (3.20)$$

$$b_i^j(X_j) = \begin{cases} b_{ij} & \text{where } i \text{ is a finished or intermediate product} \\ b_{ij}/X_j & \text{where } i \text{ is an old capital good.} \end{cases} \quad (3.21)$$

We then write, in the following, the m by n matrices $(a^1(X_1), a^2(X_2), \ldots, a^n(X_n))$ and $(b^1(X_1), b^2(X_2), \ldots, b^n(X_n))$ as $A(X)$ and $B(X)$, respectively. Of course, $a^j(X)$ and $b^j(X)$ are constant for $X^j \geqslant X_j^u$, because of the multiplicity conditions.

Similarly, instantaneous production process j is possessed of both multiplicity and indivisibility properties above and below Y_j^u, respectively, where Y_j^u is the unit activity level of process j. That is, for $Y_j \geqslant Y_j^u$, production coefficients are constant. They are a_{ij}', b_{ij}', while for $Y_j < Y_j^u$ we have:

$$a_i^{j\prime}(Y_j) = \begin{cases} a_{ij}' & \text{where } i \text{ is a material or an intermediate product} \\ a_{ij}'/Y_j & \text{where } i \text{ is a brand-new or old capital good,} \end{cases} \quad (3.20')$$

$$b_i^{j\prime}(Y_j) = \begin{cases} b_{ij}' & \text{where } i \text{ is a finished or intermediate product,} \\ b_{ij}'/Y_j & \text{where } i \text{ is an old capital good.} \end{cases} \quad (3.21')$$

Matrices of these coefficients are denoted by $A'(Y)$ and $B'(Y)$; elements of their j-th columns are constant if $Y_j \geqslant Y_j^u$ because of the multiplicity conditions, while if $Y_j < Y_j^u$, they are subject to rules of switches to (3.20') and (3.21') due to the assumed indivisibility of instantaneous production processes.

It is now clear that, in the case where returns to scale may change, price–cost conditions (3.5) and (3.5') may be put in the following forms:

$$\psi B(X) \leqslant (1+r)(PA(X) + wL)(I+Q) \quad \text{for non-instantaneous processes,} \quad (3.22)$$

$$PB'(Y) \leqslant (1+r)(PA'(Y) + wL') \quad \text{for instantaneous processes.} \quad (3.23)$$

As has been already noted, the former includes the financial cost, while the latter has no such item. The investment equation (3.10) is reproduced as:

$$V = \left[\frac{\psi}{1+r} B(X)X^0 - PB(\bar{X})\bar{X}^0 \right] + \left[\frac{\psi}{1+r} B(X)X^* - PB(\bar{X})\bar{X}^* \right],$$

(3.24)

where X^0, $\bar{X}^0$, X^*, and $\bar{X}^*$, as well as X^{0*} and $\bar{X}^{0*}$ below are defined as in (3.11). Finally, the feasibility conditions (3.1″) and (3.2″) are written as:

$$B(\bar{X})\bar{X} + B'(Y)Y \geqq A(X)X^{0*} + A'(Y)Y + D(P,w,X,Y)$$

(3.25)

$$N \geqq LX^{0*} + L'Y.$$

(3.26)

In (3.25) and (3.26), Y is not an arbitrary production vector but must be adjusted so as to satisfy these conditions. As has been explained in section 5 above and will be discussed in more detail and more explicitly later, there are interindustrial repercussions between X^{0*} and Y unless some restrictions are imposed. In chapter 4 we shall establish the existence of an equilibrium, that is, the existence of P, w, r, X and Y fulfilling conditions (3.22)–(3.26), provided that Say's law prevails in the entire economy. However, in the presence of the anti-Say's law part in the aggregate investment V, this existence theorem will be violated. To realize equilibrium and full employment is, in this general and realistic case, an impossible task.

8 Finally, a remark is made of storage and maintenance activities. It is first noted that our list of production activities includes those of storage and maintenance which enable the firms to carry over an amount of a commodity available in one period to the next. In defining these activities we follow the same strategy as we have taken when we deal with aged capital goods; that is, the stock of commodity available in the next period is regarded as qualitatively different from the same stock of commodity available in the current period. Those parts of supplies of commodities which exceed their demands, as we have inequalities in (3.1′) or (3.25), are not carried over to the next period because the list of activities $(A, L; B)$ includes those for storage and maintenance, and no outputs which are not demanded by these activities can be stored until the next period. The excessive outputs are discarded at the end of the current period, so that the rule of free goods prevails, i.e., prices are set at zero for those commodities for which strict inequality '>' holds in (3.1′) or (3.25). We then have an *ex post* equation:

$$PB(\bar{X})\bar{X} + PB'(Y)Y = PA(X)X + PA'(Y)Y + PD.$$

Therefore, by defining z as $1/(1+r)$, we obtain:

$$[z\psi B(X)X + PB'(Y)Y] - [PA(X)X + PA'(Y)Y]$$
$$= z\psi B(X)X - PB(\bar{X})\bar{X} + PD,$$

(3.27)

where $X = X^{0}*$ and $Y = Y^*$. Of course, where constant returns to scale prevail, X, $\bar{X}$ and Y in the parentheses attached to the coefficient matrices B, B', A and A', are omitted.

In this expression, the part in the first pair of square brackets represents the aggregate output, while that in the second pair the aggregate input. (Note that output and input include 'output' and 'input' of storage activities.) On the right-hand side the first term is the discounted expected value of the stocks of commodities produced at the beginning of the next period, as well as those to be carried over from the current period by storage and maintenance activities, and the second term is the value of the stocks of commodities currently held in the economy. Accordingly the difference between these two terms gives the value of investment, while the last term PD stands for the total value of consumption. Thus (3.27) corresponds to the Keynesian *ex post* accounting equilibrium condition: Net output = investment + consumption.

As has been seen in a previous chapter, we have for each product:

output − supply = the increase in the stock of the product,

and for each producer's good:

demand − input = the increase in the stock of the producer's good.

These equations are now modified because output defined below includes the amount carried over from the past by storage and maintenance activities.[22] Then the first equation is rewritten in the following way:

output − supply = stock to be carried over to the next period + residual.

Similarly, input below includes the stock to be carried over to the future and the second equation above may be written as:

(demand − input) + stock having been carried over from the past = residual.

If the residual is positive for a certain commodity, it is assumed that it will be disposed of without cost. Then the rule of free goods works: the price P_i is

[22] On the right-hand side of the above two equations, the increase in the stock of a commodity includes an unintended one which may be called the 'residual'. This is the part which is not carried over by a storage activity. Then we have:
The increase in the stock of a commodity
= the stock to be carried over to the next period + residual
− the stock having been carried over from the past.
In view of this, the two equations below are obtained immediately.

zero where the residual of commodity i is positive. Multiplying the above two equations by the respective prices obeying the free goods rule and adding them up over all commodities, we have:

the value of output − the value of input − the value of increased
                                         stocks of products and producer's goods
= supply of products − demand for producer's goods
= the total consumption.

This equation obtained under the free goods rule is nothing else than (3.27) and it implies that the net total output equals investment (i.e., the increase in the stocks of products and producer's goods) plus consumption. We also find from it that the total supply of goods equals the total demand for producer's and consumer's goods; however, this is an *ex post* equation which is valid for prices fulfilling the rule of free goods, so that it is not an identity at all. Thus it does not imply Say's law in Keynes' sense.

4   Temporary equilibrium

1 So far the argument has been made in terms of the input and output matrices, A, L and B (and A', L' and B'), of the von Neumann type in the sense that they regard intermediate products and used capital goods as inputs of some production processes and output of some other or the same processes. Von Neumann assesses each process at stationary equilibrium prices and assumes that those processes which can yield profits only at a rate that is less than the maximum rate will not be employed by entrepreneurs. Concerning the quantity aspect of the economy he concentrates his attention on a state of growth equilibrium where the activity level of each and every process expands at a uniform rate. In this state of growth equilibrium, if the commodities are produced more than they are demanded, they are in excess supply and will become free goods whose prices are zero. Excluding these free goods, von Neumann's equilibrium is a long-run steady growth equilibrium with all processes expanding at an equalized rate.

It is clear that such a state, though one may imagine it, is very far from the reality of an actual economy. It is impossible to assume that it may approximate the actual movement of the economy even in the long run, whilst it obviously does not in the short run. The actual economy is always at a transition stage from one state to another; the proportions of its sectors are subject to constant fluctuations. Moreover, his model assumes that the primary factors of production (land and labour) are available as much as they are required. This means that it is definitely inapplicable to such economies as the UK's, West Germany's and Japan's, because of the scarcity of land there, while it may perfectly fit the US economy at some stage, where land is vast and labour is imported at a constant real wage rate. It is true, of course, that there are would-be *gastarbeiter* in the third world, who are prepared to come to industrial countries at the prevailing wage rate there. But it is normal, rather than exceptional, that the elasticity of supply of labour is positive but finite with respect to real wages.

Furthermore, it must be added that the stability of von Neumann's growth equilibrium has not yet been established (perhaps not even discussed), while its existence has been confirmed by many mathematicians and economists. It is true that Solow and Samuelson[1] have shown, under some reasonable assumptions specified below, that the balanced growth equilibrium of their model is stable. But, as will be seen soon, the lag structure of their model is entirely opposite to the one of the von Neumann model. While in the latter the stocks of goods resulting from the production activities in the previous period determine the level of activities in the current period, the former gives no consideration to the constraints of limited availability of stocks of goods and simply assumes that the current activity levels of production determine outputs in the following period.

To expound this fact we may use the following notation. Let $X_i(t)$ be the output of commodity i in period t. The use of stock of good i available at the beginning of period t is assumed to be a function of $X_1(t), \ldots, X_n(t)$, that is $f_i(X_1(t), \ldots, X_n(t))$. In addition, we assume, for simplicity's sake, that the entire output $X_i(t-1)$ in the previous period is reserved for further production and made available for production in period t. We may then write:

$$X_i(t-1) = f_i(X_1,(t) \ldots X_n(t)) \qquad i = 1, \ldots, n. \qquad (4.1)$$

This is the type of lags dealt with by von Neumann.

On the other hand, assuming one period of production lag, Solow and Samuelson put production functions in the form:

$$X_i(t+1) = g_i(X_1(t), \ldots, X_n(t)) \qquad i = 1, \ldots, n \qquad (4.2)$$

and show that the path $\{X_1(t), \ldots, X_n(t)\}, t = 0, 1, \ldots, ad\ infinitum$ generated from the system (4.2) converges on the balanced growth equilibrium if functions g_i's are (1) non-negative, (2) non-decreasing, (3) indecomposable and (4) homogeneous of degree one in the non-negative region of X.[2] This theorem may be applied to the system (4.1) too because it is reasonable to assume that the demands for the stocks of goods, f_i's, satisfy the above four conditions. Then, in view of the fact that lags of the system (4.1) are in reverse to those of (4.2), we find that the von Neumann balanced growth equilibrium of the system (4.1) is unstable.

Of course, (4.1) is a very special form of the von Neumann model, so that despite the above we must refrain from deriving any conclusive conclusion about the stability of the balanced growth solutions of the model. In fact, where joint production is allowed for, one may naturally guess from the proof of the Turnpike Theorem[3] that the balanced growth equilibrium of

---

[1] R. M. Solow and P. A. Samuelson, 'Balanced Growth under Constant Returns to Scale', *Econometrica*, July 1953, pp. 412–24.

[2] See M. Morishima, *Equilibrium, Stability and Growth*, Oxford, 1964, pp. 196–210. For the definition of indecomposability of the system, see ibid., p. 198.

[3] See, for example, M. Morishima, *Theory of Economic Growth*, Oxford, 1969, pp. 190–4.

the von Neumann economy may be stable or unstable with respect to any direction, or stable with respect to some directions and unstable with respect to other directions. It is evident that, in the case of an unstable balanced growth equilibrium, the concept of such an equilibrium has no relevance to the actual analysis of the economy, regardless of it being of a long-run perspective, or just within a temporary, myopic vision.

Consequently, the von Neumann theory has to be substantially and drastically revised if it is to be useful. In the following we first of all remove his condition that all outputs must expand at an equal rate in the state of equilibrium; instead the current output vector X may be disproportional to the output vector $\bar{X}$ in the previous period. Secondly, we rule out excess demand for any good in the state of equilibrium, though it may be consistent with excess supply if the price of the relevant good is zero, i.e., the rule of free goods prevails. As the list of goods of the economy includes those goods, such as intermediate products and old capital goods, which are not generally traded in the market, but are produced in one section and handed over to another in the same firm, so the market mechanism does not work for a number of goods in the economy. For these goods too, however, excess demand has to be cleared, because otherwise the economy cannot be efficient. We thus assume that firms are organized and operate in an efficient way, so that there is neither shortage nor overabundance of these goods unless they are free goods. (It is noted that for those goods with no market accounting prices are set. They are zero where they are over-produced.) We are concerned with the establishment of an equilibrium in an economy where (1) firms are operated efficiently, i.e., sections of each firm are connected with each other in an efficient way and (2) the market works so as to link firms with each other, as well as to link firms with households, in an efficient manner.

Reflecting this fact, prices are also classified into two categories; one being the market prices and the other the efficiency prices. There needs to be no explanation of the market prices; they are of course determined in the market, while efficiency prices are accounting, or imputed, prices determined by the firms themselves for the purpose of efficient management. Although they are not published, as the market prices are, the prices of these two categories are equally significant from the point of view of running the national economy. Unless the price vector P (consisting of the prices of these two categories) is flexibly regulated, the establishment of equilibrium is impossible.

Finally, we deal with an economy with multiple primary factors of production, i.e., heterogeneous labour and heterogeneous land. Then the labour and land input coefficients of various production processes form a matrix, say L. The total demand for labour and land is represented by LX. On the other hand, the availability (or supply) of these factors is shown by a vector $\bar{N}$, which is usually considered as depending upon the prices of factors. We assume, however, for the sake of simplicity that $\bar{N}$ is constant. In the factor market the demand LX is compared with $\bar{N}$. If there is an excess demand the factor price is raised so as to remove it. In this chapter we first assume, as we do for goods, the rule of free goods for factors, in order to show the existence of temporary equilibrium. Obviously, as far as the factors of production are concerned, this is a very bad assumption which is never allowed to hold in the actual economy where wages never vanish in spite of the existence of unemployment. (Samuelson has given this rule a name, 'the neoclassical rule of shadow prices', in reference to wage determination. He has applied it to his Ricardian economy. The result is obviously unsatisfactory.[4]) In later sections of this chapter, therefore, we replace it by a more reasonable one and find out its consequences.

2 There still remains three assumptions which von Neumann made in his growth equilibrium model. The first is Say's law, so that entrepreneurs can make investments with no financial constraints. Secondly, constant returns to scale prevail in production. There is no optimum size of the production unit; by constructing exactly the same factory on the adjacent site the firm can double its size without losing efficiency. Thirdly, there is no instantaneous production process; thus A' and B' are absent. It takes one unit of time in order for each process to be completed. As has been discussed in the previous chapter, these assumptions are unsatisfactory and have to be replaced by more general ones. It seems, however, to be strategically wise to retain all of them and obtain first the standard result to the effect that there exists a point in the price-activity domain at which the economy establishes a temporary equilibrium. Beginning with this simple case, we shall in a later part of this chapter extend our analysis to a more realistic, and logically more general, case where Say's law is at least partially denied and increasing returns to scale and instantaneous production processes are allowed for.

It has already been discussed in one of my previous books that a von Neumann-like economy which is very similar to our present model has a set of temporary equilibrium solutions.[5] For the convenience of those persons who are for the first time concerned with this type of problem and thus have not yet read that part of the book, I shall reproduce the essential part of the argument concisely. To show the existence of an equilibrium we follow the proof given by such contemporary authors as Arrow, Debreu, Hahn, Gale

[4] P. A. Samuelson, 'The Canonical Classical Model of Political Economy', *Journal of Economic Literature*, 1978, pp. 1415–34. See also M. Morishima, *Ricardo's Economics*, Cambridge University Press, 1989, pp. 121–5.

[5] M. Morishima, *Theory of Economic Growth*, chapter VIII.

and Nikaido and apply the following lemma after adapting it to the model which we are now discussing.

Lemma: Where excess demand functions $E_i(P_1, \ldots, P_n)$, $i = 1, \ldots, n$, are all continuous in price $P_j \geqslant 0$, $j = 1, \ldots, n$, satisfying Walras' identity:

$$\Sigma P_i E_i(P_1, \ldots, P_n) \equiv 0, \tag{4.1*}$$

then there is a non-negative, non-zero price set, $(P_1, \ldots, P_n)$, such that:

$$E_i(P_1, \ldots, P_n) \leqslant 0, \quad i = 1, \ldots n. \tag{4.2*}$$

Furthermore, if (4.2*) holds with strict inequality '<' for some i, then the corresponding P_i is zero.

This lemma is often referred to as the Gale–Nikaido–Debreu (or GND) lemma. There is, however, an important difference between this standard case and our von Neumann-like model. While the former assumes diminishing returns to scale prevailing in the economy, the latter is concerned with an economy in which returns are constant with respect to expansion or reduction of the scale of production. Therefore, in this case the activity levels X can change independently even though prices P are fixed, so that in order to determine X it must appear in the lemma as independent variables.

In order to rewrite the lemma such that it would fit our model, let us first write the equilibrium conditions explicitly. Besides the condition on investment and savings given later, equilibrium conditions include the following three sets of inequalities:

$$PA + WL \geqslant z\psi B, \tag{4.3}$$

$$B\bar{X} \geqslant AX + D(P, W, X), \tag{4.4}$$

$$\bar{N} \geqslant LX, \tag{4.5}$$

where z represents $1/(1 + r)$; W denotes the vector of prices of the primary factors of production; $D(P, W, X)$ the individuals' demand for goods for the purpose of consumption. As we assume Say's law, there is no financial obstacle to investment and all production activities are financed by the firms' revolving fund; q_j is removed from (3.4) in chapter 3 or (4.3) above.

Excess demand for goods and primary factors of production is given by:

$$E = AX + D(P, W, X) - B\bar{X}, \tag{4.6}$$

$$F = LX - \bar{N} \tag{4.7}$$

respectively, while excess profits of production are given by:

$$G = z\psi B - PA - WL. \tag{4.8}$$

The savings of the households of workers and landowners are:

$$W\bar{N} - PD(P, W, X)$$

while net corporation savings may be defined as an excess of the firms' profits realized at the beginning of the current period, $[PB-(P_{-1}A+ W_{-1}L)]\bar{X}$, over the increase in the corporations' assets due to the reappraisal of the stock of goods, $[P-z_{-1}\psi_{-1}]B\bar{X}$, from the discounted expected prices, $z_{-1}\psi_{-1}$, to the current prices, P. (Alternatively, this appreciation of the value of the stock of commodities $B\bar{X}$ may be regarded as constituting the corporations' investment):

$$[PB-(P_{-1}A+ W_{-1}L)]\bar{X}-[P-z_{-1}\psi_{-1}]B\bar{X}$$

and their investment is:

$$z\psi BX - PB\bar{X}.$$

Then the excess of total (individual and corporational) savings over investment may be given, in view of the fact that $[z_{-1}\psi_{-1}B - P_{-1}A - W_{-1}L]\bar{X}$ vanishes because the rule of profitability holds in the previous period, as:

$$H= W\bar{N}- PD(P, W, X)-[z\psi BX - PB\bar{X}]. \tag{4.9}$$

In the state of temporary equilibrium there are no savings which are not invested, so that investment is at least as large as savings. Thus:[6]

$$H\leqslant 0. \tag{4.10}$$

From (4.6)–(4.9) it is at once seen that the sum of PE, WF, GX and H identically vanishes because the sum is equal to $(z_{-1}\psi_{-1}B - P_{-1}A - W_{-1}L)\bar{X}$ that is zero by virtue of the temporary equilibrium conditions and the rule of profitability which are both assumed to hold in the previous period. (This also means that the corporations' net savings defined above vanish as has been stated.) We then obtain:

$$PE+ WF+GX+H\equiv 0, \tag{4.11}$$

which is called the extended Walras identity.

The extension has been made in two places. First, excess profits from various processes, GX, explicitly appear in the identity, because of the assumption of constant returns to scale. Also it includes excess of savings over investment, H, as an item, because we grasp the economy in the midst of dynamic movement, so that we cannot eliminate savings and investment,

[6] Remember that Say's law is assumed to prevail; there is no financial constraint to be imposed upon investment.

as the usual static general equilibrium theorists do. The identity (4.11) plays a powerful role in the proof of the existence of temporary equilibrium below. We, nevertheless, require a few more assumptions in order to be able to embark upon the work of proof. First, we assume that expected prices ψ are continuous functions of current prices of all goods and factors; i.e.:

$$\psi = \psi(P_1, \ldots, P_n, W_1, \ldots, W_l). \tag{4.12}$$

Concerning the form of the function ψ we make no additional assumption. The continuity is just enough, despite the additional assumption in the previous work[7] to the effect that ψ is homogeneous of degree 1 in P's and W's. This condition, which has the same implications as Hicks' condition that the elasticities of expectations are all equal to 1, should obviously be irrelevant to the existence of equilibrium.

Secondly, we assume the expectation formed in the previous period about the total value of the stocks of goods of the current period is macroscopically correct, though this assumption of correct expectation may not be fulfilled microscopically, i.e., it does not hold for each kind of product. The condition for this macroscopic perfect foresight may be written in the following form:

$$\psi_{-1} B\bar{X} = PB\bar{X}. \tag{4.13}$$

We use this as the condition for determining the level of prices in spite of it being very artificial for that capacity. Nevertheless we have to use it, because in an analysis whose main purpose is not the determination of the absolute price level, the condition for determining it may be provisionally artificial. As soon as the model is linked with a serious analysis of money in chapter 6, (4.13) will be replaced by the demand–supply equation of money that determines the price level.

Finally, we assume that the demand for consumption goods from profits is negligible, while the aggregate consumption of workers and landowners does not exceed their full employment income, $W\bar{N}$; hence we obtain:

$$W\bar{N} \geqq PD(P, W, X). \tag{4.14}$$

By applying the lemma stated above we can show that there is a non-negative, non-zero set (X, P, W, r) fulfilling the temporary equilibrium conditions (4.3), (4.4), (4.5) and (4.10), because the extended Walras identity holds. We can then easily show that the absolute level of prices and wages is determined by (4.13). In the state of temporary equilibrium the rule of free goods must hold. This is seen in the following way. If the rule did not hold, we would have either $P_i > 0$ for some i for which $E_i < 0$, or $W_i > 0$ with

---

[7] See Morishima, *Theory of Economic Growth*, p. 139.

$F_i < 0$. Hence $PE + WF < 0$. This contradicts the extended Walras identity, because $GX \leqslant 0$ and $H \leqslant 0$ in the state of temporary equilibrium. Similarly, if the rule of profitability did not hold, we would have $GX < 0$, a contradiction to the Walras identity again. Thus the rule of free goods and the rule of profitability are both valid in temporary equilibrium, so that we have both $PE + WF = 0$ and $GX = 0$, which, together with the Walras identity, imply $H = 0$ (that is, savings = investment).

3 We have so far been concerned with the business of establishing an equilibrium for the model expounded in chapter 3. In doing so we have made an assumption that it includes no instantaneous production process. It is of course true that in the actual economy there are goods which are produced almost with no time lag, especially so when production which is made according to a conveyor belt system is divided into a sequence of production processes and the final stage of the sequence, taken as an independent process, is concerned. We do not assume that every process of the final stage is instantaneous; we are only interested in showing that there is no change in the result even though some processes are instantaneous.

Using the notation in chapter 3 we designate the activity levels of instantaneous processes as Y. A' and B' are the matrices of input and output coefficients of these processes and L' the matrix of their labour and land input coefficients. We then have the following sets of inequalities for temporary equilibrium:

(i) demand–supply inequalities for goods:

$$B\bar{X} + B'Y \geqslant AX + A'Y + D(P, W, X, Y),$$

(ii) demand–supply inequalities for primary factors of production:

$$\bar{N} \geqslant LX + L'Y,$$

(iii) price–cost inequalities:

(a) $z\psi B \leqslant PA + WL$;   (b) $zPB' \leqslant PA' + WL'$,

(iv) savings–investment inequality:

$$H \leqslant 0,$$

where z is defined as $1/(1+r)$, as before, while H includes profits from instantaneous processes as a part of the aggregate savings; otherwise there is no change in H. Then we can show the following *modified* extended Walras identity holds as long as the temporary equilibrium conditions (iii(a)) and the associating rule of profitability hold for non-instantaneous processes in the previous period. That is:

$$PE + WF + GX + H \equiv 0, \qquad\qquad\qquad (4.15)$$

where E and F are approximately redefined vectors of excess demand. In parallel to G we may define G' as $zPB' - (PA' + WL')$. It may then be noted that in the modified Walras identity above the term $G'Y$ is absent in spite of the presence of GX.

In spite of these changes in the model we can prove, by the use of almost the same method, that there is a point at which the conditions (i)–(iv) above are all satisfied. Then the level of temporary equilibrium prices and wages is adjusted such that expectations are correct macroscopically, so that equation (4.13) holds.

The presence of instantaneous processes does not affect our conclusion that there is a temporary general equilibrium in the economy. This is always true under Say's law. The rule of free goods and the rule of profitability are both effective in the state of equilibrium. Not only are all kinds of primary factors of production fully employed, unless they are free goods, but also there is no stock of old capital goods left unused, unless they are obsolete and, hence, free. Furthermore, there is no overproduction of intermediate products. It can be shown that the point of temporary equilibrium is a point of temporary Pareto efficiency.

However, it is possible that the equilibrium wages thus established is not high enough for enabling the workers to make a living at the subsistence level. If it is so, the workers are demoralized with the equilibrium payment; they do not supply labour of the amount that, the model supposes, they would do. They would make strong resistance against the wages' falling to such a low level and, therefore, an additional constraint that the wage rate must be at least as high as Pc, where c is the subsistence consumption bundle, must be imposed.

In order to investigate the effects of this constraint upon temporary equilibrium, we simplify the model by assuming that there are (i) two commodities (consumption goods and capital goods), (ii) one primary factor (labour) and (iii) two production processes, where input and output coefficients are $(0, a_{2j}, l_j)$ and (b_{1j}, b_{2j}), $j = 1, 2$. We assume process 1 is less labour intensive (or more capital intensive) than process 2, so that:

$$a_{21}/l_1 > a_{22}/l_2.$$

The temporary equilibrium conditions for prices are assumed to hold with strict equality for both processes:

$$b_j P^e = (1 + r^e)(a_{2j} P_2^e + l_j W^e), \qquad j = 1, 2, \qquad \text{where } b_j = (b_{1j}, b_{2j}).$$

Let us now suppose that the price of commodities remains fixed at P^e in spite of the wage rate being set at a higher value, say W^s, than W^e. W^s is set at the subsistence level. Then r^e would decline to r^s at which conditions:

$$b_1 P^e = (1+r^s)(a_{21}P_2^e + l_1 W^s), \qquad b_2 P^e < (1+r^s)(a_{22}P_2^e + l_2 W^s)$$

are shown to be fulfilled, because process 2 is more labour intensive, so that it becomes less profitable at (P^e, W^s). Therefore, activity levels must be adjusted. As process 2 is not utilized because of it being unprofitable, we have:

$$b_{21}\bar{X}_1 + b_{22}\bar{X}_2 = a_{21}X_1^s,$$

at (P^e, W^s), while:

$$b_{21}\bar{X}_1 + b_{22}\bar{X}_2 = a_{21}X_1^e + a_{22}X_2^e$$

at (P^e, W^e). We can then show that:

$$LX^s = l_1 X_1^s < LX^e = l_1 X_1^e + l_2 X_2^e.$$

Thus employment is decreased so that unemployment emerges in the labour market.[8] In the case of many kinds of labour being present, we have the relativity constraint on wage rates, in addition to the above absolute subsistence constraint. This also would create unemployment of labour.

4 We have so far assumed Say's law in its purest and narrowest form; all entrepreneurs carry out their production activities without borrowing money from bankers or other financiers. In the following we extend the concept of Say's law so as to cover more realistic circumstances where some entrepreneurs may borrow money with the purpose of getting purchasing power for obtaining the necessary means of production. Bankers are, on the other hand, assumed to be passive and adaptive. They lend money as much as they are requested and, in addition to this, they automatically lend the entire amount of money they have just received from entrepreneurs as interest, again to the same or other entrepreneurs to satisfy their demand. Under this perfectly flexible supply of money, entrepreneurs are provided by bankers with the purchasing power they need for their production activities. There is no financial restriction on investment and Say's law holds.

In this type of economy, entrepreneurs must pay the financial cost to the bankers; so that price–cost inequalities are revised so as to include the interest charged by the banks. Thus we have, instead of (iii(a)):

$$z\psi B \leqslant (PA + WL)(I+Q), \tag{4.16}$$

---

[8] As for the consumption goods its demand will increase or decrease according to whether the effect of the wage increase is greater or less than the effect of the decrease in employment. Where its equilibrium condition is violated, its price has to be adjusted.

while (iii(b)) for instantaneous processes are kept intact because we may assume that all these are financed by the revolving fund of the respective firms. In (4.16), as before, Q is a diagonal matrix with non-negative elements, standing for the respective rates of interest, on the diagonal, which are regarded as given in the following. For those processes which are operated by use of the firms' own funds, the corresponding elements of Q take on the value 0. The other amendment which we have to make to the previous system (i)–(iv) is to the excess savings H. It now includes the total amount of interest that goes to the account of banks, $(PA + WL)QX$, which is automatically available for meeting investment demand. Thus, the total savings in H is increased by $(PA + WL)QX$. Concerning all other elements, E, F, G', etc., we make no revision.

It can then be seen that the identity (4.15) which I have referred to as 'the modified extended Walras identity' still continues to hold in this new system. As we assume that entrepreneurs obtain purchasing power as much as they want to have despite the existence of banks, there is no additional constraint on the activities X. In this new system they are adjusted as freely as they were in the previous system where the problem of financing production has been ignored. With given Q, the equilibrium values of P, W, X, Y and z are obtained as the fixed point of the equilibrium conditions, though G and H are revised in the way as has been explained above. The absolute level of prices and wages is adjusted as before, such that expectations of prices are correct macroscopically.

Let P^e, W^e, X^e, Y^e, z^e be equilibrium values of the respective variables. Let us designate the equilibrium value of the rate of profit as r^e, which is equal to $(1/z^e) - 1$. It is needless to say that the full employment of all primary factors of production, the full utilization of old capital goods and the efficient provision of intermediate products are all realized provided the free goods rule holds for commodities and factors. This is the perfect state of equilibrium which neoclassical economists, such as Arrow–Debreu and Arrow–Hahn in particular, seek after. It would be worth emphasizing that Say's law is the main necessary condition for its realization and, therefore, money must be channelled where, and as much as, it is wanted. The banks should not play the role of the controller of investment. They should be adaptive to the decisions made by entrepreneurs and should never take an active part and remain passive in providing capital to the entrepreneurs. Thus the neutrality of the banking system in this sense is a necessary condition for Pareto-efficiency to be realized in the economy.

5 However, as soon as Say's law ceases to be valid, we have a completely different story. To see this, let us divide, as we have done in chapter 3 above, the aggregate investment into Say's law and anti-Say's law parts. Let us

classify, as we have done in chapter 3, production processes into two groups and designate their activity levels as:

$$X^{0*}=\begin{bmatrix}X_I^p\\X_{II}^*\end{bmatrix},\ X^0=\begin{bmatrix}X_I^p\\0\end{bmatrix},\ X^*=\begin{bmatrix}0\\X_{II}^*\end{bmatrix},\tag{4.17}$$

so that $X^{0*}=X^0+X^*$. In order to operate the activities belonging to the first group, which is the anti-Say's law group, entrepreneurs need money offered by bankers or monied men. Where this money is limited in total amount, entrepreneurs might be unable to operate the production processes at the equilibrium levels as they want to or to construct the production facilities at the scale they want to have. They can be run only at the limited levels of X_I^0. Then X_{II} and Y are set at X_{II}^* and Y^*, respectively, corresponding to the value of X_I^0, for which bankers have advanced necessary funds.

It is very difficult to find out what would happen in general, when the amount of the anti-Say's law part of investment is set lower than its equlibrium value:

$$V_I^e=z^e\psi^e B\begin{bmatrix}X_I^e\\0\end{bmatrix}-P^eB\begin{bmatrix}\bar{X}_I\\0\end{bmatrix},\tag{4.18}$$

where $\psi^e=\psi(P^e,\ W^e)$. The activity levels X_I^0 sanctioned by bankers are not necessarily proportional to X_I^e; some activities may be treated favourably by bankers, while some others unfavourably. In the following we first concentrate our attention on the case of X_I^0 being proportional to X_I^e, i.e., $X_I^0=aX_I^e$. Of course $a<1$. Furthermore, we make an assumption to the effect that the elasticity of demand for consumption goods with respect to the factor income is unity, so that $D(P, W, X, Y)$ is homogeneous of degree one in X and Y. Let $X_{II}^*=aX_{II}^e$ and $Y^*=aY^e$. We can then at once see that X_I^0, X_{II}^*, Y^* satisfy the equilibrium condition (i) in section 3 with strict inequality for goods i, for which $(B\bar{X})_i>0$. We can also see that (ii) holds with strict inequality and (iii(a)) modified as (4.16) and (iii(b)) are not disturbed as long as P^e and W^e prevail. This implies that the rule of free goods is violated, while the rule of profitability continues to hold. We can see that $PE+WF<0$ and $GX=0$ and $G'Y=0$; hence $H>0$ from the modified Walras identity. Thus, savings $>$ investment.

However, this amount of savings gives the 'notional' savings according to the recent terminology. It consists of personal notional savings, that is personal notional income *minus* personal consumption, and corporations' notional savings, that is notional profits *minus* the reappraisal of the stocks of goods. Personal notional income includes the expected income of those workers who actually turn out to be unemployed and that of those landowners whose land is not actually fully used. To remove this we must subtract the total value of the excess supply of labour and land or the lost income of unemployed factors (i.e., WF) from the personal notional income. Similarly the corporations' notional profits includes the profits from the sales which are hoped to be realized but actually turn out to be abortive. The latter is also removed if we subtract the total value of the excess supply of goods (i.e., PE) from these notional profits. Thus, $PE + WF + H$ gives the excess of *actual* savings over investment. This is evidently zero by the identity, because GX vanishes at $X = X^*$.

The above argument establishes the proposition that P^e, W^e, z^e, X_I^0, X_{II}^*, Y^* satisfy all the equilibrium conditions (i)–(iv), though the last of the conditions must be amended such that it holds not in the original notional sense but in terms of the actual savings and the actual investment. It is noted that investment too should not be the original notional one intended by entrepreneurs but the actual one which is set lower than the former because of the limitation of the amount of money made available by bankers. It is also emphasized that the rule of free goods does not hold for both goods and factors; in spite of the existence of an excess supply of a good (or a factor), its price remains positive.

The downwards rigidity of prices may be adequate for some goods and factors, but is completely unsatisfactory for others. This is seen for each type of goods and factors in the following way. There are five groups of goods: (i) agricultural and mineral products which may be used as materials for producing other goods, or as final consumption goods, (ii) the manufactured consumption goods, (iii) new capital goods, (iv) old capital goods and (v) intermediate goods. In addition to these we have (vi) labour and land. As has been observed and emphasized by P. J. D. Wiles the prices of commodities in the categories, (ii) and (iii), are rigid or at least sticky.[9] Prices of goods belonging to (iv) and (v) may not be market prices but accounting prices. Firms and other corporations set their accounting prices but these are valid only within their organizations and have no effect in the outside world. As for the primary factors of production we have already examined, though under Say's law, the effects of the downwards rigidity of wages. As for land, Marx pointed out that some positive amount of the absolute rent may coexist with the excess supply of land, by saying that 'in all civilised countries a comparatively appreciable portion of land always remains uncultivated',[10] whereas it could be utilized if the absolute rent were lower. Thus the downward rigidity generally prevails in the category (vi).

On the other hand, the prices of agricultural and mineral products are

[9] P. J. D. Wiles, *Price, Cost and Output*, 2nd edn Basil Blackwell, 1961.
[10] K. Marx, *Capital*, vol. III, Progress Publishers, Moscow, 1966, p. 757.

flexible; they are decided in the market by demand and supply, and where demand and supply are not equalized, they fluctuate as the cobweb theorem shows. Let i be a commodity in group (i), and suppose it cannot be produced instantaneously. Then, on the supply side, we have $(B\bar{X})_i > 0$ and $(B'Y)_i = 0$, so that the excess demand for i may be put in the form:

$$E_i = (AX^0)_i + (AX^*)_i + (A'Y^*)_i + D_i(P^e, W^e, X^0, X^*, Y^*) - (B\bar{X})_i.$$
(4.19)

As we have $E_i < 0$ in the state of 'equilibrium' established above, P_i will decrease so as to establish $E_i = 0$, keeping all other variables constant. Thus for the new price we have $P_i < P_i^e$.

Then, such a decline in P would violate the equilibrium conditions (iii(a)) and (iii(b)). For the processes j which produce commodity i, (iii(a)) turns out to be the one with strict inequality ' < ',[11] so that z has to be increased (that is to say, r has to be decreased) to restore (iii(a)). On the other hand, for those processes which use i as material, the cost will decrease and, accordingly, z (or r) has to decrease (or increase) in order to maintain (iii(b)). Thus the processes j producing i become less profitable, while those j utilizing i will be more profitable. X_j for the former will decrease, while X_j or Y_j for the latter will increase. These have an effect on D_i, because this depends on X and Y, in addition to the effects upon $(AX)_i$ and $(A'Y)_i$. There will be a net increase or decrease in the excess demand for i, which will create a further adjustment of P_i. It is evident that this in turn gives rise to further changes in X and Y. But those secondary adjustments are smaller than the previous ones. In this way, the excess supply of commodity i will finally be cleared.

In the particular model Keynes has been concerned with, the sectors of agriculture and mining are absent or almost negligible, so that there is no sector in which the price mechanism regulating demand and supply works. Moreover, he has assumed that it takes no time for completing the final process of producing consumption goods. Where the demands for consumption goods $D(\ldots)$ are set at a low level, there is no problem in adjusting the activity levels of production of manufactured consumption goods. Without time lag, their levels of outputs are adjusted such that outputs are equal to their demands, whereas this would give rise to an excess supply of goods in the pipelines of producing consumption goods. (We implicitly assume here that every process manufacturing consumption goods have the final stage which requires only a negligible period time in order to obtain its final product, so that it may be regarded as instantaneous.)

---

[11] We assume that ψ_i decreases wherever P_i decreases.

Thus, in Keynesian circumstances, an X_I^0 set proportionally lower than X_I^e creates a state of affairs where X_{II}^* and Y^* are also cut down from the level of X_{II}^e and Y^e in the same proportion. There is no change in prices and wages; hence no change in the rate of profit either. Then unemployment would be observed and remain in the market of primary factors of production because their prices are rigid downwards. Also, the stocks of intermediate products would, in general, be in excess supply and a part of the stocks of old capital goods too. Thus the Keynesian economy is a fixprice economy, and its equilibrium could hardly be Pareto-efficient, of course.

As has been seen above, an economy with agriculture and mining being present, which is the economy discussed by Ricardo, is not a complete fixprice economy. Where Say's law, partly or entirely, ceases to prevail in this economy,[12] prices of agricultural and mineral products are adjusted and deviate from their temporary equilibrium values, P_i^e's. This will bring about a difference in the rate of profits between these sectors and other fixprice sectors and will result in the economy being in a state of Pareto-inefficiency. Regardless of the economy being of the Keynesian or the Ricardian type, we may thus conclude that Adam Smith's invisible hand would not work as soon as the unrealistic hypothesis of Say's law is denied and bankers control at least a part of the aggregate investment.

Finally, where X_I^0 is not proportional to X^e, that is, where bankers treat some of the processes in the anti-Say's law group very favourably at the sacrifice of the other processes in the same group, it is obvious that no clear-cut relationship is proposed as reasonable, between X_{II}^* and X_{II}^e, and Y^* and Y^e. The economy will run in a direction entirely different from the temporary equilibrium under Say's law. In this case, the temporary equilibrium analysis developed in earlier sections of the present chapter cannot be considered as a model analysis which gives a norm of working of the economy. Thus, in order for the temporary equilibrium solutions to be able to provide useful suggestions concerning the actual state of the economy, we must implicitly assume that the proportions between components of X_I^0 are not diverted from those of X_I^e significantly. In any case, it is correct to conclude that the invisible hand does not work and the economy is brought into a state of Pareto-inefficiency once anti-Say's law activities are admitted.

The proposition that the temporary equilibrium is a Pareto optimum[13] is usually referred to as the first welfare theorem. It is valid under Say's law but does not in general hold if Say's law does not prevail. As it is violated in

---

[12] However, Ricardo himself has accepted Say's law.
[13] M. Morishima, *Theory of Economic Growth*, Clarendon Press, Oxford; 1969, pp. 160 ff.

the actual world, the welfare theorem cannot be regarded as being true at the temporary equilibrium point being accompanied with underemployment of the factors of production. Where the financial constraint is slackened and, hence, investment expands, then the actual point will be nearer to the temporary equilibrium point so that the degree of Pareto-inefficiency of the point will diminish.

This effect should be attributed to banks as their contributions to welfare. The conventional view, however, does not see this but emphasizes that a Pareto-optimum is realized as long as economic competition is carried out perfectly. Once Say's law which is behind this view is rejected, the problem of how much the anti-Say's law prevailing in the economy deviates from Say's law becomes relevant. Behind a given anti-Say's law there may be alternative financial systems for raising investment funds. These systems are compared in their merits and demerits, and a welfare theorem should be established by taking into consideration the following points: which system would promote investment most, which would secure the firms most and make them confident, and so on.

Although the first welfare theorem is often interpreted as a proof of Adam Smith's invisible hand thesis, it should not be forgotten that the thesis tacitly assumes Say's law. Under anti-Say's law, even if households and firms intend to act in their own interest, their schedules of action cannot be fully carried out, because of a shortage of money. The nexus between the real and monetary sectors would be vitally important for welfare.

In financing anti-Say's law activities there are at least two ways; one borrows the necessary money from banks, as is usually seen in Germany, Italy, France and Japan, and the other raises the necessary amount from the market by issuing new shares as is practised in Great Britain and America. Which is more efficient in promoting industrial activities? In spite of the importance of this question the present volume cannot deal, in full detail, with this comparative systems problem, though its later chapters discuss some aspects of the relationship between industries and banks which now prevails in Japan. (In any case, it is interesting to see that the so-called industrial countries may further be classified into two groups according to whether countries are net exporters or net importers of manufacturing products. Germany, France, Italy and Japan are clear net exporters, while Great Britain and the USA are clear net importers. Are their financial systems responsible for this fact?)

6 Let us examine, in this section, how repercussions are made from anti-Say's law activities to Say's law and instantaneous activities. For this purpose, agricultural and mineral products, manufactured final products and those kinds of intermediate products which are sold to other firms are

listed in the upper part of the input and output matrices, A, A', B and B', and the activities which produce these commodities are listed in the second half of the activity list. Then, in the lower part of the matrices presented are old capital goods as well as those intermediate products which are produced, not for sale to other firms, but for use within the firms. The activities for production of intermediate products are presented in the first half of the activity list. Old capital goods are regarded as joint products of some other processes.

Throughout the following we identify the activities in the first half as anti-Say's law activities, whose levels are fixed at X_I^0, and those in the second half as Say's law or instantaneous activities. This identification should be satisfactory, at least as a practical approximation. This is because it is reasonable to assume that the firms need the financial support by bankers for the construction and expansion of the production pipelines, so that the activities for producing intermediate products, especially those for the firms' own use, are all of the anti-Say's law type, while activities at the final stage of production, which include those bringing intermediate products at the exit of the pipeline as completed products that are sold to other firms, are self-financed by the firms' revolving fund and are classified as Say's law activities.

Because old capital goods as by-products of production processes which use new or younger capital goods only appear in the lower part of the output matrix B, we may assume that there is no joint output as far as the upper part of B is concerned. Of course, there are cases in which two or several outputs, say, mutton, sheep skin and wool, are obtained from a single action of slaughtering sheep. Neglecting all these possibilities of proper joint production and assuming that there are no alternative processes to produce the commodities listed in the upper part of B, we find that the right-hand corner of the upper part of B may be written as J, where J is an 'incomplete' identity matrix in the sense that some of the diagonal elements may take on the value 0, instead of 1, while others are 1. Similarly, the upper right-hand corner of B' has a submatrix J'. It is assumed that those commodities for which 0 is placed on the diagonal of J (that is, they are not produced by production processes with a time lag) are produced by those which are instantaneous. They, therefore, have 1 on the diagonal of J'. Conversely those products which are not produced instantaneously are produced by processes requiring time. Thus J and J' are conjugate and their sum makes the identity matrix, I, which has, of course, 1 at every place on the diagonal.

Then rows of this output submatrix are further permuted such that commodities produced instantaneously are first listed and next followed by those for which it takes one period of time to complete their final stage of production. Its columns are also identically permuted, so that instantaneous processes which are listed first are followed by the processes with production time lags of one period. On the input side, we make exactly the same arrangements. Denoting the input submatrix at the upper right-hand corner by M, the demand–supply inequalities for the completed outputs (that is to say, the intermediate products used within the firms and old capital goods as joint outputs being excluded) may be put in the following form:

$$\begin{bmatrix} Y \\ \bar{X}_{\text{II}} \end{bmatrix} \geq M \begin{bmatrix} Y \\ X_{\text{II}} \end{bmatrix} + KX_1^0 + D(P,W,X_1^0,X_{\text{II}},Y), \tag{4.20}$$

where components of $\bar{X}_{\text{II}}$, X_{II} and Y have been appropriately rearranged, K represents a submatrix of A at the upper, left-hand corner; and D is the consumption vector of the reduced dimension obtained by removing void components corresponding to the intermediate products and old capital goods used within the firms. Some particular components of D, such as those for the new capital goods and the intermediate products to be sold to other firms, are identically zero.

In (4.20) it is easily seen that those inequalities for Y, in fact, hold with equality, because Y can be adjusted so as to establish equations. It is possible, on the other hand, that some of the remaining inequalities of (4.20) may hold with strict inequality '$>$', because their left-hand sides are fixed at $\bar{X}_{\text{II}}$ and are not adjustable to the respective right-hand sides. The differences between the left- and right-hand sides of the inequalities of (4.20) for $\bar{X}_{\text{II}}$ give the unsold amount of $\bar{X}_{\text{II}}$ which could be stored for selling in the next period. Let S be the vector of residuals. In view of the fact that there is no residual for outputs produced by instantaneous processes, we may put (4.20) in the following form:

$$\begin{bmatrix} Y \\ \bar{X}_{\text{II}} \end{bmatrix} = M \begin{bmatrix} Y \\ X_{\text{II}} \end{bmatrix} + D(\ldots) + KX_1^0 + \begin{bmatrix} 0 \\ S \end{bmatrix}, \tag{4.21}$$

where the last three terms on the right-hand side stand for the vectors of consumption, the demand for investment purposes and the residuals.

As for S a comment may be desirable. I have already pointed out that our activities include not only those for production but also those for storage and maintenance. It is also implicitly assumed that commodities must be properly stored and maintained in order for them to be available for use at the beginning of the next period. Accordingly those parts of the stocks of commodities which are intended to be stored for the next period are not accounted as residuals; they should instead be regarded as inputs for storage activities. Thus the residuals include only those stocks which are not intended to be carried over to the next period and, therefore, are disposed of freely. We denote a component of S by s_i in the following.

Where the rule of free goods prevails, the price of commodity i, P_i, is set at zero if $s_i > 0$. Then the holders of the commodity will lose their assets in value, so that they will counteract in order to prevent the rule. If they themselves either buy back or destroy s_i to remove the residual, they can keep the price at a positive level. The amount needed for the buying back or for the loss of the asset by destroying s_i amounts to $P_i s_i$; of course they would maximize the value of stocks which remains after removing s_i, i.e., $u_i = P_i(X_i - s_i)$.

System (4.21) is very similar to the conventional input–output system. In the case of Say's law activities X_{II} being absent, S also disappears and (4.21) is reduced to:

$$Y = MY + D(P,W,X^0,Y) + KX_1^{()}. \tag{4.21'}$$

As Y is perfectly flexible and can establish (4.21') without any help from price adjustment, we may regard P and W as constant in (4.21). Once X_1^0 is determined, Y is obtained by solving the equation. This gives repercussions of X_1^0 upon Y.

On the other hand, in the general case of lagged variables X_{II} being present, solutions are not so simple. First, in order to establish equality between the demand for and supply of agricultural and mineral products which belong to group II because of their production lags, their prices have to fluctuate. Then, on the one hand, the consumption demand for them is increased or decreased, and, on the other, the profitability of agriculture and mining is affected. This latter obviously gives rise to a change in the activity levels of these two industries. This mechanism has traditionally been the subject of the cobweb theorem, which may be reformulated so as to fit the input–output system (4.21). The agricultural and mining activities are evidently not instantaneous, so that they constitute X_{II}, but should be distinguished from other (fixprice) members of X_{II}, because they depend on their prices. Later, we denote the set of these flexprice activities by Z and the set of non-instantaneous fixprice activities by X_{II}. For the sake of making the analysis simpler we neglect Z throughout this section, by assuming that there is neither agriculture nor mining.

As D depends on P, W, X_1^0, X_{II} and Y, we can solve the first half of (4.21) with respect to the products of instantaneous processes Y_i, $i = 1, \ldots, h$:

$$Y_i = Y_i(X_{II}, X_1^0, P, W), \qquad i = 1, \ldots, h, \tag{4.22}$$

where X_{II} consists of components $X_{h+1}, \ldots, X_n$. Substituting this into the second half of (4.21) and taking into account the fact that D_i's vanish in these equations, we may put them in the form:

$$\bar{X}_i = \sum_1^h m_{ij} Y_j(X_{II}, X_1^0, P, W) + \sum_{h+1}^n m_{ij} X_j + k_i X_1^0 + s_i \qquad i = h+1, \ldots, n, \tag{4.23}$$

where k_i's are row vectors. If we could treat s_i's as given in these equations we could solve them with respect to X_j's by regarding X_I^0 as parameters. But, unfortunately, s_i's are unknown, like X_j's.

In order to evade this difficulty, let us assume that the economy works in such a way that the total value of stocks remaining after s_i's are removed, that is, the sum of the amounts used for production and investment, $\sum u_i = \sum P_i(\bar{X}_i - s_i)$, is maximized. Naturally, the maximization is made in a decentralized way by the agent i holding $\bar{X}_i$, independently of other owners of $\bar{X}_j$'s; but in the following, we simplify the problem by maximizing $\sum u_i$ in a centralized way, subject to (4.23) and $X_i \geqq 0$, $i = h+1, \ldots, n$. Then s_i and X_i are determined, say, at s_i^* and X_i^*, $i = h+1, \ldots, n$. Once these values of X_i^* are given, we then obtain from (4.22) the value of instantaneous outputs Y_i at Y_i^*, $i = 1, \ldots, h$. These Y_i^*'s, together with X_i^*'s, constitute Y^* and X_{II}^*, respectively. Thus it is the input–output system (4.21) which decides the correspondence of Y and X_{II} to given anti-Say's law activities X_I^0.

The system, however, differs from the conventional one considerably. Its input coefficient matrix M includes inputs at the final stage of production only, while the conventional inputs for a product include inputs at its earlier stages of production as well, so that elements of M would be much smaller than the corresponding elements of the usual input coefficient matrix. In our system (4.21) the inputs at earlier stages are included in the term KX_I^0. We consider them as fixed, as we take X_I^0 as being determined in the market of financing investment, while according to the traditional input–output system they are regarded as changing in proportion to Y and X_{II}. Thus our reasoning is a complete reverse of the traditional analysis. Instead of finding the values of Y and X_{II} which correspond to given X_I^0, it finds out the values of Y and X_{II} on the assumption that the vector X_I adjusts itself accordingly as Y and X_{II} change. This difference is due to the fact that the traditional analysis assumes Say's law and ignores the problem of how the firms finance production.

Secondly, as has been mentioned before, it also ignores production lags completely as it assumes production being instantaneous. It is clear that this assumption is unsatisfactory at least for a number of sectors, where the production period exceeds 1 period, the base period on which the input–output table is constructed. The traditional theory, therefore, overestimates the total output as it takes, by assumption, outputs of sectors with large production lags as being produced within the period. It misses the fact that production is constrained by the stocks of commodities $\bar{X}_{II}$ available to the economy. In the system with lags, outputs Y and X_{II} can be obtained, in the manner as explained above, by solving the simultaneous equations (4.21) having the left-hand side partly fixed at $\bar{X}_{II}$. An algorithm to solve them has been discussed above. There remains, however, the problem of realization of equilibrium which is yet unsolved, that is, how the firms in the actual economy will reach these solutions in spite of their decentralized decision-making in competitive circumstances. This will be discussed in chapter 5 below.

Finally, let us classify goods and factors into two categories: the final products, and factors or means of production. The former consists of outputs produced instantaneously, agricultural and mineral products (though these have been neglected in the above) and other completed products including the intermediate products to be sold as 'parts' to other firms, while the latter is made up of other intermediate products used within the firms where they are produced, old capital goods and primary factors of production. It is now noted that equilibrium established in the markets of the final products does not bring forth equilibrium for factors. This is seen in the following way. Let us suppose that X_I^0 is set lower than its temporary equilibrium value X_I^e. If we first ignore effects upon X_{II}, it is certain that an X_I^0 ($< X_I^e$) yields Y^* lower than Y^e, as the conventional input–output analysis concludes. Then the demands for the factors are all lower than their equilibrium levels, so that it is clear that they result in unemployment of all factors. This is a situation which Keynes has called 'poverty in the midst of plenty', that is a Pareto-inefficient state of affairs where unemployment of labour (or poverty) coexists with an excess supply (or plenty) of all other factors of production and production facilities.

Where X_{II} adjusts itself, an X_I^0 set lower than X_I^e brings about room for expansion of X_{II}, because some amount of stocks of $\bar{X}_{II}$ is released from the production of X_I and may be used for expansion of X_{II}. It may be even higher than the temporary equilibrium value X_{II}^e; but when X_I^0 is set low, the expansion of X_{II} would absorb, at least partly, the unemployment of the factors. But it may be concluded that we would still have no full employment of any of them, provided that X_I^0 is set low and the economy is in a state of pessimism. Thus, where we deny the over-all prevalence of Say's law and assume the existence of some anti-Say's law sectors, the mechanism equilibrating demands for and supplies of commodities works only in a corner of the whole economic system. While, on the surface of the economy, the input–output equilibrium condition, though modified into the form (4.21), holds true, in its deep bottom an excess supply of intermediate products, except those which are produced instantaneously, idle stocks of old capital goods and unemployed labour and land are not removed.

7 Let us now observe how the Böhm-Bawerk, Wicksell, Hayek problem of synchronization of production is dealt with in our model. It has already been seen that the sets of production processes (A, L, B) and (A', L', B') include processes at various stages which produce final outputs at different

points of time. Let process 1 be the first stage process for producing output *a*, process 2 and 3 the second and third stages, and instantaneous process 1′ the final fourth stage, all these four completing the production of *a*. Processes 1, 2, 3 are included in the set (A, L, B) and process 1′ in (A', L', B'). In the same period 0, all these four processes are operated, process 1′ yielding product *a* in period 0, while processes 3, 2, 1 are carried out, in order to produce the final product *a* in periods 1, 2, 3, respectively.

Production must be synchronized in Böhm-Bawerk's manner, in order to produce *a* continuously in a stream of time, but the temporary equilibrium relative activities of the involved processes depend upon prices ψ which are expected to prevail in the next period 1, instead of those expected to be in consecutive periods, 1, 2, 3. Our model would, therefore, adequately be called myopic. Unless ψ's are accurately expected prices and correctly reflect the future movement of prices, there is always a danger that they would mislead economic agents, so that the processes are synchronized in the current period with wrong relativities. Then how should ψ's be formed in order to give rise to correct synchronization?

My previous work has shown that such values of ψ's are obtained by solving the equations of the model of 'perfect equilibrium'.[14] In this model we are concerned with an economy where entrepreneurs have 'perfect foresight' over all periods in the future. The economy is provided with commodities $B\bar{X}$ from the past and has the natural and human resources $\bar{N}$ with an expectation of their development $N(1)$, $N(2)$, $N(3)$, . . . in the future. The production is carried out in period 0 at $X(0)$ and $Y(0)$, the former yielding outputs $BX(0)$ in period 1. Then production will be carried out at $X(1)$ in period 1; repeating this procedure, we have an infinite sequence of activities $X(0)$, $X(1)$, . . ., $X(t)$, . . . We also have an infinite sequence $Y(0)$, $Y(1)$, . . ., $Y(t)$, . . . of instantaneous activities. In order to determine the values of *X*'s and *Y*'s, we need not only the demand–supply conditions for outputs, time-taking and instantaneous, and those for factors, but also the price–cost conditions for processes which generate the sequence of prices. In the case of time-taking production processes, as has been seen, outputs are evaluated at their expected prices ψ's, while inputs at $P(0)$ and $W(0)$. Under the assumption of perfect foresight, these ψ's should be actual input prices in period 1, $P(1)$, while outputs of the processes of period 1 are evaluated at $P(2)$, which remain to be expected prices in period 1 but turn out to be correct and, therefore, actual in period 2. In this way we obtain an infinite sequence, $P(0)$, $P(1)$, . . ., $P(t)$, . . .; similarly, $W(t)$ and $r(t)$, $t = 0, 1, . . .$

This state of perfect equilibrium is a state in period 0. It is merely an

[14] M. Morishima, *Theory of Economic Growth*.

extension of the concept of temporary equilibrium so as to take demand
and supply in the future into account. The number of inequalities to be dealt
with are enormous but the existence of equilibrium is established, in
principle, in the same way as in the case of temporary equilibrium. In fact,
some additional arguments have to be made carefully, because we are now
concerned with infinite sequences.[15] It is then easy to see that if the ψ's of the
temporary equilibrium model are equal to the equilibrium $P(1)$ of the
perfect foresight model, the temporary equilibrium in period 0 denoted by
$X(0)$, $Y(0)$, $P(0)$, $W(0)$, $r(0)$ is on the path of the perfect equilibrium over
time. It is also easy to see that processes are well linked with each other, so
that the right synchronization is observed in the state of perfect
equilibrium.

It is needless to say that the path of perfect equilibrium would prevail
only when entrepreneurs are able to foresee the future perfectly. Although
Böhm-Bawerk, Wicksell, Hayek and others have discussed the problem of
synchronization and the problem of the choice of production periods under
the assumption of perfect foresight, no entrepreneur has such an ability in
the actual world. Agents can only foresee prices in the near future; and there
is no assurance that their expectations would actually be realized in the
course of time. Thus we have, in general, $\psi \neq P(1)$. Then the actual
synchronization would be deviate from the right one to be established in the
state of perfect equilibrium. Moreover, in the next period 1, the expected
prices for period 2, the $\psi(1)$ which are formed in period 1 may not only be
different from $P(2)$ but also may conflict with those ψ formed in period 0.
That is to say, the synchronization carried out with ψ in period 0 may be
incompatible with the one with $\psi(1)$ in period 1, in the sense that some
intermediate products are in excess supply, so that either their prices have to
be adjusted or the goods in process in excess supply are destroyed in order
to prevent prices from falling to zero. Unless expected prices ψ, $\psi(1)$,
$\psi(2)$, . . . develop consistently, the production structure always has to be
adjusted; in most cases the adjustment may be mild, but in some cases, it
would be a drastic and far-reaching one.

It has been seen that the costs of time-taking production processes
include financial cost Q, but this is regarded as given in the above analysis.
In the following we shall try to sketch how a change in Q gives rise to a
change in the production structure; but preceding the sketch it must be
pointed out that between Böhm-Bawerk and Wicksell on the one side and
us on the other there is a significant difference in view about how Q is
determined. Being concerned with the real theory of capital and interest

---

[15] See Morishima, *Theory of Economic Growth*, pp. 151–7. The equilibrium sequences have
been referred to as the Hicks–Malinvaud trajectories.

they develop a model of the real subeconomy within which the rate of interest (hence Q) is determined (i.e., the so-called new wage-fund theory). Being influenced by these economists and reformulating their theory, we consider that it is the rate of profit, rather than the rate of interest, which is determined in the real subeconomy. On the other hand, however, we regard the rate of interest as being a variable to be determined in the monetary subeconomy, as will be seen in chapter 6 below, and as being a given constant as far as the real subeconomy is concerned. Nevertheless, it is clear that this does not prevent us from examining the effects upon the real economy of a change in the rate of interest.

To examine the effects rigorously, a comparative statics analysis of the temporary equilibrium, with respect to a change in Q, has to be made. We refrain from doing so in this place and are satisfied with seeing in a heuristic way how the equilibrium conditions are affected. First of all, while prices and wages are unchanged, a direct effect of an increase in Q would be a decline in the rate of profits of time-taking production processes, the instantaneous production processes yielding the profits at the same rate as before. This would induce entrepreneurs to switch their production activities from time-taking to instantaneous processes. However, the prices would be affected; those products, let us call them the X products, which are produced by time-taking processes will become relatively less abundant than those produced by instantaneous ones (the Y products), after the switch of activities from the former to the latter. Therefore, not only the prices of the X products would increase, but also their expected prices would be stimulated, while the prices of the Y products would decrease. These price changes would give rise to an increase in the rates of profits of the X processes and a decline of those of the Y processes. Where a new temporary equilibrium is re-established, the rates of profits are equalized but they would be lower than the previous equilibrium rate of profits r. Thus we observe a trade off relationship between r and Q.

Suppose now there are alternative chains of production processes of different length producing the same kind of commodity; entrepreneurs will choose the most profitable chain among them. It is assumed that before the change in Q, a particular chain is adopted. For each elementary process i belonging to it, let us assume that intermediate product i is a sole input for producing an intermediate product, $i+1$, of one stage forward; we ignore all of labour and other factor costs, as well as material costs, for the sake of simplicity. Suppose an increase in Q gives rise to an increase in $(1+r)(1+Q)$ at some rate, say g. The price of the final product will then be increased, in the next period, at the rate $(1+g)(1+\pi_1)-1$, where π_1 is the rate of increase in the price of the intermediate product at the final stage. The price of the final product in the period after the next must increase at the rate

$(1 + g)^2(1 + \pi_2) - 1$ against the price of the product before the change in Q, where π_2 is the rate of increase of the price of the intermediate product at the second stage from the last. Generally we have the formula:

$$\pi = (1 + g)^i(1 + \pi_i) - 1,$$

where π is the rate of inflation of the price of the final product in the i-th period in the future, while π_i is the current rate of inflation of the price of the intermediate product i at the i-th stage from the last. The formula shows that it will be violated unless an increasing inflation is expected.

If the above formula is not satisfied at some i because π does not reach the right-hand side of the above expression, then the production process to produce the intermediate product of stage $i + 1$ by using that of stage i is found to be unprofitable. Then that production is no longer made and the production chain will be switched to another one. Entrepreneurs will search for an alternative chain which would satisfy the formula; this would be found from among those which are shorter in length. Of course, the switch cannot be made without extra costs, so that it will not be carried out unless the old chain violates the formula greatly. In any case, in our model too, as Böhm-Bawerk and others have claimed on the basis of their models, we may conclude, from the above heuristic argument, that an increase in the rate of interest will generally shorten the production periods of commodities.

8 In previous sections of the present chapter I have shown that the absence of anti-Say's law activities implies the existence of a full employment–full-utilization temporary equilibrium for any given activities $\bar{X}$ carried out in the previous period, provided that factor prices W are subject to the free goods rule. This theorem, however, is based on the restrictive assumption that constant returns to scale prevail throughout the economy; like in the Arrow–Hahn L-economy, the increasing returns are ruled out. It remains for us to extend the result so as to allow for possibilities of setting up large indivisible facilities where productivity is higher than that of the small-scale institutions.

The problems of increasing returns has been formulated in section 6 of chapter 3 in the form of inequalities with variable input and output coefficients. In general, both instantaneous and time-taking production processes may be subject to increasing returns. In the following we assume for the sake of simplicity that returns of all instantaneous processes are constant, while possibilities of increasing returns are allowed for, only with respect to time-taking production processes. In the case of some instantaneous processes being indivisible and, therefore, being subject to increasing returns up to a certain scale of production, the following reasoning still *mutatis mutandis* holds true. A summary of the proof of existence of temporary equilibrium under the indivisibility is given in appendix II below.

Under the assumption of constant returns for instantaneous processes, the model is presented in terms of the following inequalities:
 (i) The price–cost inequalities:

$$\psi B(X) \leqslant (1+r)(PA(X)+WL)(I+Q) \quad \text{for non-instantaneous} \quad (4.24)$$
$$\text{processes,}$$

$$PB' \leqslant (1+r)(PA'+WL') \quad\quad \text{for instantaneous} \quad (4.25)$$
$$\text{processes,}$$

 (ii) the demand–supply inequalities for goods:

$$B(\bar X)\bar X + B'Y \geqslant A(X)X^{0*} + A'Y + D(P,\,W,\,X^{0*},\,Y), \quad (4.26)$$

 (iii) the demand–supply inequalities for primary factors:

$$\bar N \geqslant LX^{0*} + L'Y, \quad (4.27)$$

 (iv) the savings–investment inequality:

$$W\bar N - PD \leqslant [z\psi B(X)X^0 - PB(\bar X)\bar X^0] + [z\psi B(X)X^* - PB(\bar X)\bar X^*], \ (4.28)$$

where the part in the first pair of the square brackets of (4.28) represents the anti-Say's law part of investment and the one in the second the Say's law part. X^0 and X^*, as before, refer to the anti-Say's law and Say's law activity vectors, respectively, while X^{0*} is the mixture of them, that is to say: as now familiar to us, we have:

$$X^0 = \begin{bmatrix} X^0_{\mathrm{I}} \\ 0 \end{bmatrix},\ X^* = \begin{bmatrix} 0 \\ X^*_{\mathrm{I}} \end{bmatrix} \text{ and } X^{*0} = \begin{bmatrix} X^0_{\mathrm{I}} \\ X^*_{\mathrm{II}} \end{bmatrix}.$$

Variable production coefficients $A(X)$ and $B(X)$ are defined as in chapter 3. Namely, first $A(X)$ consists of m columns $a^j(X_j)$, $j=1,\ldots,m$, whose i-th component is designated by $a^j_i(X_j)$. For $X_j<1$:

$$a^j_i(X_j) = \begin{cases} a_{ij} & \text{for } i \text{ that is a material or intermediate product} \\ a_{ij}/X_j & \text{for } i \text{ that is a brand-new or old capital good,} \end{cases} (4.29)$$

while for $X_j \geqslant 1$:

$$a^j_i(X_j) = a_{ij} \text{ for all } i. \quad (4.29')$$

Similarly, $b^j_i(X_j)$ is the i-th component of the j-th column vector of $B(X)$. For $X_j<1$, we have:

$$b^j_i(X_j) = \begin{cases} b_{ij} & \text{for } i \text{ that is a finished or intermediate product} \\ b_{ij}/X_j & \text{for } i \text{ that is an old capital good,} \end{cases} (4.30)$$

while for $X_j \geqslant 1$:

$$b_i^j(X_j) = b_{ij} \text{ for all } i. \tag{4.30'}$$

Of course, for the processes with returns being constant with respect to a change in their activity levels, $a_i^j(X_j)$ and $b_i^j(X_j)$ remain constant at a_{ij} and b_{ij}, respectively, regardless of the values of X_j.

Let us now solve the system (4.24)–(4.28) without the restriction of anti-Say's law. We thus regard all processes as being under Say's law, so that there is no need for distinguishing activities into group I and II. Then we need not define X^0, X^* and X^{0*}. We may replace X^{0*} in (4.26) and (4.27) simply by X. In (4.28) the total amount of investment is completely free, so that there is no additional constraint requiring that the aggregate investment should not be higher than a certain level prescribed by financial organizations. Under this assumption of the over-all prevalence of Say's law we can now show that there is a full-employment full-utilization temporary equilibrium solution to the inequality system, (4.24)–(4.28).

We arrive at the same result that we have confirmed under the constant returns to scale. The economy can realize the neoclassical state of full-employment full-utilization equilibrium if there is no anti-Say's law activity. Where there is no financial constraint and all production activities are provided with funds as much as the entrepreneurs want to obtain for them, the existing stocks of natural resources, land and labour, as well as the existing stocks of intermediate products, are all employed completely, provided the rule of free goods is valid for factors. Also the available production facilities, machines and equipment, are all operated to their full capacities. We might say that the neoclassical worship of invisible hand will be rewarded because Pareto-efficiency is realized in the economy.

This has been true in the case of all processes being both divisible and multiplicable, if Say's law is fulfilled; but the gap between the ideal Say's law world and the actual anti-Say's law world is widened when technology is developed, and downwards-indivisible big plants become more and more possible. To establish large-scale plants it is evident that they must be financed by outside money. In aggregate investment the anti-Say's law part becomes larger in quantity and more essential in the role it plays. If this part is severely restricted because of the low intention of the financial organizations to support the industry, the distance of the actual economic performance from the frontier of Pareto-efficiency would be very grave and great. Whereas the actual state may be analysed in terms of input–output equations as in the previous case of industries being under constant returns to scale, the economy is in a state of underutilization equilibrium as far as the utilization of resources and facilities is concerned, and the actual state has to be described in terms of inequalities with positive prices. In controlling the gap, invisible hand cannot play the role of the Saviour. It has been and will be powerless in this respect and should, therefore, be replaced by a visible collaboration between industrial and banking sectors.

This collaboration has worked well in Japan through the postwar period. It has often been confused with collaboration between industry and government and, in fact, Japan has been accused of forming a Japan Inc. which is a serious violation of the principal code of behaviour of the free enterprise system. It has been obscured by emphasizing that Japan has invented a number of means which promote X-efficiencies in the economy, such as the permanent employment system, wage payment according to seniority, the paternalistic company-welfare system, the company philosophy, company songs, calisthenics in the working place, etc., etc. I do not deny that there is some truth in this fable. But I believe, on the other hand, that no one, except H. Okumura and a few others,[16] has properly emphasized the significance and cleverness of the Japanese financial system. All major industrial companies belong to one of, say, ten or fifteen very big enterprise groups, each of which has a big bank or a big security company as a member. An investment plan proposed by a company is discussed at a meeting of the heads of the companies of the group which are held rather regularly and frequently; if approved, the investment plan will be financially supported not only by the financial institutions of the group but also by trading houses and related industrial companies within the group. Thus a greater amount of money would *ceteris paribus* be available in Japan for investment than in other countries to a given technological project. It will be utilized efficiently as all plans are examined and compared at the group's summit meeting; the possibility of misuse of funds would, therefore, be minimized.

This way of realizing innovations is very different from the picture depicted by Schumpeter. In his world, an idea for some particular innovation is always formed by an ingenious entrepreneur and the decision is made by him in a heroic manner. The whole idea is a secret, and the entrepreneur's ingenuity, braveness and charisma are the main assets for convincing bankers that they should help him to realize his dream by providing financial support. The secrecy of the idea enables the originator to obtain monopolistic profits until the followers begin to copy him.

On the other hand, in the Japanese way of making decisions on innovations the idea is openly discussed from the start. At least, the chairmen of the companies of the same group are made aware of it. If their secretaries are included at least thirty to fifty persons are precisely informed

---

[16] Hiroshi Okumura, *Ginko to Kigyo: Sono Kikenna Kankei* (Banks and Enterprises: Their Dangerous Relationship), Toyo-keizai Shinpo Sha, Tokyo, 1978.

of the idea as soon as it is proposed and discussed in the chairmen's meeting. The secret is easily leaked, and, as this is expected by all members of the meeting, they will not discuss and conceive of the idea from the point of view of pursuing monopolistic profits that would last for a short period, but with a longer perspective of the business.[17] As the idea is an 'open secret', and more or less similar ones will be discussed, almost at the same time, by other industrial groups, the new business will meet severe competition from its cradle period. This would explain, at least to some extent, that the impact of innovations of the Japanese type is, like heavy territorial rain, concentrated, dense and speedy, so that the existing old industry has no chance to keep its foothold.

Moreover, collaborations are not limited to those between industrial firms and financial organizations. To form a new business a multitude of advance technologies is needed. This technological collaboration is easier if the new idea is discussed in a meeting attended by the chairmen of the companies producing different types of commodities. These companies will technically support the newly formed company by providing their own technical experts for a limited period or permanently. Innovations then can be performed by a group of ordinary chairmen, without any charismatic individual hero. It is certain that this reduction of heroic work to routine is one of the major sources of her economic success; and it should be noted that this reduction itself has been made possible by a number of organizational innovations carried out in the postwar Japan. In any case, the actual economy would work in Japan more or less in the way described above. As financial restraint is not severe there because of the collaboration of banks with the firms in groups, we may consider that her economy is almost in a state that is not very far from the neoclassical equilibrium.[18]

9 In the actual world, as has been stated, agriculture, forestry, fishing and mining are flexprice sectors, while manufacturing, wholesale and retail, transportation and others are usually fixprice sectors. We now, therefore, modify the model discussed above so as to accommodate flexprice sectors within it. In the model of a mixed economy, there are three broad groups of commodities, named X, Y, and Z. The X group includes all commodities belonging to the fixprice, non-instantaneous production sector. The industrialists of this group are not profit maximizing price-takers. They regulate the activity levels, X, of production of the commodities in this group, independently of the price set. As the production is not instanta-

---

[17] In fact, a chairman who proposes an idea which mainly aims to yield monopolistic profits will not be respected by the other chairmen of the group.

[18] Of course, as Okumura and others observe, where the collaboration is excessive, the existence of the enterprise groups is in contradiction to the ethics of free competition.

neous but takes time, a change in X does not bring about any change in the current outputs of the commodities in the group; it rather affects the demand for the commodities and factors which are needed for the production, while its outcome is only observed at the beginning of the next period. Where the commodities in this group are themselves used for the production of them, a change in activities X regulates the demand for these commodities. It is possible that the outputs of X commodities now supplied in the market which have resulted from the activities of the last period are not necessarily in the right proportion to the current demand, so it may happen for some commodities in the X group that the supply is not equal to the demand; in fact, there may be an excess supply of these commodities in the state of temporary equilibrium. The residuals thus brought about will be dealt with in the way already discussed.

Secondly, the Y group is made up of those commodities which are instantaneously produced. They too belong to the fixprice sector, so that their activity levels Y are regulated independently of the prices of the commodities. A change in Y affects not only the demand for the commodities which are required for the production of those in the Y group, but also the current supply of those whose production is carried out at the level of Y, because they are produced without any time lag. For the production of Y commodities, capital goods (machines, tools and equipment) are of course used. Used capital goods are treated as joint outputs of the Y production which are made available for further use at the beginning of the next period. This means that it takes one period of time for the production of joint outputs, whereas the main outputs, Y commodities, are produced instantaneously.[19] We assume, to simplify the analysis, that no Y commodity can be produced jointly with some other Y. As the supply of each Y commodity can be adjusted, with no time lag, to its demand, the supply–demand condition for temporary equilibrium holds with strict equality for any and every Y commodity.

The third, called the Z group, is a flexprice sector, consisting of those commodities whose prices are determined according to the cobweb formula. The rate of change of their prices $\dot{P}_Z$ being proportional to their respective amounts of excess demand.[20] However, it takes at least one period to produce their outputs so that the supply of the Z commodities which have been produced in the last period remains constant throughout the tatonnement process of price adjustment in the present period. The

---

[19] This is the right way of treatment of used capital goods, which is adopted in the next chapter. We have assumed, however, throughout this chapter for the sake of simplifying mathematical expressions, that capital goods are also instantly aged if they are used in instantaneous production processes.

[20] $\dot{P}_Z = dP_Z/dt$, where t is the tatonnement time defined in section 1, chapter 5 below.

process accomplishes a temporary equilibrium in the end. On the basis of current prices thus established, new production decisions are formed in order to provide the outputs in the future. Like X commodities, the outputs of Z commodities produced in the previous period are not in right proportion to their current demand. In addition to this, joint production is not ruled out in the Z sector. For these two reasons, temporary equilibrium does not mean that the supply is strictly equated with the corresponding demand in the case of Z commodities. There is a possibility of inequality.

If a Z commodity is perishable, its price will be highly flexible as we observe at the strawberry and fish markets. The rule of free goods may hold approximately, but it is not surprising to see that residuals of strawberry and fish will be destroyed to keep their prices. Storable Z commodities such as corn will be stored, but where it is considered that corn is not worth storing, we would have residual corn which will be burnt by the farmers themselves.

In determining the supply function of the Z commodities prices, $P = (P_X, P_Y, P_Z)$ are all taken as given, where P_X, for example, stands for the vector of prices of X commodities. For each existing firm belonging to the Z sector a number of production processes are available, on the basis of which its production possibility set is formed. To start production of Z commodities immediately, the firm needs primary factors of production (land and labour), new or old capital goods, goods in process and other means of production. Because it takes time to produce them within the company, the availability of them is a limiting factor for current production and, therefore, should be taken as given, unless they are at once obtainable in the market. Then the firm's production function derived from its production possibility set is subject to diminishing returns, since it first carries out production by adopting the most productive method and has then (as it is exhausted) to shift to a less productive one. Regarding the prices of X, Y and Z commodities, as well as those of primary factors and imported materials, as all given, the profits of the firm may be taken as a function of prices. It is evident that the profit maximization, subject to the production possibility set, yields the supply function $Z(P)$, by applying the theory of price-takers to Z entrepreneurs. We need not mention the prices of the primary factors of production and other imported materials as members of variables of $Z(P)$ explicitly, since they are assumed to be constant throughout this section and the following chapter.

This type of model is unique among those previously examined for stability of temporary equilibrium, because although these are concerned with some multiple-market economy, their markets are all homogeneous (usually). They all are of the flexprice type with no consideration of production lags, as they are in the Hicks–Samuelson–Arrow–Debreu–

Hahn models as well as in mine in *DKR* or in Leonteif's and Sraffian input–output models. Because of homogeneity these models are essentially one-sector models, while our present model comprises three heterogeneous sectors, i.e., two fixprice sectors with or without lags and one flexprice sector with production lags. It is obvious that such a model is much closer to reality than the conventional one with n homogeneous markets. In our time, most basic necessities are still offered by flexprice industries, while the price of the majority of industrial products are set at their cost of production which allows for reasonable mark-ups. In addition to finished manufacturing, wholesale and retail, transportation, parts, intermediate products and goods in process are all included in this category.

In addition to these product markets there are the markets for the primary factors of production as well as those for the commodities which are impossible to produce within the economy and, hence, have to be imported entirely. Throughout the present chapter we have assumed that the foreign economy is large enough and can provide the commodities, which cannot be produced in the home economy, in the amounts that are required, without any change in their prices. This means that the elasticity of supply of them is assumed to be infinitely large in the foreign economy. In the case of the primary factors of production we may make a similar assumption. We may assume, in particular, for labour that it is immigrated or emigrated accordingly as an excess demand or supply prevails in the labour market; similarly for other factors. We are thus enabled to treat all the factor prices as constant throughout the following chapter where temporary equilibrium is examined for stability.

Finally, I must add a remark on the uniqueness of temporary equilibrium. Like usual existence theorems, ours allows multiple (even infinitely many, in the worst case) equilibria being possible. There may be an additional theory explaining how the economy selects among them; but to obtain one we have to go a long way. Or it may be said that this problem of selection of an equilibrium is irrelevant or unimportant, because we are concerned with only those properties which the economy has as long as it is in equilibrium. In any case, wherever the economy chooses one equilibrium in one period, a set of temporary equilibria for the next period is determined, from among which the economy selects one in that period. Thus, provided the temporary equilibria are multiple, the paths of the temporary equilibria are also multiple. This is true because we lack a theory to select the realized one from the possible temporary equilibria, but we can still say that everything that is said in the chapters below is valid, whichever equilibrium path the economy actually follows.

5 Stability and motion

1 Let us designate the activities in the previous period as X_{-1} and the available amount of labour in the current period as N_0. A time sequence of temporary equilibria which starts from the initial point (X_{-1}, N_0), is examined in this chapter with respect to the following two points. The first is referred to by Walras as the problem of tatonnement, which is concerned with the problem of how temporary equilibrium whose existence is theoretically assured by the fixed point theorem is actually obtained (i.e., found and attained) in a market where free competition prevails. Economists, including Walras himself, usually call it the problem of the stability of the temporary equilibrium point. In fact, it examines whether the process of tatonnement starting from a point off the temporary equilibrium will converge to this last eventually.

The second is concerned with whether a time sequence of temporary equilibria initiating from a hypothetical initial position (X'_{-1}, N_0) will converge to the original sequence from the historically given initial position (X_{-1}, N_0), where $X'_{-1} \neq X_{-1}$. In this problem, the stability of the equilibrium path (or movement) is investigated; if the motion settles, in the end, at a certain point, which may be called a long-run equilibrium point, the stability of *motion* is reduced to the stability of the long-run equilibrium *point*, as it was so in the case of Ricardo who believed the existence of a long-run stationary state. Where there is no such point, the stability of the equilibrium path should be formulated in terms of the stability of motion, rather than that of an equilibrium point.

Although the stability of the equilibrium point has been discussed by many economists as Hahn's survey shows,[1] there is essentially no work concerning the stability of the equilibrium path, except my work in chapter 5 of *Dogakuteki Keizai Riron (DKR)*. It is true that Solow and Samuelson have discussed the stability of the path of balanced growth, but their analysis is, more precisely speaking, no more than a modification of the

---

[1] F. H. Hahn, 'Stability', in K. J. Arrow and M. D. Intriligator (eds.), *Handbook of Mathematical Economics*, vol. II, North-Holland, Amsterdam, 1982.

stability theory of a point, instead of that of motion, because a state of balanced growth is reduced, in terms of relative magnitudes of outputs, to a *point* where relative outputs are fixed.

Before embarking upon the work of examining how our present model works through time, it would be more convenient for the reader to have a precise definition of the stability of an equilibrium point as well as that of an equilibrium motion. First of all, let us for the sake of simplicity rule out instantaneous activities and assume Say's law. With given $\bar{X} = X_{-1}$ and $\bar{N} = N_0$, let a set of solutions to the temporary equilibrium system of inequalities, (4.3), (4.4), (4.5) of chapter 4, be designated (P_0, W_0, z_0, X_0), where the notation is obvious except for z_0 which is the reciprocal of $1 +$ the rate of profit. The set is referred to as the temporary equilibrium. To attain this point, keeping $\bar{X}$ and $\bar{N}$ throughout at X_{-1} and N_0 respectively, we start the process of tatonnement from a point (P', W', z', X') which is arbitrarily chosen and adjust some or all of its elements if they do not fulfil the conditions for temporary equilibrium. The new position $(P^{(1)}, W^{(1)}, z^{(1)}, X^{(1)})$ attained in this way is further altered to $(P^{(2)}, W^{(2)}, z^{(2)}, X^{(2)})$, unless it conforms with the equilibrium conditions. The process of adjustment will continue until the economic position finally approaches (P_0, W_0, z_0, X_0); otherwise the tatonnement is unsuccessful. Where tatonnement is sucessful, even if it starts from an arbitrary point, the equilibrium is said to be stable, so that we have $\lim_{t \to \infty} (P^{(t)}, W^{(t)}, z^{(t)}, X^{(t)}) = (P_0, W_0, z_0, X_0)$ wherever the equilibrium is stable.[2] Of course it is certain that the stability depends on how P, W, z, X are adjusted. We shall later make the adjustment rules of these variables explicit.

Secondly, the stability of temporary equilibrium motion is formulated in the following way. With $\bar{X}$ and $\bar{N}$ being given at those X_{-1} and N_0 which are obtained as the result of the economy being established in the state of temporary equilibrium in the previous period, the economy will be in temporary equilibrium in period 0 at (P_0, W_0, z_0, X_0), so that the economy is provided with X_0, N_1 at the beginning of period 1, on the basis of which it is further seen that a temporary equilibrium will be realized in period 1 at (P_1, W_1, z_1, X_1), and so on. This of course assumes that each temporary equilibrium is stable in the sense defined above. The stability of motion of this sequence through time, (P_t, W_t, z_t, X_t), $t = 0, 1, 2, \ldots$ *ad infinitum*, is tested against other hypothetical sequences of temporary equilibria (P'_t, W'_t, z'_t, X'_t), $t = 0, 1, 2, \ldots$, starting from an arbitrarily chosen, conceived initial position (X'_{-1}, N_0), which deviates from the actual one (X_{-1}, N_0). A shift in the initial position gives rise to a change in temporary equilibrium from $(P_0,$

---

[2] Here t does not stand for a historical or calendar time but for a tatonnement time within period 0 which represents the progress of tatonnement.

W_0, z_0, X_0) to (P'_0, W'_0, z'_0, X'_0) which will further create a change in the temporary equilibrium in period 1, and so on.

The path created from the actual initial position may be referred to as the actual path, which is compared with the hypothetical path generated from a hypothetical initial position. Then the stability of the actual path is obtained if the hypothetical equilibrium (P'_t, W'_t, z'_t, X'_t) approaches the actual one, (P_t, W_t, z_t, X_t), as t gets very large, for any hypothetical initial position (X'_{-1}, N_0), that is to say, if (P'_t, W'_t, z'_t, X'_t) is close to (P_t, W_t, z_t, X_t) as t tends to be large. As is easily realized, the stability in this sense does not necessarily imply the economy will settle in the end at some kind of stationary state, or a long-run equilibrium, as Ricardo or other classical economists have claimed.

It is now at once seen that the two stability theories are formulated in terms of two different concepts of time. One is time within a period, that has been called a tatonnement time in footnote 2 above, the other being time over periods. In order for the two theories to collaborate with each other in developing a dynamic economic theory, the two concepts should be consistent and compatible with each other. Especially we must clarify at the beginning the meaning of the proposition that time within a particular period tends to infinity. Is it possible to stay in the same period when the time within the period becomes larger and larger without limit? My *DKR* has been concerned with this issue; its solution is as follows. Let the beginning and the end of a period be represented as τ_0 and τ_1, respectively, by the calendar time. A point of time within the period is expressed by τ. It must be noted that the end of the first period (say, a week), i.e., 24.00 hours Sunday, is the beginning of the second week, i.e., 00.00 hours Monday. To avoid such overlapping we must exclude the point of time 24.00 hours Sunday from one of the weeks and include it in the latter, or *vice versa*. In this way we may avoid overlapping but, if we do so, then either the first week has no week end or the second week has no beginning. We shall include 24.00 hours Sunday in the beginning of the second week as 00.00 hours Monday. Therefore in our economy each week has a beginning but no week has an end.

We then have a semi-open set of points of time belonging to a week which has the power of continuum. Such a set can be made to correspond to real numbers from 0 to infinity in a one-to-one relationship, keeping the order; that is to say, the calendar time from the beginning of one week until the beginning of the next week can be made to correspond the real number t from 0 to infinity. Without using calendar time we can alternatively express the point of time by the week to which it belongs and by the position of that point within the week. We call the latter the tatonnement time. Because tatonnement is carried out during the week its progress can be expressed in terms of the tatonnement time t. Where t tends to infinity, time is approaching the week end and *vice versa*.

2 In dealing with these problems, let us first begin with the case of anti-Say's law activities being absent, i.e., $X_1^0 = \emptyset$. (The case of financial restriction being imposed on production activities, that is, the case of the presence of anti-Say's law activities, will be discussed later in section 7.) Let P_X refer to the vector of prices of the commodities produced by the X activities; P_Y and P_Z are defined similarly. We assume these sets of products of activities X, Y and Z as being distinct from each other. Let $P^0 = (P_X^0, P_Y^0, P_Z^0)$, X^0, and Y^0 be a set of equilibrium prices and activity levels. For examination of its stability we conceive of two alternative cases below, because, it seems, fixprice sectors need to be treated somewhat carefully.

First we are concerned with the case where their prices P_X and P_Y are fixed and remain constant at P_X^0 and P_Y^0. In this case, referred to as case I below, the price–cost inequalities for the X and Y activities include P_Z as the only variables, depending on which the profits of all activities X, Y, Z will fluctuate as they employ commodities Z for production. The levels of activities, X and Y, will be increased or decreased accordingly as their profit rates are above or below the equilibrium one. When P_Z ceases to fluctuate and settles at its equilibrium value, the equilibrium price–cost inequalities are established for X and Y; hence there would be no further adjustment of X and Y via this channel. However, the X and Y thus determined do not necessarily establish the demand–supply equilibrium conditions for X and Y commodities. But, because all X and Y activities are now equally profitable, the entrepreneur is indifferent between expanding some or other X by reducing some or other Y, or *vice versa*, from point of view of pursuing profits. The activity levels of those X and Y commodities which are in excess supply or excess demand will be reduced or increased until their equilibrium conditions for demand and supply are finally fulfilled.

In case II, on the other hand, P_X and P_Y are not necessarily set at their equilibrium values at the commencement of the tatonnement process. Then adjustments of P_X and P_Y are inevitable, and there arises a rather self-contradictory situation where fixprices are flexible.[3] It must be noted, however, that the most essential feature of our fixprice industries, as distinguished from the flexprice industries, does not lie in the rigidity of the prices of their products but their charging reasonable profits to the

---

[3] The tatonnement in case II is a method of groping for the prices at which the fixprice system works as such. Once those prices have been established, the excess demand or supply for the products of these industries, caused by an exogenous shift in demand, are removed by adjusting their activity levels only, provided roundabout effects through factor markets are neglected; no further changes in prices occur.

products, instead of extracting maximum profits from the business.[4] Prices are adjusted in these industries such that the equal rate of profits will eventually be established at the time when tatonnement comes to an end, whereas the rate of profits differs from one firm to another, depending on the relative position of the supply and demand curves, in the case of the flexprice industries Z.

For the purpose of finding equilibrium fixprices P_X and P_Y, we increase or decrease the prices, during the searching process, accordingly as there is an excess demand or supply in the market of the goods produced by X and Y. Thus the system has a dual adjustment mechanism concerning X and Y. The activity levels of X and Y are regulated by the excess profits of the respective activities, while the prices of the products by the excess demand for them. Consequently, where there is an excess demand for a product in the X or Y group, its price goes up and, therefore, the activities which produce it become more profitable, so that the industry producing that commodity will expand. This will then give rise to an increase in the supply of the produce in the case of the commodity being in the Y group (as it is produced instantaneously), while there is no immediate effect upon supply if it is an X commodity because of a production lag.

This is seen in more detail in the following way. First we examine the case of the products of X or Y being consumer goods. Let D_X and D_Y be the demands for them; of course $D_X = 0$ if the commodity is a producer's good. Similarly for D_Y. Where P_X rises, the consumer demand D_X declines, while where X expands, D_X increases, because an increase in X gives rise to an increase in wages and profits as more labour is employed and more profits accrue. Similarly, D_Y changes when Y expands. It is thus seen that an increase in P_X (or P_Y) resulting from an excess demand for X (or Y) creates two effects working in opposite directions, one being the direct effect of P_X (or P_Y) upon D_X (or D_Y), and the other an indirect one through the expansion effect upon X (or Y) caused by a rise in P_X (or P_Y). (There would also be an indirect effect upon D_Z.) Provided that the negative effect dominates the positive one, the demand for the product of X (or Y) diminishes, at least as far as the part of the consumer demand in the total demand is concerned. Thus the increase in price due to an excess demand for a product of X (or Y) tends to decrease its demand; it works, therefore, as a stabilizer as long as the proviso just mentioned is satisfied.

Let us next see what happens to the demand for producers' goods produced by X, when some elements of P_X are set too high. It is obvious,

[4] This is the usual way of defining fixprice industries; the term 'fixprice' does not imply that the price of the product is fixed, but it means that it does not change once it is fixed, while it may clearly change during the process of groping for the point where it is fixed.

first of all, that the corresponding X's profitability is higher than the other activities. In this case these X will be expanded while all the others are reduced. These have effects on the demand for consumers' goods D_X, D_Y and D_Z which have been examined in the above. They also disturb demands for producers' goods, produced by the activities of the X group, which may be increased or decreased as some X's increase and others decrease, while their supplies are undisturbed because of the production lag. Where negative effects are dominant, we may expect an excess supply or a decrease in excess demand in the market of these producers' goods. The P_X originally set too high is now revised to a lower one, or the rate of increase of P_X is decreased; we may thus observe a tendency towards a temporary equilibrium. Of course, in the case of positive effects being dominant, we have an opposite result; it works as a destabilizer.

In the case of some of the elements of P_Y being set too high, the mechanism just observed for X, either consumers' or producers' goods, works, *mutatis mutandis*, for the products of these Y activities. In addition to these, an increase in Y gives rise to an increase in the current supply of the products, because there is no production lag for Y. Thus, in the case of Y, there is an additional reason that we may expect a positive excess supply in the market of the producers' goods produced instantaneously, after the adjustment of the activities levels. Of course, there are many other channels of repercussions, some being favourable but others adverse. For instance, an increase in P_Z as a result of an excess demand for the products of Z activities will give rise to a decrease in the rates of profits of those activities of the X group which employ the products of the Z activities as materials. Therefore these X's will be decreased, so that we would have an excess supply of the producers' goods which are used by the X's. We have similar repercussions through Y's where the profitability of Y is affected by an increase in P_Z. In the analysis of stability of temporary equilibrium, the tatonnement process must be rigorously specified and carefully examined, by taking all possible repercussions into account. This will be done in later parts of this chapter.

It is evident that the time path of prices and activity levels (P, X, Y) generated by the tatonnement procedure should always remain in the non-negative orthant; negative prices and negative activity levels are obviously meaningless. This important problem has usually been neglected in stability analysis, because in conventional systems, like our model of case I, it can be shown that any price begins to increase once it hits the boundary of $P_i = 0$. (Thus the price never becomes negative.) This is because demand would be huge, so that an excess demand would be positive, if $P_i = 0$, and the commodity i is not free. Thus in conventional systems, where all commodities are of the flexprice type, excess demand always exists on the boundary, so that prices will never be negative.

In systems, like case II above, which include fixprice commodities, the problem of non-negative solutions becomes substantial and is, therefore, of real significance. Where constant returns to scale prevail, excess profits per unit activity are independent of the level of production, so that at $X_i = 0$, the excess profits of the i-th activity can easily be negative, provided prices are set inappropriately. Then by virtue of the adjustment rule $\dot{X}_i < 0$; so $X_i < 0$ may be obtained if the tatonnement adjustment equation is simply or blindly solved mathematically. To prevent X_i from taking on a negative value, the regime must be switched at the point $X_i = 0$ from the one described above to another, say, X_i remaining to be 0 even if, at $X_i = 0$, the activity i yields negative excess profits. There is no change in X_i, in spite of the pressure to push X_i downwards existing at that point.

As for P_i with i belonging to the X or Y products group, a force to keep P_i non-negative works automatically, if i is a consumption good, because the consumer demand for i at $P_i = 0$ is large enough to make its excess demand positive; thus P_i begins to increase again if it falls sufficiently. For other commodities which consumers do not buy, such as intermediate products, goods in process and used and new capital goods, such a force to sustain the positiveness of the price does not prevail at the boundary of $P_i = 0$. Because only producers are concerned with such a commodity i and no consumer would buy it, its excess demand would depend on activity levels X and Y, but be independent of the price P_i. The excess demand, therefore, may take on a negative value at $P_i = 0$. The price would fall to a negative value from its level of 0, unless a constraint is imposed, in order to prevent P_i from getting to negative. To do so, the pricing procedure of the tatonnement must be switched to the one according to which the price of commodity i is kept constant at 0 even though its excess demand is negative. As is easily observed, such a system involving switching is non-linear. Where the temporary equilibrium point is an interior point with P^0, X^0, and Y^0 all being positive, the switching does not matter at all when we study whether the temporary equilibrium is *locally* stable. But where it is on the boundary of the non-negative orthant so that at least one component of vectors P^0, X^0 and Y^0 is zero, the switching problem has a real significance, even if we are only concerned with its local stability.[5] As X and Y include all possible production activities, some of them will not be utilized in the state of

[5] Regarding previous studies in switching, see H. Uzawa, 'Gradient Method for Concave Programming, II', *Studies in Linear and Non-Linear Programming*, ed. K. J. Arrow *et al.*, Stanford University Press, 1958, pp. 127–32; M. Morishima, *Equilibrium, Stability and Growth*, Oxford University Press, 1964, pp. 38–43. The mathematics discussed there applies to our present model.

temporary equilibrium; this means that it is not an interior point.

3 Throughout the following, wherever it is possible, we shall stick to the same notation as I used in chapter 4 on temporary equilibrium. However, we have to complicate the notation so as to make characters of sectors of the present model distinct. Apart from instantaneous production activities, there are non-instantaneous ones which take time to yield outputs. The latter are further classified into two subgroups, i.e., the group of activities whose intensities are decided by consulting the levels of prices of their outputs (namely, the activities of the flexprice (Z) sectors) and the group consisting of those of the fixprice (X) sectors whose intensities are determined independently of prices. The intensity vectors of these two are denoted by $Z(P)$ and X, respectively, while the one of the instantaneous group by Y.

The input coefficient matrix of A of the industries of Z and X groups is, then, partitioned into the following form:

$$A = \begin{bmatrix} A_{ZZ} & A_{ZX} \\ A_{XZ} & A_{XX} \\ A_{YZ} & A_{YX} \end{bmatrix}, \tag{5.1}$$

where the first subscript applied to A represents the sector in which the input commodity is produced and the second the sector where it is used. For example, A_{ZX} represents, in matrix form, the input coefficients of the fixprice (X) sectors concerning commodities produced by the flexprice (Z) sectors. The output matrix B and the factor input matrix L are similarly partitioned.

The input coefficient matrix A' for instantaneous production activities is also partitioned into the form:

$$A' = \begin{bmatrix} A_{ZY} \\ A_{XY} \\ A_{YY} \end{bmatrix}. \tag{5.2}$$

It is noted that the primes applied to the above expression designate the fact that the relevant commodities are used by the instantaneous production (Y) sectors, while the same distinction is not made for submatrices A_{iY}, etc. as it is clear that they stand for coefficients of Y sectors.

Concerning output coefficients, it may be convenient in the analysis below to specify the distribution of zero elements in the output matrix by making the following assumptions. First, outputs of the Z sector (agriculture, forestry, fishery and mining) cannot be produced as joint outputs of the X and Y sectors (manufactures, construction and other fixprice industries). Also the assumption that there is no joint production within the Z sector is safe and acceptable as it may be taken as the one for a first approximation to reality; so we may in fact observe that apples and pears cannot be jointly produced, whereas we may be able to point out a number of joint agricultural outputs, such as meat and hide, let alone a vast number of fish which are simultaneously caught in a single net. Secondly, we assume that some outputs of the X sector may be produced as by-products of the activities of the Z, X and Y sectors, since there are second-hand or used durable goods and scraps and waste, such as steel scraps and waste cotton, which are produced and recycled in the production process. Thirdly, the Y commodities produced instantaneously are not by-products of the Z and X activities. We may also assume, as we do, that no joint production prevails within the Y sector; we, in fact, regard instantaneous production as being exceptional and unusual, so we consider that it is even more difficult and very unlikely for a single activity to bring forth plural kinds of products instantly. Of course, as has already been pointed out, there are examples of instantaneous activities of joint production, such as sheep slaughtering producing many products, meat, wool, hide, etc.; in the following we rule out all these from our list of Y sectors.

So far output coefficients are all undated. As already has been stated repeatedly, there is a one period production lag in the Z and X sectors; their outputs of activities in period τ are only available in period $\tau + 1$. This means that these outputs in period τ are the results of the activities in period $\tau - 1$; therefore, they remain constant throughout the tatonnement process in period τ, only flexibly variable outputs being those of the Y sector. Thus the one appearing on the supply side of the equilibrium condition of period τ is not the whole output matrix but only the instantaneous part of the matrix, that is:

$$B^* = \begin{bmatrix} 0 & 0 & 0 \\ 0 & 0 & 0 \\ 0 & 0 & I_Y \end{bmatrix},$$

where I_Y is an identity matrix which is of the same order as that of the vector Y, while the lagged output matrix B^{**} takes the form of:

$$B^{**} = \begin{bmatrix} I_Z & 0 & 0 \\ B_{XZ} & B_{XX} & B_{XY} \\ 0 & 0 & 0 \end{bmatrix},$$

where I_Z is an identity matrix. As was stated at the end of the previous chapter, it is appropriate to assume that, for the activities in the group Y, the main outputs are produced instantaneously, while their by-products (used capital goods, etc.) are made usable at the beginning of the next period after the Y activities have been accomplished, so that B_{XY} is a submatrix of B^{**}, while I_Y belongs to B^*. Clearly, $B^* + B^{**} = B + B'$.

Let $\tilde{Z}(\tilde{P})$, $\tilde{X}$, $\tilde{Y}$ be the three activity vectors in the previous period $\tau - 1$, and $Z(P)$, X, Y those of the current period τ, where $\tilde{P}$ and P are the equilibrium flexprices in the respective periods. Then the flexible and fixed parts of the total supply are given, for period τ, by:

$$ B^* \begin{bmatrix} 0 \\ 0 \\ Y \end{bmatrix} \text{ and } B^{**} \begin{bmatrix} \tilde{Z}(\tilde{P}) \\ \tilde{X} \\ \tilde{Y} \end{bmatrix}. $$

On the other hand, in period $\tau + 1$, they are given by:

$$ B^* \begin{bmatrix} 0 \\ 0 \\ \tilde{Y} \end{bmatrix} \text{ and } B^{**} \begin{bmatrix} Z(P) \\ X \\ Y \end{bmatrix}, $$

where $\tilde{Y}$ is obviously the vector in period $\tau + 1$. This implies that the total supply, including both flexible and fixed parts, is expressed, for period τ or $\tau + 1$, as:

$$ B^* \begin{bmatrix} 0 \\ 0 \\ Y \end{bmatrix} + B^{**} \begin{bmatrix} \tilde{Z}(\tilde{P}) \\ \tilde{X} \\ \tilde{Y} \end{bmatrix} $$

or

$$ B^* \begin{bmatrix} 0 \\ 0 \\ \tilde{Y} \end{bmatrix} + B^{**} \begin{bmatrix} Z(P) \\ X \\ Y \end{bmatrix}, $$

respectively. It cannot be simply represented, as in the usual von Neumann system, by a product of the undated output matrix B and the undated activity vector, because of the simultaneous presence of instantaneous and non-instantaneous production in our system.

As has already been explained, the activity vector of the flexprice sector, $Z(P)$, depends on the prices of the outputs of the sector, while the intensities of the fixprice activities, X and Y, are regarded as independent, flexible variables. The consumer demand functions of the outputs of the three sectors are designated by D_Z, D_X, D_Y, all of them, as has already been observed, depending upon flexible prices P, as well as on wages and profits of the industries. Because these last two obviously depend upon all the industrial activities, $Z(P)$, X and Y, the demand functions may be written, for example, in the form:

$$D_Z = D_Z(P, Z(P), X, Y),$$

because wage rates W are assumed to be kept constant in the following. It is now clear that P, X and Y are the ultimate variables of these functions; we may then put them in the following simple form:

$$D_Z = D_Z(P, X, Y), \quad D_X(P, X, Y), \quad D_Y = D_Y(P, X, Y).$$

Next we assume below that these functions are analytic and expandable into Taylor series. They may, therefore, be approximated by a linear expression in a small neighbourhood of the temporary equilibrium point (P^0, X^0, Y^0). Thus:

$$D_Z = D_Z^0 + D_{ZP}^0(P - P^0) + D_{ZX}^0(X - X^0) + D_{ZY}^0(Y - Y^0),$$
$$D_X = D_X^0 + D_{XP}^0(P - P^0) + D_{XX}^0(X - X^0) + D_{XY}^0(Y - Y^0), \quad (5.3)$$
$$D_Y = D_Y^0 + D_{YP}^0(P - P^0) + D_{YX}^0(X - X^0) + D_{YY}^0(Y - Y^0),$$

where D_Z^0, D_X^0 and D_Y^0 stand for the consumer demands for the outputs of the three sectors at the point of temporary equilibrium. The coefficients such as D_{ZP}^0, D_{XP}^0, etc., are partial derivatives of the demand functions for those commodities which are products of the sectors represented by the first subscript of the coefficients, with respect to the variables signified by the second subscript. Superscript 0 attached to them implies that they are evaluated at the equilibrium point.

Let us draw our attention to the vector of investment activities which are intended to be carried out during the current period. Let X_I be the vector of the levels of such activities. We assume that each of its elements is fixed at some particular level, so that it remains at X_I^0 throughout a process of tatonnement. It creates demands for commodities of the three sectors of the amounts $A_{ZI}X_I^0$, $A_{XI}X_I^0$, $A_{YI}X_I^0$, respectively, where A_{ZI}, A_{XI}, A_{YI} are input coefficients regarding the investment activities. They are naturally submatrices of A_{ZX}, A_{XX}, A_{YX}, because I is a subset of the fixprice activities X. These investment demands, together with the consumer demands and the intersectoral demands for producers' goods, are added up to form the total demand:

$$\begin{bmatrix} A_{ZZ} & A_{ZX} & A_{ZY} \\ A_{YZ} & A_{XX} & A_{XY} \\ A_{YZ} & A_{YX} & A_{YY} \end{bmatrix} \begin{bmatrix} Z(P) \\ X \\ Y \end{bmatrix} + \begin{bmatrix} D_Z \\ D_X \\ D_Y \end{bmatrix} + \begin{bmatrix} A_{ZI} \\ A_{XI} \\ A_{YI} \end{bmatrix} X_I^0,$$

where and throughout the following we write the complement of X_I^0 in X simply as X and the complements of A_{ZI}, A_{XI}, A_{YI} in A_{ZX}, A_{XX}, A_{YX} simply as A_{ZX}, A_{XX}, A_{YX}.

In order to attain an equilibrium, these have to be adjusted, during the process of tatonnement, such that they do not exceed the corresponding supplies. Where, in the last period, a temporary equilibrium is established at prices $\check{P}$, for the Z industries and at intensities $\check{X}$ and $\check{Y}$ of the X and Y sectors, respectively, we may write their supplies as:

$$B^* \begin{bmatrix} 0 \\ 0 \\ Y \end{bmatrix} \text{ and } B^{**} \begin{bmatrix} \check{Z}(\check{P}) \\ \check{X} \\ \check{Y} \end{bmatrix},$$

Y being the intensity vector of the Y sector in the current period. Evidently, $\check{Z}(\check{P})$, $\check{X}$ and $\check{Y}$ are regarded as constant, while $Z(P)$, X, Y are flexible according to the rules of tatonnement. The neoclassical law of prices does hold for the flexprice sectors, that is P_i takes on the value of zero wherever the i-th demand–supply equilibrium condition holds with strict inequality. However, the same law does not hold for any fixprice commodity in the X or Y category in the state of equilibrium. We, in fact, assume that the price does not fall but is kept unchanged, even though supply exceeds demand for this commodity. Residuals are discarded to keep prices.

4 Let us now introduce adjustment functions of prices and intensities of activities, in order to examine the temporary equilibrium of week τ for stability. We begin with the price adjustment equation for the Z sector. As we confine ourselves to the tatonnement analysis for a particular period (or week) only, in this section and the next, we omit thereinafter all the subscripts referring to the week τ in which tatonnement is carried out. A set (P^0, X^0, Y^0) gives the temporary equilibrium of the week. At the equilibrium point the supply–demand conditions hold for the Z industries (agriculture, forestry, etc.) in the form of equation, rather than inequality, because joint production possibilities are ruled out for them and the prices of the commodities are adjusted until the equality is established. That is:

$$A_{ZZ}Z(P^0) + A_{ZX}X^0 + A_{ZY}Y^0 + D_Z(P^0, X^0, Y^0) + A_{Z1}X_1^0 = \check{Z}(\check{P}), \quad \text{(E1)}$$

where $\check{Z}(\check{P})$ is the output of Z commodities available in the week, which is the result of the production activities in the previous week, as it is so in the cobweb theory. We can show that $P^0 > 0$, and the switching problem mentioned above does not arise with regard to the adjustment of P discussed below.

Now let S be the excess supply, that is an excess of supply, $\check{Z}(\check{P})$, over demand, that is the sum of the production demands, $A_{ZZ}Z(P)$, $A_{ZX}X$, $A_{ZY}Y$, the consumer demand, $D_Z(P, X, Y)$ and the investment demand, $A_{Z1}X_1^0$. Of course S takes on the value of 0 at the equilibrium point. This means that output of no Z commodity is left over to the market of the next week, as it is cleared, because of the absence of joint production activity, at the end of the current week when the tatonnement process is terminated. However, in the midst of the process, at the moment when an excess supply S appears in the market, it would be considered to be carried over to the market in the next week, so that the total quantities of the Z commodities include S and amount to $Z(P) + S$. This may exceed or fall short of the output of the next week, $Z(P^0)$, that is obtained when the equilibrium is established in the current week.

We assume throughout the following that the prices P of the Z commodities are adjusted according to the formula (5.4) below, which implies that P decreases, during the current week, whenever the $Z(P) + S$ is expected to exceed $Z(P^0)$ in the next week, and *vice versa*. Thus:

$$\dot{P} = a_1[Z(P^0) - (Z(P) + S)], \tag{5.4}$$

where a_1 represents the adjustment coefficient which is a diagonal matrix with positive numbers on the diagonal. Viewing the definition of S and taking account of the assumption that the consumer demand function for Z commodities is expandable into a Taylor series and may, therefore, be approximated by a linear expression in a neighbourhood of the temporary equilibrium point, we may then rewrite the adjustment equation in the following form:

$$\begin{aligned}
\dot{P} = a_1[&A_{ZZ}(Z(P) - Z(P^0)) \\
&+ A_{ZX}(X - X^0) + A_{ZY}(Y - Y^0) \\
&+ D^0_{ZP}(P - P^0) + D^0_{ZX}(X - X^0) \\
&+ D^0_{ZY}(Y - Y^0) - (Z(P) - Z(P^0))].
\end{aligned} \tag{5.4'}$$

Note that $\bar{Z}(\dot{P})$ and the investment demand are constant.

The reader may notice a difference between the adjustment function (5.4) above and the usual one due to Samuelson. The latter assumes that P is regulated by the excess supply S only and independent of whether output $Z(P)$ falls short of (or exceeds) the equilibrium output $Z(P^0)$. In examining the difference between the two adjustment formulas, we must be aware of, in addition to the prima-facie distinction, the fact that there is another important distinction between them. That is to say, while there is one period of production lag in our model, it is assumed by Samuelson that production is instantaneous. In the case of no production lag we should have $\bar{Z}(\dot{P})$ in place of $Z(P^0)$ in (5.4); therefore, (5.4) reduces to:

$$\dot{P} = a_1[-S'], \tag{5.4''}$$

where S' is an excess supply in the case of supply being instantaneous and flexible, that is, an excess of supply $Z(P)$ over total demand. Thus, in the case of a production lag being present, our (5.4) implies the same type of price adjustment as Samuelson's (5.4″) does in the case of no lag. We may therefore conclude that (5.4) and (5.4″) are essentially equivalent, their apparent difference being ascribed to whether we allow for a time lag in production or not.

Let us next turn to the X sector. As this is a fixprice sector and the prices of X commodities are all decided by the factories or suppliers and kept constant throughout the tatonnement process, adjustment is consequently made in quantity. We assume that the activity level X is increased if it is below its equilibrium level X^0, while it is decreased if it is above X^0. Thus we have, for X other than X_1^0 which are fixed, the formula of adjustment:

$$\dot{X} = a_2(X^0 - X), \tag{5.5}$$

where X^0 stands for an equilibrium value of X. The adjustment (5.5) is different, in an essential way, from the usual one (discussed before) which assumes that $\dot{X}_i$ positively depends on the corresponding excess profits. In the latter case, while excess profits for process i is negative, $\dot{X}_i$ is negative as long as $X_i > 0$ but it should be zero at $X_i = 0$. This switching of the adjustment formula is necessary in order to keep X_i in the non-negative region. No switching is needed, on the other hand, where we assume (5.5), because with $X_i^0 = 0$, the movement of X_i generated by (5.5) stops at $X_i = 0$ and never gets into the negative region. This is also true for the adjustment rule (5.6) discussed below.

X^0 satisfies the equilibrium condition:

$$A_{XZ}Z(P) + A_{XX}X + A_{XY}Y + D_X(P, X, Y)$$
$$+ A_{XI}X_1^0 \leqslant B_{XZ}\tilde{Z}(\tilde{P}) + B_{XX}\tilde{X} + B_{XY}\tilde{Y} \tag{E2}$$

provided P and Y are set at P^0 and Y^0, respectively, and hence $Z(P) = Z(P^0)$. Obviously, on the right-hand side of the above inequality, $\tilde{Z}(\tilde{P})$, $\tilde{X}$, $\tilde{Y}$ are the temporary equilibrium activity levels of $Z(P)$, X, Y in the previous week. In (5.5) a_2 is a diagonal matrix with positive elements on the diagonal. Where the part in the parentheses of (5.5) takes on a positive value, that is to say, where $X^0 > X$, X increases, so that the difference between X^0 and X will shrink. It will also decrease in the opposite case of $X^0 < X$. Therefore, X will finally approach the equilibrium X^0 at the end of the tatonnement.

Finally, in the case of the Y group too, we may confirm a similar convergence of its intensity vector Y towards the equilibrium level Y^0. Because Y commodities are all produced instantaneously, both supply and demand sides are flexible in their case, and, furthermore, as it is assumed that joint production is absent in the sector, it is seen that the temporary equilibrium condition holds with equality for each Y commodity. Thus we have:

$$A_{YZ}Z(P) + A_{YX}X + A_{YY}Y + D_Y(P, X, Y) + A_{Y1}X_1^0 = Y, \qquad (E3)$$

which will be established at $Y = Y^0$ provided that P and X are also set at P^0 and X^0. To obtain $Y = Y^0$, a quantity adjustment has to be made. We assume that Y will change according to the formula:

$$\dot{Y} = a_3(Y^0 - Y). \qquad (5.6)$$

Evidently, like a_2, the coefficient a_3 is a diagonal matrix with positive elements on the diagonal. Clearly, (5.6) means that Y decreases or increases wherever Y exceeds or falls short of its equilibrium level Y^0. In the same way that I have shown X's approach to X^0, we can observe that Y will eventually arrive at Y^0 when the market is closed at the end of the week. Hence the conditions for temporary equilibrium (E2) and (E3) will be established, regardless of the behaviour of P. Of course, (E1) is obtained when P is stable; the stability of the Z sector is crucial for the general temporary equilibrium (E1)–(E3).

In this way our analysis of the mixed economy is finally reduced to the one having the Z sector in the centre, the other X and Y sectors adjusting themselves in quantities, independently of what is happening in the market of Z commodities. It is clear that the influences of X and Y on the Z market become negligible when X and Y sufficiently approach X^0 and Y^0, so that on the right-hand side of (5.4′) only those terms which relate to $Z(P) - Z(P^0)$ and $P - P^0$ remain effective, all the other terms relating to $X - X^0$ and $Y - Y^0$ being considered as insignificant in the final stage of tatonnement. In the following section, therefore, we isolate the Z sector from the rest of the mixed economy and concentrate our attention upon an unalloyed multiple market economy which singles out Z commodities only, in order to examine it for stability.

5 To inquire into the problem of stability we assume that the supply function of each Z commodity is analytic and apply a Taylor expansion to $Z(P)$, which may, therefore, be approximated, in a small vicinity of the temporary equilibrium point P^0, by:

$$Z(P) = Z(P^0) + R(P - P^0).$$

R is a matrix of derivatives of $Z(P)$ with respect to P, evaluated at P^0. Remembering that we rule out joint production in the Z sector, we see that partial cross derivatives $\partial Z_i/\partial P_j$, with $i \neq j$, would be all non-positive,[6] but we assume they are small in magnitude. Moreover we assume, in the following, that $Z_i(P)$, for all i, are normal, so that each of Z commodities has a positive direct derivative, $\partial Z_i/\partial P_i$. These result in a near diagonal matrix with positive diagonal elements. Substituting, we may simplify (5.4') in the following form:

$$\dot{P} = a_1[(A_{ZZ} - I)R + D_{ZP}^0](P - P^0) \tag{5.7}$$

because whenever we reach the final stage of tatonnement in which X and Y have already settled at X^0 and Y^0, or at least in a small neighbourhood of them, all other terms of (5.4') are negligible.

In order to examine the tatonnement path generated by (5.7), the idea which immediately occurs to those who have worked in the field of economic stability is to impose the following assumptions on the matrices $A_{ZZ}R$ and $D_{ZP}^0 - R$. First, because R is near diagonal with positive elements on the diagonal and A_{ZZ} is non-negative, $A_{ZZ}R$ is also a non-negative matrix. Secondly, as diagonal elements of D_{ZP}^0 may be assumed to be all negative as income effects may be considered to be negligible, it is certain that $D_{ZP}^0 - R$ is a matrix with negative elements on the diagonal. Then we are concerned with a case where these diagonal elements are large enough to dominate other elements; that is to say, the matrix:

$$M = A_{ZZ}R + (D_{ZP}^0 - R)$$

is a dominant negative diagonal matrix in the sense of Arrow *et al.* that there is a positive vector u such that:

$$|m_{ii}|u_i > \sum_j |m_{ij}|u_j \qquad \text{for all } i \tag{5.8}$$

where m_{ij}'s are elements of M. If the absolute values of the diagonal elements of $D_{ZP}^0 - R$ are large enough to dominate other elements of M, (5.8) is always fulfilled, and M is said to be dominant negative diagonal. Then, defining the Liapounoff function Γ as:

$$\Gamma = \max_j |\dot{P}_j|/u_j,$$

---

[6] We may derive this supply function in the following way. As we assume that production of Z commodities is not instantaneous, their outputs do not depend on their current prices. They are functions of the prices the producers expect to prevail in the market when their products are ready to be sold. But these expectations are formed on the basis of the information of the current output prices, so that the expected outputs of flexprice commodities depend on their respective current prices. In addition, they depend on prices of inputs (materials, etc.). As the prices of fixprice commodities P_X and P_Y are assumed to be constant, the only variable prices of inputs are P_Z, the prices of flexprice commodities. Naturally, where an element of P_Z, say P_j, is increased, the output $Z_i(P)$ will decrease, as long as i uses j.

Arrow, Block and Hurwicz have shown that wherever $d\Gamma/dt$ exists it is negative except at equilibrium point where $\dot{P}_j = 0$ for all j.[7] This means that provided P is set in a small neighbourhood of P^0 initially, it will change such that the distance Γ of $\dot{P}$ from the equilibrium point $\dot{P} = 0$ diminishes at all times, until it finally settles at it. In this way, though it depends on rather restrictive assumption of dominant negative diagonalness, the local stability of the temporary equilibrium prices P^0 is established. Hence $Z(P)$ also approaches $Z(P^0)$. As has already been seen, X and Y too approach X^0 and Y^0. Thus we see that the economy comes nearer and nearer to the equilibrium point as the tatonnement proceeds.

6 Let us now assume that each temporary equilibrium in the historical sequence is stable. It is also assumed that the economy is supplied with an ample amount of financial funds for investment, so that there is no substantive restriction upon the investment activities X_1^0, all activities being freely expandable or reducible. Then, as has been observed in chapter 4, it is true that we have a temporary equilibrium of the type that the existing factors of production are all fully employed and the existing stocks of capital goods are also fully utilized, unless they are free goods. Before we examine the case of the financial restriction being effective in section 7 below of this chapter, we concentrate our attention upon a time sequence of such temporary equilibria and investigate whether it would trace out a stable motion.

Let $\bar{V}^T = (\bar{Z}(\bar{P})^T, \bar{X}^T, \bar{Y}^T)$ be the activity level vectors carried out in the last period (or week); the T applied to a vector signifies its transposition. Then the economy is provided with the endowment of the consumption goods, capital goods and intermediate products of the amounts $B^{**}\bar{V}$ at the commencement of the present period. In the state of temporary equilibrium we have:

$$B^*U + B^{**}\bar{V} \geqslant AX + A'Y + D(P, X, Y), \qquad (5.9)$$

where X and Y are activities, for the present period, of time-taking and instantaneous production, respectively. We write $U^T = (0, 0, Y^T)$. A and A' are input coefficient matrices of time-taking and instantaneous production processes, respectively, while B^* and B^{**} are dated output coefficient matrices defined before. $D(P, X, Y)$ is, of course, the consumer demand vector.

As for the factors of production, $\bar{N}$ represents the vector of their supply, and L and L' matrices of factor input coefficients. Where some of the

[7] K. J. Arrow, H. D. Block and L. Hurwicz, 'On the Stability of the Competitive Equilibrium II', *Econometrica*, 27, 1959, pp. 82–109.

elements of $LX + L'Y$ exceed the corresponding elements of $\bar{N}$, production at the levels X and Y is not feasible; hence the following is required for the feasibility of production:

$$\bar{N} \geqslant LX + L'Y; \tag{5.10}$$

where the neoclassical rule of free goods holds for products. The price of commodity i is zero if (5.9) holds for i with strict inequality ' $>$ '. Similarly, factor i is a free good and its price is zero if (5.10) holds for i with ' $>$ '. Activities assessed at the equilibrium prices must satisfy the following conditions:

$$(z\psi_Z I_Z + z\psi_X B_{XZ}, \ z\psi_X B_{XX}) \leqslant (PA + WL)(I + Q),$$
$$z\psi_X B_{XY} + zP_Y I_Y \leqslant PA' + WL' \tag{5.11}$$

where B_{XZ}, B_{XX} and B_{XY} are the submatrices of B^{**}, ψ_Z, ψ_X are the vectors of expected prices and z is the reciprocal of $1 +$ the rate of profits of the X commodities; so $z\psi$ stands for the vector of discounted expected prices. W is the vector of factor prices. If there is a production process which satisfies either the first or the second condition of (5.11) above with the reversed inequality ' $>$ ', it brings forth positive excess profits; then entrepreneurs will increase the activity level of such a process by decreasing the levels of other processes which they use. In the state of a temporary equilibrium there should not be such a process; hence (5.11) is a necessary condition for equilibrium.

At the outset of the next period the economy has the endowment of the amounts $B^{**}V$ resulting from the activities in the present period, where $V^T = (Z(P)^T, X^T, Y^T)$. The supply of factors of production in the next period may be different from the present one. Accordingly, in (5.9) $\bar{V}$ will be replaced by V and in (5.10) $\bar{N}$ by a new vector prevailing in the next period. Then with Q given, it is seen that the new equilibrium conditions, designated by (5.9′), (5.10′) and (5.11′), are fulfilled by new X, Y, P, W, denoted by X', Y', P', W', respectively. Thus we have a sequence, $\bar{X} \to X \to X'$ and $Y \to Y'$. From X' and Y', the economy moves to X'' and Y'' in the third period. We have $P \to P' \to P'' \ldots$ and $W \to W' \to W'' \to \ldots$, too.

These sequences, especially that of $\bar{X} \to X \to X' \to \ldots$, are compared with alternative sequences. Suppose now that an invention is made and a new method of production (or a number of related new production processes) becomes available in the present period. The input matrices A and L and the output matrices are expanded, horizontally and vertically, to accommodate these new processes and the new commodities used or produced by them. In the present period and afterwards, entrepreneurs will choose their best activities from among the expanded set. (We assume, for the sake of simplicity, that the newly invented methods are all non-instantaneous ones, so that there is no expansion in the instantaneous set.) However, the invention disturbs not just the quantity equilibrium conditions (5.9) and (5.10), but the price conditions (5.11) too. Although repercussions among them are simultaneous, the initial stimulus appears in the price conditions and is propagated from it to the quantity conditions. This is because it is the price system which is first put out of the previous position by invention. The price conditions (5.11) will take the role of the menu of methods of production listing the values of all processes available, old and new, and entrepreneurs will make their orders from among them. Their choice must be feasible, so that they must satisfy (5.9) and (5.10) with the enlarged new matrices.

With this availability of new processes, it may become possible to produce some commodities at drastically cheaper prices. These may be commodities which have been produced previously by old methods, or may, in many cases, be new commodities. They are, however, not entirely new goods, in the sense that among academics, technologists and entrepreneurs it has been familiar for a certain period of time how they could be manufactured; for example, the TV system was such a case, fifty or sixty years ago. They all knew how to produce these commodities but did not do so because the business was found to be not commercially viable. However, after the introduction of some new methods of production it becomes possible for entrepreneurs to produce these commodities at commercially acceptable prices. A new business will start for them, and they are no longer merely a dream only known in a science book but are actually traded on the market.

Once these commodities become available at cheaper prices those processes which use these commodities and have so far been judged as unprofitable, because of the use of these expensive commodities as means, now become economical. Then in other, related, fields of production, there will be a shift in technology; a number of production processes which have been known but not used in the past are now actually adopted. There will then be innovation in these areas, in the sense that traditional methods are completely wiped out and replaced by new ones. This is an immediate or direct trigger effect which has been given rise to by the original inventions; this would happen in the first period after the original innovation. In the second period, there will be second round or indirect effects that the inventions, together with the induced first round trigger effect, will create. As time goes by, trigger effects become larger and larger, and will spread more and more.[8] The price structure will change into a very different one.

[8] The trigger effect was first analysed by H. Simon statically and then dynamized by the present author. See H. A. Simon, 'Effects of Technological Change in the Leontief Model', in T. C. Koopmans (ed.), *Activity Analysis of Production and Allocation*, New York, Wiley, 1951, pp. 260–81. M. Morishima, *Equilibrium, Stability and Growth*, Oxford, Clarendon Press, 1964, pp. 116–22.

The economy will choose production processes at any point of time in the future which are entirely different from those which would have been chosen without the new inventions. In parallel to the change in the activity set, X, adopted, there will be a drastic change in the list of commodities produced. In this way, culture and indeed the quality of life have been changed throughout history, with every major invention which brought widespread, large-scale and far-reaching trigger effects. In this sense, the sequence of temporary equilibria, $\bar{X} \to (X, Y) \to (X', Y') \to \ldots$, is unstable with respect to the development of technical knowledge; that is to say, it will diverge from the original sequence that would be obtained if no innovation were carried out.

Even though we have no invention or no other exogenous stimulus, trigger effects may be brought about. The following example will illustrate how a self-generated endogenous trigger action may start. Consider an economy whose working population is getting old. Labour is thus becoming more scarce and getting relatively more expensive. At one stage, activities using robots will be found in such an economy to be more profitable than those using human labour, so that robotization will progress at a large scale. Once the demand for robots becomes considerably large, these will be more produced and, consequently, its cost of production and hence its price will decline greatly. This creates an acceleration in the trend of substituting robots for human labour.

We may then observe its immense trigger effects. First of all, robotization will create a large number of robot correlated industries, such as robot repairing stations and firms dealing with robot and computer software. Moreover, there are many production activities which have so far been either abortive or have been given up for the reason that they are very dangerous; these have, therefore, been judged as not economically feasible. In the age of robots being widely available, however, entrepreneurs need not incur high costs for securing safety. Investment opportunities will then be increased in almost every corner of the economy. In this way, as soon as investment is made in this new area, additional new opportunities will be opened and investment will be accelerated. For instance, the ocean or sea bed which has so far been very difficult to use economically is now turning into a treasure house for future developments since the advent of various kinds of robots. It is very likely that the ocean will eventually be put under human control as developments at the initial stage which have just started will certainly trigger off various, ambitious innovations under the sea. Evidently similar things are happening in space too.

In the age of robotics, the form of the firm and the principle by which it is managed and administered will greatly differ from the ones of the present day. The firm raises its profits, not by exploiting human labour, but by arranging the production system such that robots of the firm are efficiently operated. There will be no Labour Standards Law to be applied to them; they will work twenty-four hours a day. This will result in making competition between firms very severe, and workers will have to defend themselves in some way or another from robots' cold-hearted, tireless attacks upon them and their unions. In spite of their efforts, workers will be driven to the wall and will have to share a position in the firm with their colleagues, robots. Otherwise, in order to be a master of robots, they will have to return to universities or other higher educational organizations several times during their working lifetime, so as to learn and rehearse newly developed production techniques.

It seems, moreover, that the small, family-based enterprise will in the future become an increasingly popular form of enterprise. (In fact, as is seen below, a sign of this is observed in a few parts of the world.) First of all, robots are suited to the production of several kinds of goods which are different in size or form, each in small quantities. For that reason, when they produce certain goods for a number of companies, the good for each company being produced with subtle differences in specifications, robots can demonstrate a high degree of efficiency. Moreover, it is evident that those industries which have robotized have very small labour forces, and it is possible for a single family to establish a highly productive firm by hiring only a very few workers.[9] The family which serves as the basis of production is not necessarily a large, extended family; even a nuclear family can start an enterprise by using robots with the assistance of a few workers. Since these companies can supply components of the products for sevoreal large companies, the risks from any one of the large companies falling into difficulties are dispersed. Large companies achieve the finished product by purchasing and assembling various components from small companies.

By delegating a certain number of production processes which have so far been carried out within the large companies to small companies, they will be able to reduce their scale of production to an immense degree. The large-scale factory production system of the present day may be replaced, in the future, by a collectivity of small, family-based enterprises, and the atmosphere of production may become, in the future, far more paternalistic, warm, loose and flexible (perhaps far less Protestant) than is the case at present under the cold, rigorous and impersonal mass production regime.

---

[9] Japan held 50% of the robots produced in the world in 1982 and more than 44% throughout the 1970s; see OECD, *Industrial Robots: Their Role in Manufacturing Industry*, 1983. The industrial success of Japan in the 1970s and 1980s is mainly due to her advancement in the robotization, by means of which Japanese small businesses have been improved enormously. Italy is also a good user of robots in the world and has advanced greatly in productivity.

Thus, even the so-called tendency towards mass production or monopolization (due to Marx) may be stopped, or there is a possibility that it will be at least hindered greatly, by robots. If so, then the usual model of the capitalist economy will be inappropriate for analysing this sort of economy; more suitable is a model which is perhaps nearer, in the labour relationship, to Marx's model of simple commodity production, where the producer himself owns the requisite machinery (robots) and tools, and acts as a worker. In areas where robots can be used, this form of production is likely to be the most efficient unit of production. Thus, a process of robotization, initiated because of a shortage of labour due to the working force becoming aged, may finally lead to even a change in the regime of the economy, at least partially in its corner. If this happens, the path of economic development (or the sequence of temporary equilibria) will be totally unstable.[10]

7 The analysis has so far proceeded on the assumption that there is no financial restriction in choosing X's. As has been emphasized in previous chapters, however, it is impossible to carry out some production processes, especially those in connection with major investment projects, such as incorporation of new companies, construction of new production systems, introduction of anti-pollution facilities, and so on, without the collaboration of financiers or bankers. We have classified such processes as those belonging to class I, denoting them by X_I. The elements of vector X_I are not free variables in the system; they are fixed at a point X_I^0 by agreement with financiers. The amount of money needed for carrying out these activities at the level X_I^0 is promised by financiers to be provided to the producers.

Where X_I is restricted to X_I^0, it is, in general, impossible to realize a temporary equilibrium at the level of full employment of labour and full capacity utilization of capital and resources. Where some of the conditions of (5.9) and (5.10) are violated with inequality ' < ', inflation is inevitable in terms of P or W, or both. Where the conditions of (5.9) and (5.10) hold with strict inequality ' > ', either capital goods are underutilized or some factors are unemployed. Where the rule of free goods does not hold, the underemployment of capital goods and factors is involuntary, corresponding elements of P and W being kept positive. The full employment is impossible because of a shortage of investment that follows from the insufficiency of financial support.

[10] Another example of the success along the line described above has been vigorously discussed by Julia Bamford. Besides the industrial zones such as Turin, Genoa and Milan, based on the basis of large factories, Italy has a recent addition that is called Terza Italia (Third Italy) where small firms based on farming families have been developed after 1970. Emilia Romagna and Tuscany are well-known examples of Terza Italia. See J. Bamford, 'The Development of Small Firms, the Traditional Family and Agrarian Pattern in Italy', in R. Graffee and R. Scase (eds.), *Entrepreneurship in Europe*, Croom Helm, 1987.

Let us now compare two sequences of temporary equilibria: one starting from a low level of X_I, say X_I^0, while the other is the one from a higher X_I, say X_I^*, in the following way. Suppose more investment projects are approved and supported by financiers in X_I^* than in X_I^0. This would create a new demand for bricks; then the activity of production of the brick industry, which is a member of X_{II}, will be increased. Then the brick industry's demand for clay will, in turn, increase in the present period, or in the future. The production of clay too will be expanded. This would happen, sooner or later, unless the excess supply of bricks and clay are very large in the current period. These types of repercussions or multiplier effects, which may be ascribed to Schumpeter, as footnote 11 below evidences, should be distinguished from Keynes' consumption multiplier process.

From this point of view, we may now interpret Ricardo, Keynes and Schumpeter as being concerned with the following cases, respectively. First we call X_I^0 anti-Say's law activities, their levels of intensities being fixed by investment decisions, while X_{II} Say's law activities which are flexible variables. Ricardo has assumed that there is no anti-Say's law activity, so that his sequence of temporary equilibria may be more or less similar to the one discussed in the previous section. On the other hand, Keynes may be interpreted as having assumed (a) that there is no Say's law activity, that is $X_{II} = \emptyset$, and (b) that all consumption goods are produced instantly. He makes no discussion concerning repercussions from X_I^0 to X_{II} and confines himself in the analysis of repercussions from X_I^0 to Y. On the other hand, Schumpeter has been concerned with a more general case with X_I^0, X_{II} and Y, all existing in the economy. Repercussions from X_I^0 to X_{II} may be grasped as trigger effects, by means of which we may answer in our own way to one of Schumpeter's main problems: 'Why do entrepreneurs appear . . . in clusters?'[11] It is clear that the trigger effects of an anti-Say's law process upon other processes are brought forth by parallel trigger effects of the creation of one entrepreneur upon many other entrepreneurs. It is not surprising to see that such a problem has never been asked either of Ricardo or of Keynes. Under their assumptions stated above, it is impossible to ask this question because of the absence of the repercussion from X_I^0 to X_{II} in their models.

The reader might have found that this book bears a resemblance, in a number of points, to Schumpeter's *Economic Development*. It is true that I have been greatly stimulated and influenced by it, but this does not mean

[11] J. A. Schumpeter, *The Theory of Economic Development*, Harvard University Press, 1951, p. 228. He himself considers that 'the successful appearance of an entrepreneur is followed by the appearance . . . of some others' (p. 229). They appear not only in the same industry as the original pioneer's but also in other related branches. This repercussion of profit opportunity from one branch to another might be explained by our trigger effect, though there is no such analysis by Schumpeter himself.

that there is a sympathy between this volume and his, even in the points where the reader would find his marks. I must emphasize that there are places where his influence has the opposite effect: I even completely oppose him on some of these points, two of which I would like to call the reader's attention to in the following.

As has been indicated in a previous chapter, Schumpeter's theory of innovation is based on his interpretation of Walras' general equilibrium theoretic view of the development of the economy. Schumpeter describes the dynamic process caused by an entrepreneur's innovative behaviour, by taking the case of the introduction of looms as an example, in the following manner.

[N]ew businesses are continually arising under the impulse of the alluring profit. A complete reorganisation of the industry occurs, with its increases in production, its competitive struggle, its supersession of obsolete businesses, its possible dismissal of workers, and so forth. . . .[T]he final result must be a new equilibrium position, in which, with new data, the law of cost again rules, so that now the prices of the products are again equal to the wages and rents of the services of labour and land. . . ./Consequently, the surplus of the entrepreneur in question and of his immediate followers disappear.' (Schumpeter, *The Theory of Economic Development*, pp. 131–2.)

We may easily excerpt many other passages to the same effect from Schumpeter. For example:

[T]he swarm-like appearance [of entrepreneurs] necessitates a special and distinguishable process of absorption, or incorporating the new things and of adapting the economic system to them, a process of liquidation or, as I used to say, an approach to a new *static state*. (ibid., p. 231; italics by MM.)
[T]he depression leads . . . to a new equilibrium position . . . Of course the position reached in the end never completely corresponds to the theoretical picture of a system without development, in which there would no longer be income in the form of interest . . . Nevertheless, an approximation to a position without development always occurs, and this, being relatively steady, may again be a starting point for the carrying out of new combinations. [W]e come to the conclusion that according to our theory there must always be a process of absorption between two booms, ending in a position approaching equilibrium . . . (ibid., pp. 242 and 244.)

These imply that Schumpeter believes the existence of a static equilibrium in correspondence to each given state of technology. He also believes this long-run equilibrium point is stable. Such a vision clearly contrasts with its prototype, that is Walras' view. According to him:

Finally, in order to come still more closely to reality, we must drop the hypothesis of annual market period and adopt in its place the hypothesis of a continuous market [or that of a sequence of temporary equilibria] (inserted by MM).[12]

[12] Leon Walras, *Elements of Pure Economics*, London, George Allen and Unwin, 1954, p. 380.

This sequence does not in general approach to a long-run equilibrium because the economy 'has to renew its efforts and start over again, all the basic data of the problem, e.g., the initial quantities possessed, the utilities of goods and services, the technical coefficients, the excess of income over consumption, the working capital requirements, etc., having changed in the meantime'.[13] Therefore, even if no new combination is introduced at any point of time, the basic data other than the technical coefficients and the working capital requirements do not necessarily remain stationary. The initial quantities of commodities will never cease to fluctuate. They will grow forever even with no innovation. For Walras it is impossible to apply the stability theory of point to the sequence of temporary equilibrium. In this respect, the present volume is nearer to Walras than Schumpeter. In fact, Walras can to the utmost examine the sequential equilibria from the viewpoint of the stability of motion only, though he had not, in fact, completed such a theory.[14] It is impossible for him to discuss the existence and stability of long-run stationary equilibrium, because it contradicts his basic idea of 'the continuous' market where exogenous data are ever changing.

Thus we may say that we are very much like Walras (but unlike Schumpeter) on the point where we investigate the economy in the process of economic or technical progress, making no assumption concerning whether it finally settles at a certain position of stationary equilibrium. In other respects, however, we are much nearer to Schumpeter than Walras, who distinguishes 'economic' from 'technical' progress[15] and concentrates his attention upon the former. As his analysis abstracts from the latter, it is unclear how he would have dealt with it. But it may be likely that he, like many contemporary Walrasians, would have formulated a production function in a form which allows for technological changes, such as the one with Hicks or Harrod neutral, or biased invention. Such a formulation, however, is not amicable with the idea of technological innovations, which are unexpected, irregular and idiosyncratic and cannot be described by a continuous and systematic shift of the existing production function. Under the name of innovation 'what we are about to consider is, in fact, that kind of change arising from within the system *which so displaces its equilibrium point that the new one cannot be reached from the old one by infinitesimal steps'.*[16]

As Schumpeter has correctly pointed out, the vast majority of innovations or new combinations will not grow out of the old firms, but are carried out by completely unrelated new firms as his example of the transition from the stagecoach to the railway system shows. Thus new

[13] Walras, ibid., p. 383.
[14] This spirit of Walras was maintained by La Volpe and Hicks in the volumes quoted before.
[15] Walras, *Elements*, p. 383.   [16] Schumpeter, *The Theory*, p. 64n, italics by him.

combinations are not made by improving or adapting the production function of the old firms. For new combinations new firms are formed by new entrepreneurs, but these do not take the place of the old firms immediately and coexist side by side and compete with them.[17] The replacement is completed when the old firms surrender to the new. (As newly established projects must draw at least some of the factors of production from the old concerns – factors left unemployed are usually inferior – competition for getting able workers and managers is inevitable. The neoclassical formulation of technological change cannot examine this process of competition.)

Moreover, innovations bring about various effects on related sections of the economy. A new combination (railway) has its own allied industries which are different from those of the old combination (stagecoach). The victory of railway over stagecoach gives rise to a substantial and drastic change in the allied industries. A typical recent example is a switch from station hotel to motel which would not have been realized unless the motorcar won the competition against the railway. The neoclassical growth theory is not concerned with this process of trigger action.

The process, however, can be examined in terms of the activity vector, X and Y; the elements corresponding to the old firms which have been positive in the past will now take on the value of 0 and those of the new firms which have so far been zero now become positive. Innovations are interpreted and grasped as such structural changes in X or Y. The competition between old and new methods of production which neoclassical economists usually neglect is the subject of Schumpeter. By taking a similar way of reasoning we have reached in this chapter a view that the economic path traced out by sequential temporary equilibria is unstable. In addition to this, it has also been seen that even without innovation, an endogenous cause such as an increase in the ratio of the retired generation in the total population may create a pathbreaking new departure in the course of economic development. In this respect, we may say that this volume is unSchumpeterian because Schumpeter himself has assumed, as has been seen above, that the long-run equilibrium exists and is stable.

Finally, it is pointed out that to carry out an innovation the problem of how it is financed is most essential. This aspect of technological change is entirely ignored by many of the contemporary economists and is a subject of the next chapter. We shall tackle this problem, using the Modigliani–Miller theorem, though this is valid only under restrictive assumptions. In other situations , the M-M property (the second equation of (6.11) below) has to be replaced by a more general one concerning Q and r'.

---

[17] Schumpeter, *The Theory*, p. 226.

6 Innovations and financing

1 We now proceed to the problem of how to finance the business and examine the monetary aspects of the economy. In the previous chapters we have been concerned with the real or physical aspects of an economy; we will now investigate how the purchasing power is provided to the firms in this economy and how money and other means of finance and transaction are circulated among the firms and households.

We assume a general economy in which money may circulate in the markets and be deposited with a bank; the firms may borrow money by issuing bills or bonds – but they can borrow only for one period. When they return the money, interest must be paid to the lender. Where one wants to borrow some amount of money for a longer period (say two periods), he must issue bonds of the necessary amount and reissue them at the beginning of the second period, after having paid back the bonds for the first period at the end of the same period. In this way we simplify bonds of various durations into a single sort of bond for the shortest duration. Also, it is true that bonds issued by different subjects are treated as different commodities because some have good credit, but some others not so much. Thus, in general, bonds yield different amounts of interest. But we shall ignore this problem and simplify the matter by assuming that there prevails a uniform rate of interest in the market of bonds.

It is assumed that the firms and banks are stock companies. They all issue shares and, occasionally, additional new shares. They are held not only by households but also by the firms and possibly by banks. But again, we assume, for the sake of simplicity, that they are all held by households. Although the problems regarding institutional shareholdings are increasingly becoming more important in the practical world, we shall entirely ignore these in the following. The primary purpose of the present chapter is to provide the theoretical, monetary foundation to the general equilibrium system. We do not assume that shares are homogeneous. Dividends from them may be different from one company to another, and their prices too may be different.

Now we shall explain the notation. Let subscripts h, f, b refer to household, firm and bank. Let $\bar{M}_i$ and M_i be the money held by subject $i(=h, f, b)$ in the last and present periods, respectively. Similarly, $\bar{B}_i$ and B_i are the bonds held by i in the last and present periods. For $i=f$, they take on negative values because the firms issue bonds; otherwise they are positive. $\bar{T}_i$ and T_i are time deposits held by i in the two periods; for $i=b$ they are liabilities of the banks, so that both $\bar{T}_b$ and T_b take on negative values. As for shares $\bar{\theta}_i$ ($i=f, b$) stands for the total amount of shares issued by i until the end of the last period, and $\Delta \bar{\theta}_i$ ($i=f, b$) the new shares issued in the current period. Both of these are represented by negative amounts. Naturally $\bar{\theta}_i + \Delta \bar{\theta}_i$ gives the initial amount for the next period, that is the shares issued by i until the end of the current period. Finally, $\bar{\theta}_{ih}$ and θ_{ih} are the shares of the firm or bank i held by household h in the last and the present period, respectively. It is noted that we assume for the sake of simplicity, that shares are entirely held by households, that is to say, there is no institutional shareholder.

Each subject of these three categories makes its decision concerning consumption (or production) as well as finance, subject to its budget equation. First, we have for a household:

$$\bar{M}_h + \bar{B}_h(1 + \bar{r}') + \bar{T}_h(1 + \bar{r}'') + \sum \theta_{ih} d_i$$
$$+ \sum q_i \bar{\theta}_{ih} + W\bar{N}_h = M_h + B_h + T_h + \sum \Delta \bar{\theta}_{ih} + \sum q_i \theta_{ih} + PD_h \qquad (6.1)$$

which is an extension of the inequalities (4.14) of chapter 4 to the case of money and other financial means being present. Note that the summation $\sum$ means that relevant variables are summed up over all households, firms and banks. In the above equation $\bar{r}'$ is the rate of interest accruing from the bonds of the last period and $\bar{r}''$ is the interest rate of the time deposits of the same period. We then denote the respective rates of the current period by r' and r''. On the right-hand side of (6.1) above $\Delta \bar{\theta}_{ih}$ represents the household h's acquisition of the new shares of the firm or bank i. q_i is the price of the old shares of the same i, and d_i the rate of dividend of i. $W\bar{N}_h$ signifies the value of the supply of primary factors of production of h and PD_h that of the demand for consumption goods of h.

Secondly, for the firm f, we assume that f is involved in operating several production processes. We have already seen in the previous chapters that some of the outputs of process i are not sold to other firms but retained within the firm f in order to be used by some other processes of the same f. Thus the firm need not purchase the whole necessary input goods from other firms; some of them are provided within itself. Let A^0 and B^0 be input and output coefficient matrices of the commodities to be purchased from, or sold to, other firms. They are, of course, obtained by putting elements zeros to the places of A and B for those goods which are only transferred within the firm without payment.

The budget equation for the firm f may be written as:

$$\bar{M}_f + \bar{B}_f(1+\bar{r}') + \bar{\theta}_f d_f - \Delta\bar{\theta}_f + \sum_i PB_i^0 \bar{X}_i$$
$$= \sum_i PA_i^0 X_i + \sum_i WL_i X_i + M_f + B_f, \tag{6.2}$$

where it is noted that $\bar{\theta}_f$ denotes the shares issued by the firm in a negative quantity, d_f the rate of dividend of f, and $\Delta\bar{\theta}_f$ takes on a negative value whenever new shares are issued, otherwise it is zero. It is noted that (6.2) assumes f holding no shares of banks and other firms. $\bar{X}_i$ and X_i are the intensities of the process i operated by f in the last and present periods, respectively. The summations applied to $PB_i^0 \bar{X}_i$ and $PA_i^0 X_i$ and $WL_i X_i$ are made over all processes i which f operates, where A_i^0 and B_i^0 are the i-th columns of A^0 and B^0; L is the matrix of input coefficients of primary factors of production and L_i its column. Where the surplus of f to be realized in the current period:

$$U_f = \sum PB_i^0 \bar{X}_i - \sum PA_i^0 X_i - \sum WL_i X_i,$$

is negative, it must be filled up by financial means: either the firm diminishes the cash balance M_f or issues the bonds, so that B_f takes on a negative value. If the surplus U_f is positive, it may be used for acquiring financial assets; thus there may be no need to issue new shares, and both M_f and B_f, or even d_f, may even increase. We assume, the firm makes no time deposits.

As for the banking business we make a simplifying assumption to the effect that banks need no physical inputs, such as desks, land and office buildings. Labour is the sole factor of production employed by the bank. The wages it pays is denoted by wL_b. Let us write: $b_b = B_b/L_b$ and $t_b = T_b/L_b$. The former represents the amount of bonds held by the bank b (i.e., its lending) per bank worker, whereas the latter indicates the time deposits the bank owes per worker. As T_b is negative, t_b is also negative. Let ρ be the row vector of the lending and borrowing interest rates, r' and r'', of the bank in the current period, and β the column vector consisting of b_b and t_b. Then the bank's profit for the current period per worker may be written as:

$$\pi w = \rho\beta - w,$$

where π is the rate of profits of the banking sector, that is, the ratio of the profits, $\rho\beta - w$ to the cost w. This can be put in the form:

$$w = \zeta\rho\beta,$$

where ζ is the reciprocal of $1 +$ the rate of profits π. This is very similar to the corresponding condition (i.e., (4.3) of chapter 4) for the firm. The budget constraint for the bank is:

$$\bar{M}_b + \bar{B}_b(1 + \bar{r}') + \bar{T}_b(1 + \bar{r}'') + \bar{\theta}_b d_b - \Delta\bar{\theta}_b$$
$$= wL_b + M_b + B_b + T_b,$$

(6.3)

where d_b is the rate of dividend of the bank b and $\bar{\theta}_b$ (a negative value) the shares issued by b, and $\Delta\bar{\theta}_b$ ($\leqslant 0$) its newly issued shares. The budget equation is the same as the one for the firm, except that there is neither physical outputs nor physical inputs for the bank and no time deposits for the firm. The bank's realized surplus in the current period is:

$$\bar{r}'B_b + \bar{r}''T_b - w\bar{L}_b,$$

while its profits accruing from its current activity has been defined as:

$$\pi wL_b = r'B_b + r''T_b - wL_b.$$

One of the major tasks of monetary theory is to explain supply and demand for bonds, shares, time deposits and money. For that purpose we need new concepts such as uncertainty, risks, liquidity, etc., which do not usually play crucial roles in the value and production theory, as it may be formulated without them. Varieties of the theory of choice under uncertainty and the theory of portfolio selection have already been provided by many specialists. This aspect of the monetary theory has relatively been advanced. In this chapter we are, therefore, not concerned with the derivation of the supply and demand functions with regard to financial means; we regard them as if they are given functions of economic variables including prices of physical commodities, activity levels of production processes, the rates of profits, the borrowing and lending rates of interest, the prices of shares and the rates of dividend of the joint-stock companies.

2 We have the following market equilibrium conditions for monetary goods. First, for bonds:

$$\sum B_b + \sum B_h + \sum B_f = 0,$$

(6.4i)

where the summations are taken with respect to the respective subscripts. The bonds are issued by the firms, so that B_f's take on non-positive values, while bankers and households will buy them; hence B_b and B_h are non-negative. Similarly, the temporary equilibrium condition must hold for bonds in the previous period.
   Thus:

$$\sum \bar{B}_b + \sum \bar{B}_h + \sum \bar{B}_f = 0.$$

(6.4i')

Secondly, we assume that each firm is a joint-stock company and its shareholding is opened to the market. There are as many kinds of shares as the number of the existing firms. They are exchanged in the market and we have the following equilibrium condition for the shares of each firm:

$$\sum \bar{\theta}_{fh} = \sum \theta_{fh} \quad \text{for each } f, \tag{6.4ii}$$

where $\bar{\theta}_{fh}$'s and θ_{fh}'s are summed up with respect to their second subscript h standing for shareholders (householders). Evidently, the left-hand side of this equation equals the total number of shares of the firm f held by households, so that we have:

$$\bar{\theta}_f + \sum \theta_{fh} = 0 \quad \text{for each } f, \tag{6.4ii'}$$

where it is noted that the number of shares *issued* $\bar{\theta}_f$ is represented by a negative quantity.

Some of the existing firms may issue in the current period a certain amount of new shares, so that the shares of, say, firm f may increase $-\Delta \bar{\theta}_f = -(\theta_f - \bar{\theta}_f)$, where θ_f is the total (negative) number of shares after the increase. The equilibrium conditions for the new shares are given by:

$$\Delta \bar{\theta}_f + \sum \Delta \bar{\theta}_{fh} = 0 \quad \text{for each } f, \tag{6.4iii}$$

where the summation is taken with respect to h. This applies not only to the firms which issue new shares but also to those which do not. For the latter we have $\Delta \bar{\theta}_f = 0$ and $\Delta \bar{\theta}_{fh} = 0$, of course. Moreover, it applies to newly established firms too, for which there are no shares in the previous period, so that $\bar{\theta}_f = 0$. Therefore $\Delta \bar{\theta}_f = \theta_f$ and $\Delta \bar{\theta}_{fh} = \theta'_{fh}$, thus (6.4iii) reduces to $\theta_f + \sum \theta'_{fh} = 0$, a form parallel to (6.4ii'). θ'_{fh} is the new shares held by h.

The banks are also joint-stock companies; for the shares issued by them we obviously have the conditions equivalent to (6.4ii) and (6.4iii). They are written as:

$$\sum \bar{\theta}_{bh} = \sum \theta_{bh} \quad \text{for each } b \tag{6.4iv}$$

$$\Delta \bar{\theta}_b + \sum \Delta \bar{\theta}_{bh} = 0 \quad \text{for each } b \tag{6.4v}$$

respectively. As for the time deposits it is assumed that households are indifferent and deposit money at any bank; so we have a single equilibrium condition:

$$\sum T_b + \sum T_h = 0 \tag{6.4vi}$$

for the current period and:

$$\sum \bar{T}_b + \sum \bar{T}_h = 0 \tag{6.4vi'}$$

for the previous period. As has been said before, $\bar{T}_b$ and T_b are negative, because time deposits are liabilities for the banks.

146   Capital and credit

Finally we have for money:

$$\sum \bar{M}_b + \sum \bar{M}_h + \sum \bar{M}_f = \sum M_b + \sum M_h + \sum M_f.$$

Transferring the first term on the right-hand side to the left, this is put in the form:

$$\left(\sum \bar{M}_b - \sum M_b\right) + \sum \bar{M}_h + \sum \bar{M}_f = \sum M_h + \sum M_f. \tag{6.4vii}$$

On the left-hand side the sum of the second and third terms represents the total amount of money held by non-bank agents which is customarily designated by M in the usual Keynesian economic textbooks, while the first term in the parentheses refers to the amount of money released by the banks, ΔM, during the current period. The right-hand side of (6.4vii) represents the total amount of money non-bank agents intend to hold, that is usually signified by L in Keynesian terminology. Thus (6.4vii) is equivalent to $M + \Delta M = L$.

3 In addition to these there are two equilibrium conditions: The first is the law of equal rates of profits which should be established between industrial and banking sectors, while the second is the macroeconomic equilibrium condition making total savings to be equal to total investment.

As for the former we have seen in the previous chapters that the rates of profits are equalized at r, through the whole production process. If there are some whose rates of profits are lower than the maximum rate, those processes are not utilized in production, that is to say, the rule of profitability prevails throughout the entire processes. On the other hand, the rate of profits of banks, π, has been defined above as $\pi = (\rho\beta - w)/w$. It is natural to assume that the productivity of the workers in the banks is proportional to the level of prices, so that $\beta = p\beta^*$, where β^* is a constant vector. In the state of equilibrium we should have:

$$r = \pi = \rho\beta^* p/w - 1. \tag{6.4viii}$$

Otherwise either industrial firms or banks will disappear. In fact, if either of the two is the case, the economy cannot be in the state of equilibrium. Where industrial firms disappear, there would be excess demands for manufacturing products, while, where banks disappear, firms are not provided with money, so that they cannot carry out production. Thus condition (6.4viii) should be fulfilled in order to establish a general equilibrium.

To spell out the condition of savings = investment, we must begin by defining savings and investment precisely. First, for each household, savings are an excess of income over consumption. Its total income consists of the income from the supply of the factors of production, $W\bar{N}_h$, the dividend from the shares it holds, $\bar{\theta}_{fh}d_f$, and the interest income from bonds and time deposits, $\bar{B}_h\bar{r}' + \bar{T}_h\bar{r}''$. On the other hand, consumption amounts to PD_h. In view of the budget equation (6.1) for the household, the savings of each household S_h may be written in the form:

$$S_h = W\bar{N}_h + \sum\bar{\theta}_{ih}d_i + \bar{B}_h\bar{r}' + \bar{T}_h\bar{r}'' - PD_h$$
$$= (\sum q_i\theta_{ih} - \sum q_i\bar{\theta}_{ih}) + \sum\Delta\bar{\theta}_{ih} + (B_h - \bar{B}_h) \qquad (6.5)$$
$$+ (T_h - \bar{T}_h) + (M_h - \bar{M}_h).$$

The right-hand side of this equation shows that the savings are made in the form of the acquisition of old shares (the first term), new shares (the second) and the bonds (the third). Also they are made in the form of acquisition of time deposits (the fourth term) and money (the final term).

The firm f's savings are the net surplus which remains after deducting the repayment of interest for old loans, $\bar{B}_f\bar{r}''$, and the dividend to the shareholders, $\bar{\theta}_fd_f$, from its current surplus U_f. Bearing the definition of U_f above in mind, we have from (6.2):

$$U_f + \bar{B}_f\bar{r}' + \bar{\theta}_fd_f = (B_f - \bar{B}_f) + \Delta\bar{\theta}_f + (M_f - \bar{M}_f).$$

Note that $\bar{B}_f$, B_f and $\bar{\theta}_f$ take on negative values and $\Delta\bar{\theta}_f$ non-positive. The first term on the right-hand side stands for the increase in the firm's liabilities in a negative amount; thus the savings equal the amount of the acquisition of money – the increase in liabilities in the form of bonds + the increase in the firm's own capital. It must be noticed that the corporate savings defined in this manner do not make allowances for savings (or investments) in terms of physical goods. Let I represent that part. Then the total savings of the firm f may be put in the form:

$$S_f = I + (B_f - \bar{B}_f) + \Delta\bar{\theta}_f + (M_f - \bar{M}_f), \qquad (6.6)$$

where:

$$S_f = U_f + I + \bar{B}_f\bar{r}' + \bar{\theta}_fd_f.$$

For banks there is no investment in physical goods because we have assumed for the sake of simplicity that banks need not make any physical input; neither computers nor even buildings are used. The manpower is the only factor needed for banking. Then the savings of a bank b is seen to be equal to its profits *minus* the dividend to the shareholders; taking (6.3) into account it is put in the following form:

$$S_b = \bar{B}_b\bar{r}' + \bar{T}_b\bar{r}'' - wL_b + \bar{\theta}_bd_b$$
$$= \Delta\bar{\theta}_b + (B_b - \bar{B}_b) + (T_b - \bar{T}_b) + (M_b - \bar{M}_b). \qquad (6.7)$$

In adding up the definitional equations (6.5), (6.6), (6.7) for savings S_h, S_f, S_b over h, f, b, respectively, we find that the aggregate savings S of the economy may be written as:

$$S = I + \sum(\sum q_i \theta_{ih} - \sum q_i \bar\theta_{ih}) + (\sum\sum \Delta\bar\theta_{ih} + \sum \Delta\bar\theta_f$$
$$+ \sum \Delta\bar\theta_b) + (\sum B_h + \sum B_f + \sum B_b) + (\sum T_h + \sum T_b) \qquad (6.8)$$
$$+ (\sum M_h + \sum M_f + \sum M_b - (\sum \bar M_h + \sum \bar M_f + \sum \bar M_b)),$$

where the terms, $\sum \bar B_h + \sum \bar B_f + \sum \bar B_b$ and $\sum \bar T_h + \sum \bar T_b$, are omitted because of
(6.4i') and (6.4vi'). On the right-hand side of this expression, the second and
third terms vanish because in the case of the second term the equilibrium
conditions (6.4ii) and (6.4iv) and in the case of the third term (6.4iii) and
(6.4v) hold. The remaining three terms too vanish under the equilibrium
conditions, (6.4i), (6.4vi) and (6.4vii), respectively. Therefore we obtain:

$$S = I \qquad (6.9)$$

in the state of temporary equilibrium. Thus the macroeconomic condition
of savings being equal to investment is no more than a reflection of the
equilibrium established in the markets of old and new shares, bonds, time
deposits and money.

Let us now make a closer examination concerning investment. First,
$PB\bar X$ is the total value of the commodities produced by the activities in the
past period; they include both those which are sold in the markets and those
which are kept within the same firms for use in the future. The former are
evaluated, of course, at market prices, while the latter at efficiency (or
accounting) prices. With the use of these prices we obtain $PB\bar X$ which gives
the total value of the stocks of commodities available at the beginning of the
current period. In the same way PBX gives the total value of the stocks of
commodities to be made available in the next period. Note that these stocks
to be used in the future are valued at current prices P, but they may
alternatively be valued at discounted expected prices $z\psi$, where ψ depends
on P, and $z = 1/(1 + r)$, r being the rate of profits of the industry. The
increase in the capital stock during the period is given by $PBX - PB\bar X$ (or
$z\psi BX - PB\bar X$), that is investment in physical goods. Thus we have:

$$I = PBX - PB\bar X \text{ or } z\psi BX - PB\bar X \qquad (6.10)$$

so that it depends on prices P and production activities X. Note that
expected prices have been assumed to be functions of P.

On the other hand, in view of the definitions of S_h, S_f, S_b given by (6.5),
(6.6), (6.7), together with the definition of the surplus U_f, we see that the
aggregate savings S may be written as:[1]

[1] There is a slight difference between (6.8') and the corresponding equation (4.9) of chapter 4
in terms of H. First, note that the latter is obtained under the assumption $Q = 0$. Where
$Q \geqq 0$, the corporation net savings are re-defined so as to include interest payments to
banks. Then the total excess savings including interest payments to banks (i.e., banks'
income), denoted by H':

$$H' = H + (PA + WL)QX$$

$$S = W(\bar{N} - LX) + (PB^0\bar{X} - PA^0X - PD) + I, \qquad (6.8')$$

where $\bar{N} = \Sigma \bar{N}_h$ and LX is the total demand for factors of production including the employment of labour by banks, ΣL_b. Note that the other terms related to $\bar{B}_i$'s, $\bar{T}_i$'s, $\bar{\theta}_{ih}$'s disappear because of the equilibrium conditions established in the past (6.4i'), (6.4ii') and (6.4vi'). In the state of equilibrium, supply equals demand for the factors of production, or the rule of free goods prevails in the factor markets, thus the part in the first parentheses on the right-hand side of (6.8'), pre-multiplied by W, is equal to zero, and the outputs are either sold to the firms or to the households and, therefore, the part in the second parentheses is also zero. Hence $S = I$ from (6.8'), which plays a role of fundamental importance in connecting the real and monetary subeconomics.

Thus we have seen that there are two ways to establish the aggregate equilibrium condition (6.9). First it is obtained wherever the markets of monetary commodities, such as shares, new shares, bonds, time deposits and money, are all in equilibrium. Secondly the same is true wherever products' and factors' markets are in equilibrium. These two must be consistent with each other; we are concerned with the case in which products and factors are in equilibrium wherever monetary goods are so, and *vice versa*.

4 We can now show that there are general equilibrium solutions to the above monetary system, if it is associated with the real economic system discussed in chapter 4. We have already seen that, under the condition of macroeconomic perfect foresight (4.13) of the same chapter, the real economy has general equilibrium solutions. It has also been stated there that we are unhappy with the condition (4.13); so let us remove it. Then the real system has one degree of freedom (or one degree of indeterminacy).

At this point of the argument the reader's attention has to be drawn to the fact that the diagonal matrix of the borrowing rates of interest to be applied

is shown to be equal to:

$$W(\bar{N} - LX) + P(B\bar{X} - AX - D) + [(PA + WL)(I + Q) - z\psi B]X.$$

The three terms of this expression represent, respectively, $-WF$, $-PE$, $-GX$ of chapter 4. If we assume that supply equals demand for goods in process produced within each firm, as well as capital goods installed in it, the second term may be written as $P(B^0\bar{X} - A^0X - D)$. Thus we obtain:

$$H' = S - I - GX.$$

This means that there is a difference between the definition in terms of H or H' of chapter 4 and that in $S - I$ of this chapter. But it does not matter much because GX vanishes where the rule of profitability holds. Needless to say, the difference disappears if the excess savings H' are redefined such that firms' income includes the excess profits GX.

to the various production activities, Q, has been regarded as given throughout the discussion of the real economy. He may accordingly consider that the real economy has two degrees of freedom. But Q cannot be arbitrary. To see this, let us assume, for simplicity, that the same rate is applied to all activities, on the assumption that the banks are indifferent between the entrepreneurs who borrow the money needed for carrying out production activities, as long as the banks approve their production projects. Then $Q = r'I$. As the rate of interest is determined, as will be seen below, in the monetary economy, the Q of the real economy has to be set at a level corresponding to the monetary equilibrium rate of interest, because we are concerned with a state which establishes an general equilibrium in the two economies, real and monetary, simultaneously. By this reason Q cannot be free, and thus the real system has only one degree of freedom.

On the other hand, as will be seen below, the monetary system has one degree of overdeterminacy, unless we regard the price level p as one of its variables. Excluding the equilibrium conditions for the previous period, the monetary system consists of the following sets of equations, (6.4i)–(6.4viii), (6.9) and (6.10). Let the number of firms be f^* and that of banks b^*. Then the system contains $f^* + b^*$ share prices, q_i's, and the same number of the rate of dividends, d_i's. In addition it has, besides savings S and investment I, the rate of profits of banks π, the two rates of interest, r' and r'', of bonds and time deposits, respectively, provided P, W, X, r are determined in the real economy. Thus the total number of variables are $2(f^* + b^*) + 5$. On the other hand, the sets of equations (6.4ii) and (6.4iv) altogether include f^* and b^* conditions and the sets (6.4iii) and (6.4v) too have the same number of conditions, $f^* + b^*$. (6.4viii) has two equations, while other sets each consist of a single condition. Hence the total number of conditions of the system are $2(f^* + b^*) + 7$ which exceeds the variables in number by two.

But, in fact, the excess is only one, because these equations are dependent on each other as they are connected by the identity (6.8). As has been stated, the savings–investment condition (6.9) follows from the real equilibrium conditions, so that one of the conditions of monetary markets for shares, new shares, bonds, time deposits and money follows from the rest in the the state of monetary equilibrium. This establishes a proposition that the monetary system has one degree of overdeterminacy. One way to avoid this is to introduce one more variable into the monetary economy; Fortunately, the real economic system leaves the absolute level of prices p completely undetermined, and in fact, as has often been claimed, we may assume that the demand for money depends on p. Thus we are allowed to bring p into the list of variables of the monetary system; it then has the same number of variables as its equations, after the elimination of one equation by use of the Walras law-like identity (6.8). We can show then the existence of a set of solutions to the system by using the existence theorem due to Arrow and others.[2]

Let L_b be negligible. Then the above means that the real and monetary systems, linked to each other by the two bridging conditions:

$$r = \pi \text{ and } Q = r'J, \tag{6.11}$$

constitute two conjugate parts of the whole system. As a whole it determines the entire list of variables, the prices of commodities P, the prices of factors of production W, the activity levels X, the two rates of profits r and π, the rate of interest of the bonds r' and the rate of interest of the time deposits r'', the rates of dividends d, and the prices of shares q. Between the two subsystems, real and monetary, we observe a duality proposition: Not only are the two systems bridged by two equations (6.11), but also they have dual identities (6.8) and (6.8') for establishing the same $S = I$. The variable p left undetermined, because of the one degree of underdeterminacy of the real system, makes the one degree of overdeterminacy disappear from the monetary system, so that the whole system has an enough number of conditions to determine all variables.

Moreover, neither of the subsystems is self-contained. The real subsystem presumes that the rate of interest determined in the monetary sector prevails in the real sector, and conversely, the price level p of the monetary system adjusts the rates of profits such that the rate of profits of banks corresponding to it is equal to the general rate of profits of the industry determined in the real system. Therefore, the dichotomy of the whole economy into the two subeconomies is impossible, unless we construct a real economic model which is independent of the rate of interest, and ignore the balance between the rate of profits of the industrial firms and

---

[2] I have pointed out in my *Walras' Economics*, Cambridge University Press, 1977, p. 18, that the theorem established by Arrow–Debreu, Gale, Nikaido and others, referred to as the GND lemma, is not strong enough to prove that there is an *essential* equilibrium to each general equilibrium system, where the essential equilibrium is defined as an equilibrium in which at least some transactions are made in the case of the general equilibrium of exchange, the one in which some production is carried out in the case of that of production, the one in which a positive capital accumulation is made in the case of that of capital formation and credit, and finally the one in which the price of money is positive in the case of that of money and circulation. Thus the equilibrium whose existence has been established by the 'powerful' theorem may reduce to an empty state of no transaction, no production, no growth and no money, unless the theorem is strengthened by imposing some additional appropriate conditions. It is Hahn who has first discussed this possibility with respect to the monetary general equilibrium.

Walras' conclusion (*Walras' Economics*, p. 108) that there may exist no [essential] equilibrium of exchange in some peculiar cases is correct. The Arrow–Debreu existence theorem is valid only if an equilibrium with no exchange is regarded as an equilibrium of exchange.

152   Capital and credit

banks, as economists of the dichotomy school usually do. This impossibility enables us to say that the conventional general equilibrium theory concentrating attention on the real economy compartment has been unable to provide an entire view of the working of the whole economy.

We must say, nevertheless, that we have not been totally ignorant of this duality. We all vaguely know of it. When it is stated that relative prices are determined by the real economic equilibrium conditions and the price level by the money equation according to the so-called dichotomy into real and monetary economics, we are implicitly concerned with an economy that consists of n real commodities and the two monetary goods, bonds and money. The bond market is eliminated because other markets are in equilibrium. In the real economy relative prices are determined but the absolute level of prices is left undetermined because of its under-determinacy. To these relative prices there corresponds an equal rate of profits of the industries, but the rate of profits of banks is left totally unexamined. The remaining equation for money determines the price level since it is the only one variable which remains undetermined. Walras expounded this view in his general equilibrium model of circulation and money, but no bank appears in his system explicitly, so that he has no idea of the equilibrium between firms and banks in terms of the rate of profits.[3]

Within this framework the conventional Keynesian theory may be examined in the following way. First of all, Keynes and Keynesians, like Walras and Walrasians, have not clearly noticed the duality between (6.8) and (6.8′) as well as the bridging equation (6.11) or (6.4viii). If Keynes had got the idea of (6.11), he might have discussed it in the following way. Neglecting old and new shares of firms and banks, for the sake of simplicity, we then have three main monetary equilibrium conditions for bonds, time deposits and money; (6.8) enables us to eliminate one of these, say, the condition for time deposits, because $S = I$ is established in the real economy. The remaining two conditions for bonds and money would determine the rate of interest r' and the price level p.

From the bridging equations, on the other hand, we would obtain the rate of interest for time deposits in the following way. First, remembering that variables of the real economy have been obtained by taking Q as a parameter and considering the expression $Q = r'J$, we find that they all depend on r'; in particular, the rate of profits r of the firms and the relative price p/w, both are functions of r'. Secondly, substitute these into (6.4viii). Remembering that ρ is a vector with components r' and r'', we finally obtain

[3] L. Walras, *Elements of Pure Economics*, 1954, Homewood, Illinois, Richard D. Irwin, pp. 315–74.

a relation between r' and r'' from (6.4viii). Thus we get r'', once r' is determined elsewhere.

Following Keynes, we may now assume that the demand for money is a function of the national income Y and the rate of interest r'. Then we have:

$$\bar{M} + \Delta M = L(Y, r') = L(wY_w, r'),\qquad(6.12)$$

where $Y = wY_w$ with Y_w standing for the income in wage unit and the L function for the demand for money in Keynes' notation. Bearing in mind that Y_w is determined in the real subeconomy, depending upon r', and assuming that L is homogeneous of degree one in the variable w, the above equation may be written:

$$\bar{M}_w + \Delta M_w = L(Y_w(r'), r'),$$

where $\bar{M}_w$ is the initial amount of money in wage unit and ΔM_w its increment. This equation will determine the rate of interest. It evidently expresses the liquidity theory of interest, but it should not be forgotten that it is a version which has been strengthened and validitated by applying the duality theory to a simple monetary economy. From this peculiar theory of interest, however, follows a peculiar theory of price level which means that the price level is determined in the bond market.

5 It should be emphasized that the general equilibrium obtained in this manner establishes the full employment of factors of production (labour and land). Their supply vector $\bar{N}$ consists of components representing the existing quantities of factors of production. It is implicitly assumed that the owners of the factors do not reserve, partly or totally, the factors they have, for their own use according to the utilities of the reservations; that is to say, we assume that their supply curves are vertical at the point of existing quantities of the factors $\bar{N}$. In equilibrium full employment $\bar{N}_i = (LX)_i$ is realized for each factor i, unless it is a free good. This allows that there may be a factor such that $\bar{N}_i > (LX)_i$, with its price W_i being zero. Therefore, the resultant equilibrium is in conflict with Keynes' view that there is a persistent equilibrium accompanying a substantial amount of unemployment of labour.

This assumption of vertical supply curves of factors of production is of course far from reality and should be replaced by a more realistic one that takes account of reservation demand for factors. In the case of labour, its supply may be assumed to be determined at a point where the marginal disutility of labour is equal to the utility of real wages obtained for the marginal work the worker offers. The supply $\bar{N}_i$ for labour i depends on its real wage rate; the former will increase where the latter rises. In general we have the vector of the functions of supply of factors $\bar{N}$ which depend on wages W and prices P.

This, however, hardly improves the situation. It is true that we can avoid the case of $W_i = 0$ for some i, that is, no factor can be a free good, because N_i would be zero where $W_i = 0$, so that $\bar{N}_i(W, P) < (LX)_i$ at $W_i = 0$; hence equilibrium factor prices should be positive. But this means that the resultant equilibrium is a full employment equilibrium, equating the supply $\bar{N}(W, P)$ with the demand LX. Of course, there may be discrepancies between the existing quantities of the factors $\bar{N}$ and the actual supply, $\bar{N}(W, P)$ but they are voluntary reservations (or, as called by Keynes, voluntary unemployment) of the factors. Most of the actual unemployment is involuntary. How can we explain the phenomenon of involuntary unemployment?

This is, of course, Keynes' main problem in the *General Theory*. In tackling this problem it is evident that, where involuntary unemployment exists, the marginal disutility of labour is not equal to (in fact, lower than) the utility of the real wages paid for the marginal work. Keynes, therefore, denies the proposition that these two are necessarily equal to each other, the proposition he calls the second of the classical postulates. It is indeed sensible and realistic to reject it, because no worker, other than an independent farmer or a freelancer, is in a position to be able to decide for himself his supply of labour, so as to fulfil this postulate. For example, let us consider a factory worker. At the end of a working day, his marginal disutility may still be lower than the marginal utility of income for extra work, but he cannot continue to work because of the work regulations. There are obviously cases where overtime work is allowed and welcomed, but apparently not up to the point that is decided by the classical postulate.

Behind the regulations there are social customs, conventional practices and laws supported by political and social power allocated among individuals and institutions. These regulations are being revised in a manner which is more and more favourable towards workers accordingly as the working class obtains more power. The working hours are shortened, so that the discrepancy between real wages and the marginal disutility of labour becomes larger. Between the incomes of various occupations there is a problem of relativity. If the wages are judged to be out of the range of the traditional relativities, those that are unfavourable among them are concluded to be unfair and will be corrected. Thus we cannot deny that strong inertia works in the determination of relative wages. Even now the relative incomes of certain occupations reflect their reputations decided in the feudal age, and conversely present reputations are supported by their relative incomes. It goes without saying that the relative reputations in the feudal period were determined by the social power of the classes.[4] Thus tradition plays a significant role in wage determination.

Economists have expressed the social elements working in the labour market simply in terms of the 'downwards rigidity of wages' but have never provided a theory explaining why or by what forces wages lost perfect flexibility.[5] Where the domain within which the wage rate is socially allowed to move does not contain the equilibrium wage rate, some amount of involuntary unemployment is inevitable. Nevertheless, it is very difficult to give a clear definition of the domain within which the wage rate is socially acceptable, but it is still true that some social power, as symbolized by trade unions, works in the labour markets; and strikes, mass demonstrations and civil movements are organized and carried out. It is impossible for wages to be adjusted to the supply and demand situation in the labour market as freely as prices adjust themselves in the commodity markets. Many personal elements are involved and the market always faces the dangers of nepotism. Many complicated constraints, which are sometimes very restrictive and even mutually contradictory, are socially imposed on wages. The labour markets are not simple institutions which obey the rule of free goods; they are subtle, delicate and complicated in construction because the modern labour market is constructed so as to distinguish itself distinctly from the slave market and should not give any hint of it in spite of both dealing with human labour and playing a similar role in the process of reproduction of the economy.

Similarly, land markets are also so complex that we may still be able to observe the legacy of the feudal age there. Customs and traditions, which are often different from country to country, have to be respected. In some countries, mafia, yakuza and other organizations of similar sorts play the role of intermediator in the land markets. Consequently, we can hardly expect that rents and land prices are settled at their equilibrium values. Where they deviate from these, the deviations are transmitted to other

---

[4] It was Yasuma Takata who emphasized the social elements working in the factor markets. He published many books on this subject, all in Japanese unfortunately. For example *Seiryoku Ron* (On Social Power), Nippon Hyoron Sha, Tokyo, 1940, *Seiryoku-setsu Ronshu* (Essays in Power Theory of Economics), Nippon Hyoron Sha, Tokyo, 1941. He criticized Keynes from the point of view of this power theory in his *Keynes Ronnan* (Criticisms on Keynes), Yuhikaku, Kyoto, 1955. It is Takata's view that the theory of distribution should be constructed in a way entirely different from the theory of exchange. The former is concerned with factor markets, which is human and social, while the latter is impersonal. Recently social elements in the determination of wages such as relativity and unfairness have been emphasized by Hicks and Solow. See John Hicks, *A Market Theory of Money*, Clarendon Press, Oxford, 1989; R. M. Solow, *The Labour Market as a Social Institution*, Basil Blackwell, Cambridge, USA, 1990.

[5] This was one of Takata's criticisms of Keynes.

markets. There are repercussions from factor prices W to other variables of the distribution theory, the rates of interest r' and r'', the rates of dividends d's and the prices of shares q's. In addition, there are repercussions from W to the variables of the theory of exchange and production, commodity prices P, the levels of production activities X and the equal rate of profits of the industry r.[6] Moreover, these two sorts of repercussions cannot be independent. They must be consistent with each other, because the condition bridging the two subsystems, real and monetary, (6.4viii), must be more or less fulfilled in any circumstances; otherwise, capital will quickly move out from industries, or banks, to the other. Thus all economic variables deviate from their respective equilibrium positions. Besides this we have the problem of social power. Not only is purely economic analysis impossible for the factor markets, but also the direct and indirect effects of the social elements on other sectors of the economy are very difficult to be ascertained and spelt out.

6 Although Keynes did not make any serious analysis of the effects of the social power of the working class or other social factors upon employment, it is unfair to say that he entirely disregarded these elements. In fact, he mentioned the 'unemployment due to the refusal or inability of a unit of labour, as a result of legislation or social practices or of a combination for collective bargaining, or of slow response to change, or of mere human obstinacy, to accept reward corresponding to the value of the product attributable to its marginal productivity',[7] but he included such unemployment in the category of voluntary unemployment. Of course, this is a matter of definition, but, as long as we stick to Keynes' definition in terms of the marginal disutility of labour, the unemployment due to the factors mentioned above (say, for example, unemployment due to legislation) is involuntary as long as the worker himself is prepared to work on the basis of the utility calculation he has made. And, because of this peculiarly extended definition of voluntary unemployment, such that it includes unemployment due to social elements, no social power is taken into consideration in Keynes' theory of *in*voluntary unemployment.[8]

[6] This is the second point of emphasis made by Takata in his power theory.

[7] J. M. Keynes, *The General Theory of Employment, Interest and Money*, 1936, London, Macmillan, p. 6.

[8] Throughout my previous works (*Walras' Economics, Ricardo's Economics* and *The Economics of Industrial Society*), I have concluded, as Keynes did, that if and only if Say's law is valid, no involuntary unemployment exists. As will be seen below soon, Say's law which implies the flexible adjustment of I to S implies the perfect flexibility of P, r and X. Takata would say that these authors take W to be flexible by assuming that social power is economically ineffective.

He took a completely different approach. Under the implicit assumption of no frictional element he declared at the very beginning of the *General Theory*: 'These three assumptions [the second of the classical postulates, the absence of involuntary unemployment and Say's law] amount to the same thing in the sense that they all stand and fall together, any one of them logically involving the other two.'[9] Among the three assumptions, the equivalence of the first two is almost obvious. This is because where there is no involuntary unemployment, labour is reserved by the worker after the marginal disutility of labour reaches the utility of the real wages, so that the second postulate is fulfilled. Conversely, where there is involuntary unemployment, the marginal utility of wages is higher than the marginal disutility of labour, so that workers are ready to work at the prevailing wages. Thus the second postulate does not hold. Consequently, the main business of the theory of unemployment consists in establishing the identity between Say's law and full employment.

According to Keynes, Say's law means that even though the aggregate savings are set at any arbitrary level they create the aggregate investment of exactly the same amount. It implies that savings and investment are not independent of each other, the latter quickly adjusting itself to the former, however high or low the former is. This means that, in the definitional equation of investment (6.10), prices, the rate of profits and the activity levels are perfectly flexible, so that they are adjusted, under Say's law, such that $S \equiv I$. This is true only where there is no independent schedule of investment. No entrepreneur or no firm f has any intention of restricting the activity level X_f, that he can command, within a certain planned range; this results in X_f being freely adaptable to the mechanism of the markets. In cases where there are restrictions on the choice of X_f's and, therefore, investment moves independently from savings, the law is denied, and we say that an anti-Say's law prevails. Keynes was concerned with an economy which has an independent aggregate investment function; thus he denied the third postulate of classical economics.[10]

In what circumstances do the elements which directly influence investment in the definitional equation (6.10), that is, P, r and X, lose perfect flexibility and are hindered from reaching their respective equilibrium positions? We have already pointed out social elements that work in the factor markets and influence P, r and X; we shall later discuss financial

[9] Keynes, *The General Theory*, p. 22.
[10] Concerning Say's and anti-Say's laws, see my *Ricardo's Economics*, pp. 149–67 and pp. 189–208. Also see M. Morishima and G. Catephores, 'Anti-Say's Law versus Say's Law: a change in paradigm', in H. Hanusch (ed.), *Evolutionary Economics, Applications of Schumpeter's Ideas*, Cambridge University Press, 1988, pp. 23–70.

constraints to which investment decisions have to be subject. In this place we just mention the following proposition which is proved soon later in the remaining part of this section: Wherever some components X_i of X are set at a level, say X_i^0, which is lower than its temporary equilibrium level, X_i^e, it is then inevitable that the economy suffers from underemployment.

We may then summarize our conclusions as follows: The full employment equilibrium assumes the perfect flexibility of the variables of the system, P, W, X, etc. If one of them, for example X, is restricted within a certain domain, say by anti-Say's law, then the full-employment equilibrium is not realized. Similarly, where a restriction is imposed on W, by virtue of social pressure, we obtain unemployment. That is to say, in order for labour to be fully employed, the real wages are required as low as W^e/p^e; then where a level of the real wages, W/p, which is higher than W^e/p^e is insisted on by workers, unemployment of labour is inevitable. This is the type of unemployment emphasized by Takata. Thus the frictions due to social power in the factor markets can be an independent cause of unemployment, regardless of whether Say's law is satisfied or not.

Let us now establish the above-mentioned proposition. It is first pointed out that effects of a decrease in X_i from X_i^e to X_i^0 upon other X_j's are not necessarily all positive, and we, therefore, allow for negative repercussions.[11] We arrange X_i's in the following way. When X_i^0's are all set to be lower than the corresponding X_i^e, those X_j which are determined to be higher than X_j^e are grouped in class II and those which are equal to or less than X_j^e, in class III, while those which are set at X_j^0, of course, belong to class I. Then the repercussions from I to II are negative (or variable in the opposite direction), while those from I to III are positive or zero (or weakly positive or, let us simply say, positive). In this case the repercussions are in the same direction. Let us assume that class I consists of investment processes, class III of investment related processes, and class II of non-investment processes.

Suppose now the following inequality is fulfilled:

$$\frac{\sum P_k a_{kj}}{l_j} > \frac{\sum P_k a_{ki}}{l_i} \tag{6.13}$$

for any j in II and any i in I and III, where l_j, l_i are labour input coefficients of the processes j and i. This means that non-investment processes are more capital intensive than investment or investment-related processes.

Let h be a process in I or III for which we have:

$$\frac{\sum P_k a_{kh}}{l_h} \geqslant \frac{\sum P_k a_{ki}}{l_i} \tag{6.14}$$

[11] The proposition can easily be proved when repercussions are all positive.

for all other i in I and III. With this definition of h it is obvious that (6.13) holds for $i = h$ too.

Let us next investigate whether the fixation of X_i's for i in class I at X_i^0's create unemployment or not, that is to say, whether:

$$\sum l_i \Delta X_i < \text{or} > 0, \tag{6.15}$$

where the summation is taken over all i in classes I, II and III, and $\Delta X_i = X_i - X_i^e$ for i in classes II and III, while $\Delta X_i = X_i^0 - X_i^e$ for i in I. As we may assume that supply equals demand for goods k in the case of activities of class I being set at X_i^0, as well as in the case where they are free, so that X equals X^e, we have

$$\sum a_{ki} \Delta X_i = 0 \text{ for all } k \tag{6.16}$$

because supply, $\sum b_{ki} \bar{X}_i$, remains constant, and demand is given by $\sum a_{ki} X_i$ for non-consumption goods k. (Note that (6.16) holds trivially for consumption goods k because they are not used for production, so that all a_{ki}'s are zero for these k.) (6.16) may be written as:

$$\sum \frac{\sum P_k a_{kj}}{l_j} l_j \Delta X_j = 0.$$

Taking into account the fact that (6.13) holds for any j whose $\Delta X_j > 0$ and (6.14) holds for j whose $\Delta X_j < 0$, we obtain the following inequality:

$$\frac{\sum P_k a_{kh}}{l_h} (\sum l_j \Delta X_j) \leqslant 0.$$

It is obvious that this must hold with strict inequality, when class II is not empty. When it is empty, all ΔX_i's are non-positive and some of them are negative. Hence (6.15) is negative in any case. Thus, where the capital intensity condition (6.13) is fulfilled, we may conclude that the restriction of investment activities at levels lower than the equilibrium ones (that is, $X_i^0 < X_i^e$) creates some positive amount of unemployment of labour.

Of course (6.13) is not always true, but we may consider it to be a plausible assumption. First we may assume, as it is usually assumed in two-sector growth theory, that investment and investment-related processes which produce, rather than use, capital goods directly or indirectly use relatively lesser amounts of capital than the non-investment processes which use capital goods in order to produce non-investment, or consumption, goods. Then (6.13) holds true. On the other hand, (6.14) is not an additional assumption. It is nothing else but a definition of the process h. Thus the plausibility of the assumption is established and the above conclusion has to be accepted. The restriction making activity levels of investment processes to be below X^e implies unemployment of labour. As

Keynes insisted, we have confirmed that, where anti-Say's law prevails, full employment will not be realized.

7 Why is X_i set at X_i^0? Why is it not flexible? The answer is simple: it is because of lack of money. To carry out investment activity, X_i, one unit, the firm must buy commodities of the amount A_i^0 for input and employ factors of production L_i, so that it needs money of the amount, $PA_i^0 + WL_i$ per unit of the activity level, that is designated by Ω. If the firm wants to carry out the investment at the level X_i, the total amount it needs is:

$$\Omega X_i = (PA_i^0 + WL_i)X_i.$$

Where the firm does not have its own fund, it has to raise this amount either by issuing shares at the stock markets or by issuing the bonds to a bank to borrow the money. The usual strategy to be taken by the firm may differ from one country to another, but in the following we confine ourselves to the case of the banks lending money by creating credit to the firms.

Then how will X_i^0's be fixed? If there is no effective financial constraint (i.e., Say's law prevails), the firms' X_i's will be fixed at their full-employment, full-capital-utilization equilibrium X_i^e's. With regard to a particular investment process i, the firm f which is willing to carry out this investment programme will propose to a bank b to borrow the necessary amount of money:

$$\Omega X_i^e = (PA_i^0 + WL_i)X_i^e.$$

On the bank's side, b examines its own lending ability and calculates how much it is able to invest on this project. Of course it is not a rigorously fixed amount. If the bank considers the programme to be very promising, it may turn down many other investment proposals and concentrate a very big amount upon the particular project i. Then at what level of X_i can the bank offer support to the firm?

Let us now make explicit the assumption that the money of our model is of the M1 category and includes cash and deposit money (or current deposits) held by the private sector excluding the banks. Let us write:

$$M_h = C_h + D_{h*}, \qquad M_f = C_f + D_{f*},$$

where C_h and C_f are cash held by household h and firm f, while D_{h*} and D_{f*} are the total amounts of current deposits held by h and f, respectively. It is clear that:

$$D_{h*} = \sum D_{hb}, \qquad D_{f*} = \sum D_{fb},$$

where D_{hb} is the part of D_{h*} which is deposited to bank b; similarly for D_{fb}. In the above, obviously, the summations taken over all b are designated by the respective asterisks.

Let C_b be the total amount of cash the bank b holds. Banks are under an obligation to retain a fixed proportion (σ) of their current deposits in the form of cash, so that the following inequality must be satisfied:

$$C_b \geqslant \sigma D_{\cdot b} \qquad\qquad\qquad (6.17)$$

where $D_{\cdot b} = \Sigma D_{hb} + \Sigma D_{fb}$, the summation taken over all h and f, respectively, that is the total amount of current deposits held by b. If this holds with strict inequality, $D_{\cdot b}$ can be increased up to that point where the equality is established.

Suppose (6.17) holds with strict inequality; then there is room for expansion for the bank b to increase current deposits. Suppose the bank buys some amount of bonds issued by the firm f for raising the funds in order to carry out the investment programme i. Let the amount be B_b. The bank will not make the payment in cash but pay it into f's account of current deposits. Then D_{fb} will increase; the gap between C_b and $\sigma D_{\cdot b}$ will be reduced.

The firm f for which funds are advanced in this way will use this newly created purchasing power to buy physical capital goods, raw materials, etc., A_i^0, and factors of production, L_i, so that f can implement the investment plan on the scale X_i^* such that:

$$B_b = \Omega X_i^* = (PA_i^0 + WL_i)X_i^*.$$

A part of the current deposits thus created is soon converted into cash, while the remainder is paid out in the form of cheques to workers or to other factories for the purchase of capital goods, raw materials, etc. The created but still remaining current deposits of the firm f will be drawn out by workers and entrepreneurs who have received f's cheques. It takes some time until f's current deposits have been drawn out completely. Some amount remains in its deposits before it finally exhausts.

On the other hand, those who have drawn out money from f's account will either deposit the whole or a part of it into bank b or into other banks, or spend the remaining to buy consumption goods, etc.; those shops or factories which have sold them the goods may deposit a part of the amount they have received into bank b. In this way, b may expect an increase in deposits, but it is not large enough to off-set the amount originally drawn out from b. Hence the gap between the cash b holds and the cash reserve for current deposits is decreased immediately after the lending has been made to firm f but is slackened afterwards. It may then decrease again in the period of time during which the repercussions of the original lending take place. If the bank b's cash reserves are insufficient and the lending constraint is violated, it is impossible for the bank to support the investment programme of f.

Individual programmes proposed by various firms to the bank are diverse in their qualities. Entrepreneurs, managers and workers involved in the programmes are of different qualities. Technological prospects are different from project to project; some are revolutionarily advanced and innovative, while others may be judged to be of ordinary quality and not unusual at all. Market prospects are also different from product to product. Some may be expected to meet a large demand and are suitable for mass production; but others attract only a small group of buyers. Those which involve dangerous work will have naturally a very high rate of accidents. There are risky projects as well as safe and sound ones. Therefore, investment proposals have to be carefully examined and rigorously assessed on a case by case basis by the bank itself. They should be classified and ranked in the order of their adjusted rates of profits, after their risks, precariousness and vulnerabilities have all been taken into account.

In choosing proposed programmes, X_i's, the bank may, subject to its lending constraint, diversify its choice among various X_i's, or may concentrate upon a few X_i's by neglecting less profitable X_i's entirely. The level of selected X_i's will be higher if more other X_i's are ignored. For some investment programmes the amount of funds needed per unit of activity level, that is Ω, may be enormous, and in order to support them at the proposed levels, a huge amount of money is required. It is, therefore, impossible for a single bank, to afford the entire amount. A consortium has to be formed and the funding will be made by a number of banks jointly.

The X_i's decided by the bank b, X_i^*, will be compared with the firms' X_i^e's. Usually we have:

$$X_i^* \leqslant X_i^e.$$

If this holds with strict inequality, negotiations are made between the firm and the bank and finally they would agree at X_i^0 which is at least as high as X_i^* but would probably be less than X_i^e. In a lending and borrowing market of this type, negotiations are made face to face personally, so that it is entirely different from the Walrasian, open, impersonal commodity market based on the tatonnement principle. It is a very personal market; the trust between the banker and the entrepreneur is a most significant element of the negotiation. They each would rigorously examine their opposite number. Once an agreement is formed, the relationship between them is not temporary; they must collaborate with each other over a long period, at least as long as the project is in progress.

8 A type of determination of investment, similar to the above, has been examined by Schumpeter.[12] In discussing economic development he

---

[12] J. A. Schumpeter, *The Theory of Economic Development*, Cambridge, MA, Harvard University Press, 1934, pp. 65–74.

neglects a spontaneous change in consumers' tastes and assumes them as given. He justifies this by the fact that such a change is in general small. He writes; 'innovations in the economic system do not as a rule take place in such a way that first new wants arise spontaneously in consumption and then the productive apparatus swings round through their pressure'.[13] But the opposite is the case. The producer initiates economic changes and consumers are taught to buy and enjoy the new commodities produced. Thus, like Keynes, he too emphasizes the importance of investment as the driving force of the economy. Innovations are not, according to Schumpeter, usually carried out by the same entrepreneurs who control the existing processes but by different persons who appear independently from them, compete with them and finally displace them. He points out an adequate example such that 'in general it is not the owner of stagecoaches who builds railways'.[14] He also points out that, after a certain stage of economic development has been reached, economic organizations have grown up to be those of enormous scale, and innovations are internalized and become major concerns of the giant firms, combines or industrial groups themselves.

As a rule the production processes for innovations obtain the necessary factors of production and other means from the existing processes. For the innovators to be able to do so, it is necessary that they are given a certain amount of purchasing power by financial organizations, say banks. Although the traditional, rudimental theory of economic growth[15] always considers that investment is determined by savings (that is to say, it is based on Say's law), it is Schumpeter who has emphasized that the crucial factor in growth theory is investment which gives rise to an adjustment in savings and leads the economy in a new, different direction. In this sense, Schumpeter evidently denied Say's law.[16]

Innovations (or new combinations in Schumpeter's terminology) cannot, like the existing production processes, be financed by a revolving fund or by returns from the production processes in the previous period. 'Financing' or 'obtaining credit' is inseparable from carrying out innovations. Schumpeter writes: 'since all reserve funds and savings today usually flow to him [the banker] and the total demand for free purchasing power, whether existing or to be created, concentrates on him, he has either replaced private capitalists or become their agent; he has himself become

[13] Ibid., p. 65.   [14] Ibid., p. 66.

[15] A refined version of the rudimental theory is provided, for example, by R. M. Solow, 'A Contribution to the Theory of Economic Growth', *Quarterly Journal of Economics*, 1956, pp. 65–94.

[16] Schumpeter also states that the nature of creation of credit 'consists in creating a new demand for, without simultaneously creating, a new supply of goods'. (Schumpeter, *The Theory*, p. 106.) This is a clear denial of Say's law.

the capitalist par excellence. He stands between those who wish to form new combinations and the possessors of productive means.'[17] It is, therefore, impossible to formulate the theory of innovation without a banker in exactly the same sense that a theory of the firm without a capitalist is impossible. In the same place where the above passage appears, Schumpeter says that the banker is 'the ephor of the exchange economy'.

To carry out an investment plan an entrepreneur needs credit which enables him to obtain purchasing power. As he himself has no such power, he must borrow it. 'He can only become an entrepreneur by previously becoming a debtor.'[18] And because Schumpeter implicitly assumes that the creation of credit is made in the state of full-employment equilibrium X^e, the increased purchasing power gives rise to an inflation, a credit inflation. In this respect our analysis above is completely different from Schumpeter's. We rather follow Keynes, and are concerned with each X_i^0 being set at a position lower than the corresponding X_i^e. Schumpeter, on the other hand, is concerned with establishing his theory of economic development, and seems to be interested in a circumstance with $X_i^0 > X_i^e$ for investment processes i. Then, because of the purchasing power thus created, other production activities have to be carried on at a lower level. This is so because they can now only use smaller amounts of factors of production, because investment processes use them in such amounts that are greater than those which establish the full employment of the factors. Then we shall observe in a number of markets an increase in prices, due to the shortage of products. Thus inflation is a consequence. In our case of underinvestment with $X_i^0 < X_i^e$, however, inflation, though it may arise, is rather mild but not serious.

Schumpeter also points out that in addition to the quantity of money held by the bank there may be some other considerations which are taken into account when the bank decides to give credit. In his own words: 'if the solvency of the banking system in this sense is not to be endangered, the banks can only give credit in such a way that the resulting inflation is really temporary and moreover remains moderate'.[19] This is automatically met in our case of $X_i^0 < X_i^e$. We are applying Schumpeter's idea to Keynesian circumstances, so that involuntary unemployment is created and inflation, even if it is brought about, is a minor one and temporary. We are, therefore, allowed to ignore the additional condition imposed by Schumpeter that no serious inflation is produced by credit creation. The condition for maintaining the necessary reserve of money (6.17) is the sole one that the banks must obey in creating credit. It also goes without saying that C_b in (6.17) is always changing, so that banks have to be careful in their decision-

[17] Ibid., p. 74.   [18] Ibid., p. 102.   [19] Ibid., p. 102.

making on credit creation by paying constant attention to condition (6.17) to see whether it is still comfortably fulfilled or not.

9 It has been seen that, under anti-Say's law involuntary unemployment is unavoidable, so that condition $\bar{N} \geqslant LX$ holds with strict inequality for at least one primary factor of production. If the rule of free goods were valid for this factor, the terms $W(\bar{N} - LX)$ of (6.8') would vanish in the state of underemployment equilibrium. This would, however, create an obvious difficulty, because there is no incentive for workers to be employed because they would not receive any wages regardless of whether they were in employment or not. Thus the rule has to be denied, as Keynes did by assuming downwards rigidity for the wage rate or of course because of the social pressure; then we obtain $W(\bar{N} - LX) > 0$. This means that savings S should be larger than investment I in the identity (6.8'), because the part in the second parentheses of (6.8') cannot be negative by virtue of the condition for feasibility of transactions of commodities. Consequently, Keynes' condition $S = I$ is violated under anti-Say's law.

This is the problem of 'dual' decision-making, in which the condition is re-established by the following procedure. First, we begin by distinguishing the actual savings from the notional ones. In the definition of household h's savings (6.5) above, the value of the total supply of factors $W\bar{N}_h$ is counted as its income. It is nothing else but its 'notional' income; the h's actual income may differ from it, because the factors h supplies may be unemployed, so that some part of $W\bar{N}_h$ may be abortive.

Let $\bar{N}_h^*$ be the h's supply of factors which actually have found employers. Replacing $W\bar{N}_h$ by $W\bar{N}_h^*$, the same formula (6.5) gives S_h^*, which is the actual savings of household h. In the same way, if the part in the second parentheses of (6.8') is positive, namely, if some parts of the outputs are unsold, we must distinguish the notional sale, $PB^0\bar{X}$, from the actual one, $PB^0\bar{X}^*$; corresponding to this procedure, we have the actual savings of firm f, S_f^*, which is different from the notional one that (6.6) gives. As we have obtained the formula of the aggregate notional savings (6.8') from (6.5), (6.6), (6.7), we can derive the following formula of the aggregate actual savings:

$$S^* = W(\bar{N}^* - LX^*) + (PB^0\bar{X}^* - PA^0X^* - PD) + I, \qquad (6.11^*)$$

where $\bar{N}^* = \Sigma\bar{N}_h^*$, the summation being taken over all h. As the first and second terms on the right-hand side vanish, it is at once seen that $S^* = I$, that is, the actual (or *ex post*) savings equal the investment.

We have so far seen the problem of deviation of the actual savings from the notional ones, from the side of the real production economy. Evidently, this deviation gives rise to some alterations in the agents' schedules of demand for shares, new shares, bonds, time deposits and money. With S_h^*, the condition (6.5), for example, is now rewritten as:

$$S_h^* = \left(\sum q_i \theta_{ih}^* - \sum q_i \bar{\theta}_{ih}\right) + \sum \Delta \bar{\theta}_{ih}^*$$
$$+ (B_h^* - \bar{B}_h) + (T_h^* - \bar{T}_h) + (M_h^* - \bar{M}_h). \tag{6.5*}$$

Similar revisions are made for savings of other agents. Then, in place of (6.8), we have:

$$S^* = I + \sum \left(\sum q_i \theta_{ih}^* - \sum q_i \bar{\theta}_{ih}\right)$$
$$+ \left(\sum \sum \Delta \bar{\theta}_{ih}^* + \sum \Delta \bar{\theta}_f^* + \sum \Delta \bar{\theta}_{ib}^*\right)$$
$$+ \left(\sum B_h^* + \sum B_f^* + \sum B_b^*\right) + \left(\sum T_h^* + T_b^*\right)$$
$$+ \left(\sum M_h^* + \sum M_f^* + \sum M_b^* - \left(\sum \bar{M}_h + \sum \bar{M}_f + \sum \bar{M}_b\right)\right). \tag{6.8*}$$

The condition that the actual demand equals the actual supply holds for each monetary commodity, so that the parts in the five pairs of parentheses of (6.8*) will all vanish in the state of monetary equilibrium. This is consistent with the condition that the actual savings equal investment, which has been obtained in the real economy.

In this place we should mention the idea of 'rationing' which has been proposed by a number of economists in connection with dual decision-making. It is true that 'rationing' is carried out in the factor and commodity markets in the sense that some parts of the notional supplies are cut off according to the principle of 'first come, first served', or something else, in the case of the supply being unable to find enough demand. Where this happens in the savings-investment market, the notional savings are not fully realized, the agents having to be satisfied with a smaller amount of the actual savings. But there is no need for rationing in the monetary subeconomy. This is so because as soon as S_i's switch to S_i^*'s, agents spontaneously change their demands for monetary commodities from the notional to the actually feasible schedules, θ_{ih}^*, $\Delta \bar{\theta}_{ih}^*$, B_i^*, etc.

These demands are equated to the respective supplies without rationing as share prices, the rate of interest, etc., are adjusted. There is no need to have an additional two-stage decision rule which applies to the monetary subeconomy. Thus the single decision rule in the monetary subeconomy is compatible with the double decision rule in the real subeconomy. Nonetheless, this does not mean that a monetary general equilibrium is easily realized; as will, in fact, be seen in chapter 7 below, a monetary disequilibrium, if it once happens, tends to persist over time and aggravate itself by accelarating inflation. Finally, it is noted that the above argument *mutatis mutandis* holds true for the case of involuntary unemployment arising from frictions due to social power.

Finally, I make a note on my view of the idea of 'rationing' which has recently been developed by general equilibrium (or disequilibrium) theorists with the purpose of giving a reasonable interpretation to Keynesian thought. To simplify the argument let us be concerned with a simple case which has been referred to as case I in chapter 5. We classify commodities into three subgroups X, Y, Z and assume the prices of the first two, P_X and P_Y, being set at their respective equilibrium prices P_X^e and P_Y^e. The Z sectors are flexprice sectors, such as agriculture and mining, where markets of the Walrasian type work, and P_Z approaches P_Z^e, the temporary equilibrium prices of Z commodities; this brings about $Z = Z(P^e)$. At P_X^e, P_Y^e, P_Z^e, the equilibrium conditions for prices are fulfilled, because factor prices are also set at their equilibrium values W^e in case I. Entrepreneurs, therefore, choose activities X and Y according to the rule of profitability.

Case I is thus an economy where prices P and W, and hence, the rate of profits r, are all fixed. If anti-Say's law activities X_I^0 happen to be set at their equilibrium levels X_I^e, then other activities are also settled at their temporary equilibrium values X_{II}^e, Y^e. A full employment will be realized in factor markets. However, if $X_I^0 < X_I^e$, then production will be carried out at X_{II}^0 and Y^0, such that $X_{II}^0 < X_{II}^e$ and $Y^0 < Y^e$, so that underemployment of factors is inevitable. Then the supply of factors has to be rationed to a lower level of demand, $LX^0 + L'Y^0$.

Up to this point, there would seem to be no difference in view between me and other 'disequilibrium' theorists. Nevertheless, if we are further asked, how unemployment is rationed or distributed among all the suppliers, then they and I would appear to be very much divided. I have simply said in the above that 'it will be rationed according to the principle of "first come, first served", or something else'. But the sophisticated modern theorists would not accept such a 'naive' view and have, in fact, developed a series of advanced ideas and highbrow theories such as quantity signals, efficient rationing, the microeconomic theory of determination of effective demand and supply, the theory of non-Walrasian price formation, and so on. I regard all these as examples of oversophistication which enrich the theorists' imaginary world. In spite of all these inventions, I believe, nothing else other than the naive rule, such as the one of first come, first served, would work in the actual world.

I also add a note in this place to the effect that a state of affairs established at the end of a particular period is a temporary equilibrium, even though it may bring about some unemployment, because in a perfectly competitive economy no market power works to shift the established state of the economy to a different one within the time span of the same period. But it may change from one period to another, and in this sense it is a state of disequilibrium. I do not believe that an analysis concerning states of absolute and entire disequilibrium is possible at the present stage of development of economics; this is simply because, where no regularity is yet observed, there is no theory. Also we add that although equilibrium conditions have been rigorously spelt out, they must be generously interpreted in practical applications, so as to allow some deviations from them. The rates of profits are not exactly equalized through activities, and the mark-up ratios differ from one sector to another. Nevertheless we must say that there would be no general equilibrium where the rates greatly diverged from each other. Lastly it is noted that what has been said above in this section will exactly apply to the part of the next chapter where Say's law ceases to hold and anti-Say's law prevails.

7   Monetary disequilibrium

1 Regarding monetary theory, two alternative approaches are possible. The first (like Keynes, in the liquidity preference theory of interest) may regard the quantity of money available as a parameter and the rate of interest as a variable to be determined. There is another approach, on the other hand, which considers that the monetary authorities peg down the interest rate and adjust the quantity of money flexibly. In the latter the quantity of money thus determined is taken as the factor determining the level of prices, as the quantity theory of money asserts to do. I consider the second approach to be more appropriate than the first, as it is extremely difficult to satisfy either of the two premises of the first approach: (1) to keep the quantity of money constant and (2) to adjust the rate of interest promptly to the quantity of money so as to establish the Keynes–Hicks LM condition.

The reason is: as for the first premise, if the monetary authorities do not increase the quantity of money in a situation of there being an excess demand for money, various kinds of money substitutes such as bills, drafts or credit cards are produced and anarchism would prevail in the monetary world. The central bank would prefer to adjust the quantity of money to the demand for it rather than to keep it constant. Secondly, the rate of interest for the central bank's loan to the commercial banks, which is called the bank rate, or the discount rate, and plays the most basic role in the system of interest rates, is determined by the committee of the central bank by taking various policy effects into account. It is, therefore, kept constant as long as the same policy is maintained and implemented. Throughout this chapter we assume that the quantity of money is adjusted to the given rate of interest, in contrast to the liquidity-preference theorist's view that the interest rate is determined such that demand for money is equated with its supply. This is the platform on which Knut Wicksell has built his theory of the 'cumulative process' which may be summarized in the following manner.

Wicksell assumes that the quantity theory of money is valid, but recognizes that this theory itself has no ability to determine the level of prices, because it does not explain at all at which level the quantity of money is fixed but it merely explains that the quantity of money and the absolute level of prices are proportional. In order to show whether the price level fluctuates or remains unchanged, we need to explain in what circumstances the quantity of money will fluctuate or be constant. Otherwise we cannot show where and how the price level will settle at a particular level in the actual economy. Wicksell solves this problem by taking the height at which the interest rate is pegged down as given in the analysis. For this purpose he introduces the concept of the natural rate of interest. He defines it as the rate of interest at which the whole aggregate savings are invested. In Keynesian terminology it is the marginal efficiency of capital at which all existing savings are invested. The interest rate that the monetary authorities pegs down is called the money rate of interest. If the money rate equals the natural rate, there is no extra demand for money for the purpose of financing investment, and the existing savings are enough, so that the price level does not tend to increase or decrease. A monetary equilibrium is established in such a situation. This is because wherever the money rate of interest prevails at this level, savings equal investment, and, therefore, the purchasing power of all goods (i.e., the aggregate demand price of consumption and investment goods, $C + I$) is equal to the aggregate supply price (or income Y); thus there is no tendency for the aggregate prices (or the absolute price level) to fluctuate. In parallel to this it is observed that there is no change in the quantity of money at which an equilibrium is established in the money market. In addition, the price mechanism works in the stock market. The bond market is also in equilibrium at the money rate, being equal to the natural rate.

Where the money rate is set lower than the natural rate, the bond market will be in a state of excess supply. (As the interest firms pay is lower than the marginal productivity of capital they borrow money for investment by issuing bonds, while the demand for the bonds is small because their yields (interest) are small.) This abundance of bonds will be cleared by the central bank as the lender of last resort; in fact, the money rate cannot be kept constant unless the central bank buys all the bonds which are in excess supply in the bond market. Thus the amount of money circulating among the private, non-bank sectors is increased whenever the money rate is lower than the natural rate. And this creation of money results in an increase in the price level. Similarly, we see a decrease in prices in the opposite case.

Where we obtain an increase in all prices which is proportional to the increase in the quantity of money, there would be no real change in the economy, provided that the expected prices are all increased proportionately. Then we have the same relative prices and the same natural rate of interest. As long as there is no change in the money rate, it is obviously still lower than the natural rate. The same process as we have seen above will be repeated; hence the quantity of money is expanded and the price level is increased. In this way we have a continuing process which Wicksellians have called 'cumulative'.

Evidently, this process occurs where there is a disequilibrium between the real economy and the monetary economy. If the natural rate, which is the interest rate that the real sectors can afford, is higher than the money rate prevailing in the financial markets, money will flow out from the monetary to the real side of the economy. In the opposite case money flows back from the real sectors and is absorbed into the central and commercial banks. An equilibrium is maintained only in the case of the two interest rates being equal. Moreover we can say that this equilibrium is unstable or, we may say, on a knife-edge with respect to the price level. A downwards (or upwards) deviation of the money rate from the natural rate creates an upwards (or downwards) cumulative change in the price level.

The situation in the initial period 0 is summarized in the following way. First, the money rate of interest is fixed at a level lower than the natural rate; then the monetary equilibrium conditions discussed in the previous chapter are not all satisfied. We have, in particular, an excess supply in the bond market. This disequilibrium will be resolved by the central bank's lending of money to the city banks which would in turn clear the excess supply of bonds in the market by using the money thus acquired. Through this channel money flows out from banks to industries. This increase in the amount of money circulating among non-bank sectors will dissolve a disequilibrium (an excess demand for money) in the money market. Such an increase, however, will give rise to an increase in prices – a proportional increase in all prices, so that the natural rate of interest at the beginning of period 1 will be the same as in period 0 and, hence, is higher than the fixed money rate. The same effort to resolve the disequilibrium of financial markets as has been made in period 0 will be repeated in period 1. Then this will put the economy in a state of disequilibrium at the beginning of the following period.

It is important to note that the change through periods, observed above, is cumulative. Let the quantity of money be increased from 10 units to 15 units in the initial period. Suppose the price level is increased, in parallel, from 1 to 1.5 in the same period. Due to inflation, the shortage of money is increased, from $5 (= 15 - 10)$ in the previous period, to $7.5 (= 5 \times 1.5)$ in the first period, so that the quantity of money will be increased from 15 to 22.5 $(= 15 + 7.5)$ and the price level from 1.5 to 2.25 $(= 1.5 \times 1.5)$. Similarly we have an expanded creation of money in the second period, which results in a continuation of price inflation at the constant rate. The inflation will remain at that rate as long as the money rate of interest remains constant. Moreover, it seems, we have to conclude that inflation or deflation is almost inevitable even though we control the money rate of interest most carefully because the natural rate will change irregularly and unexpectedly, because of technological changes and for other uncontrollable reasons.

2 Wicksell's argument is based on the assumption that the full employment of the available factors and resources is realized in the 'real' side. This has been clearly pointed out by Wicksell himself as well as by the interpreters of his theory. Moreover, it implicitly assumes that the full-employment equilibrium is stationary, so that there is no change in the real aspects of the economy throughout the process of monetary cumulation. It has so far remained unexamined whether his theory is compatible with the case of the moving full-employment equilibrium as has been discussed by von Neumann in his balanced growth theory, or Solow and others in the neo-classical theory of growth. It is interesting to inquire whether the assumption of full employment can be entirely removed from the theory or not.

This problem is closely related to the problem of Say's law, because, as we have already seen, full employment is generally assured if and only if Say's law holds. Where it does not hold the full employment equilibrium cannot obtain the general assurance for existence. As I have pointed out,[1] Wicksell renounced the law on the one hand and supported the propositions implying it on the other. It is nevertheless very clear that he, unlike Keynes, never associates Say's law with the problem of full employment. As I completely support Keynes in this respect, it is extremely important for me to re-establish the analysis of the cumulative process under anti-Say's law and, by doing so, free it from the assumption of full employment.

In the following sections we try to generate the Wicksellian cumulative process within the framework of the general equilibrium system. It is true that a similar attempt has already been made with regard to Walras' model,[2] but I believe the following will still be worth presenting. It generates the cumulative process in the complete general equilibrium system consisting of the dual (real and monetary) subsystems. It is a substantially improved version over its predecessors and, at least, more comprehensible than the latter, because it discusses the effect of the full-employment equilibrium being not stationary but moving, as well as the effect of removing Say's law, upon the cumulative process. Although the present version too is based on the usual assumption of the elasticities of expectations being all unity, it is not difficult to show that the same argument *mutatis mutandis* holds for the case of elasticities being more (or

---

[1] See my *Ricardo's Economics*, Cambridge University Press, 1989, pp. 200–2.
[2] See my *Walras' Economics*, pp. 163–9.

less) than 1. Where the money rate is set at a lower (or higher) value than the natural rate, the rate of inflation (or deflation) will be accelerated or decelerated, respectively, accordingly as the elasticities are greater or less than 1.

There has once been presented an interpretation of the cumulative process by Hicks from the point of view of general equilibrium theory.[3] His view is very negative. First of all, he takes the concept of the natural rate of interest as mysterious, because there is no explicit place for the savings–investment equation in his own system of general equilibrium consisting of the demand–supply equations, one for each commodity. But this verdict due to this misunderstanding need not be taken up seriously. As Walras, in fact, has shown, savings and investment are legitimate members of the general equilibrium system of capital formation; the model developed in chapter 4 above also confirms the same effect. Hicks has reproduced, within his *Value and Capital* framework, what he considers as the Wicksellian cumulative process and has found that, if all elasticities of expectations are unity, the general equilibrium is neutral, in the sense that the economy can be in equilibrium at any level of absolute prices.

This interpretation, however, is very far from what Wicksell wanted to show; it clearly contradicts the fact that Wicksell was an adamant supporter of the quantity theory of money, insisting that the price level is determined in proportion to the quantity of money. Hicks is completely wrong in considering that 'Wicksell's price-system consists of a perfectly determinate core – the relative prices of commodities and the rate of interest – floating in a perfectly indeterminate aether of money values'.[4] He has entirely misled us as to the essential mechanism of the Wicksellian mechanism. Wicksell insists that in a system in which the monetary authorities increase (or decrease) the quantity of money elastically so as to satisfy the excess demand for (or supply of) money, (1) the price level is increased (or reduced) after the expansion (or contraction) of money and (2) after the price change the same excess demand for (or supply of) money reappears on an enlarged (or reduced) scale so that a further price change has to be made; this cumulative process continues as far as the money supply is elastic. Hicks' cumulative process is a phenomenon which may happen within a single temporary equilibrium system with a given amount of money (or in a moneyless economy), while Wicksell's is a phenomenon which may occur through time as the quantity of money is created (or reduced) from period to period.

Thus the elastic supply of money is also an indispensable component of the Wicksell theory. After having pointed out that the money rate of

---

[3] See Hicks, *Value and Capital*, pp. 254–5.   [4] Ibid., p. 253.

interest which is lower than the natural rate gives rise to an excess demand
for money and, therefore, tends to increase itself until it reaches the natural
rate, if the money supply is unadjusted, he states that an elastic supply of
money could make the money rate remain constant at the original low level.
In his own words:

When the money rate of interest is relatively too low all prices rise. The demand for
money loans is consequently increased, and as a result of a greater need for cash
holdings, the supply is diminished. The consequence is that the rate of interest is
soon restored to its normal level, so that it again coincides with the natural rate.
At the same time it is clear that in an elastic monetary system, . . . a fairly constant
difference between the two rates of interest could be maintained for a long time. . .'

This means, in modern terminology, that there prevails the quantity
adjustment mechanism in the market of money loans, while its price
variable, the interest rate, is kept constant. As long as the quantity is
variable, that is, the quantity of money supplied is adjusted in a perfectly
elastic manner, the quantity adjustment is perfect, but, where the supply
exceeds a certain critical amount, it loses its elasticity and the interest rate
starts to increase. Where it becomes inelastic, the money rate of interest
may change considerably and may even leap over the natural rate.[5]

Finally, a comment is made on Hicks' remark on the duality which, he
says, exists between the Wicksell–Lindahl model of the cumulative process
and the Harrod-type model of instability.[6] He says, the former is a flexprice
model, while the latter a fixprice and there is a duality between them 'in
something like the sense that linear programming theory has made clear'.
But the duality which the theory of linear programming is concerned with is
the duality which exists between the quantity aspect and the shadow price
aspect of the *same* problem. There is no such relationship between Wicksell
and Harrod. They are not concerned with different aspects of the same
economy. Moreover, as has been seen above, Wicksell's model is not a
flexprice model; in the market of money loans the price variable that is the
money rate of interest is fixed and adjustment is made between demand and
supply by regulating the quantity of money, so that it is also a fixprice
model. The two theories just illustrate that two models of the quantity
adjustment type may both produce an unstable movement.

[5] This interpretation of the cumulative process is coherent and consistent with Patinkin's. In
his words: 'even if the discrepancy between real and market rates were to be maintained
during subsequent periods, prices could not continue to rise unless [the supply of money in
the form of] bank credit continued to expand'. See D. Patinkin, *Money, Interest and Prices*,
Row, Paterson and Company, Illinois, p. 428.
[6] John Hicks, *Capital and Growth*, Oxford, Clarendon Press, p. 121. In this book too he does
not make clear the role of creation of money in the cumulative process.

3 Let us now be concerned with generating a cumulative process within our monetary economic model expounded in the previous chapter. To do so we begin by removing the assumption which has been taken for granted throughout that chapter, namely that the quantity of money is kept constant; and, therefore, the central bank has not played any explicit role there. This is a very difficult assumption to be realized in the actual world. Even though we could keep the quantity of money constant, money substitutes would increase and play the role of quasi-money, if money is considered to be in serious shortage. In such circumstances, in fact, various kinds of private bills or notes are issued and circulated. Money substitutes are very disturbing factors in the economy, because the monetary authorities would not be able to control this vast and hidden black market of monetary substitutes. The conditions of the economy would by no means be healthy, if they are allowed for.

The central bank c is the bank to the commercial banks. It lends them money when their cash reserves are inadequate. To get money from the central bank c, let us suppose that banks sell a part of the bonds B_b they hold to c. Let B_c be the bonds c acquires from b's. Then the amount of money paid by c to b's is B_c. Let $\bar{B}_c$ be the bonds which the central bank has had in the previous period; they mature in the current period, so that b's have to pay $\bar{B}_c$ and interest $\bar{r}'\bar{B}_c$ to c. This means the net creation of money by c amounts to:

$$\delta M_c = \delta B_c - \bar{r}'\bar{B}_c, \tag{7.1}$$

where $\delta B_c = B_c - \bar{B}_c$. In this equation it is assumed that wage payments to the employees by the central bank are ignored. If they are taken into consideration, there is an additional release of money by the amount wN_c. As $\bar{r}'\bar{B}_c$ is given and wN_c more or less fixed, δM_c may be controlled by putting δB_c, that is the increase in central bank deposits during the period, under some rule.

Including the central bank, the bond market is cleared wherever:

$$\sum B_h + \sum B_f + \sum B_b + B_c = 0. \tag{7.2}$$

It is noted that, unless otherwise stated, we use the same notation as we have adopted in chapter 6; that is to say, subscripts h, f, b, for example, stand for household, firm and bank, respectively.

A similar condition holds in the previous period; so we have exactly the same equation with a bar on the top of every B. Then we have, in view of (7.1), the formula for the creation of money:

$$\delta M_c = -\left(\sum \delta B_h + \sum \delta B_f + \sum \delta B_b\right) - \bar{r}'\bar{B}_c, \tag{7.3}$$

where $\delta B_h = B_h - \bar{B}_h$, etc. We assume that $\bar{B}_c = 0$; namely the commercial banks bought up, in the previous period, the total net amount of bonds the firms wanted to sell, without any help from the central bank. Let r'^0 be the value of $\bar{r}'$ which established, in the previous period, the equation:

$$\sum \bar{B}_h + \sum \bar{B}_f + \sum \bar{B}_b = 0.$$

Then we say that the creation of money is neutral wherever the central bank increases (or decreases) the quantity of money such that the excess supply of (or demand for) bonds of the private sectors (households, firms and commercial banks) is cleared with no change in the prevailing rate of interest; then the r' in the current period is kept to be equal to r'^0. Then with $\bar{B}_c = 0$ the neutral creation of money is obtained as $\delta M_c = \delta B_c = B_c$ from (7.2) by fixing B_i's, $i = h, f, b$, at the values corresponding to r'^0.

The monetary subsystem of the economy has the following markets: the stock (or share) markets, the markets for new stocks, time deposits and bonds and the money market. The supply and demand are equated in the stock markets by adjusting the prices of shares, q_i's, while in the time deposit market by the rate of interest r''. In the former the adjustment is quick and perfect, so that we may assume that these markets are always in equilibrium. As for the latter, commercial banks are at all times ready to accept the entire amount that is deposited; so this market too may be assumed to be never out of equilibrium, the demand always being equal to the supply. The demand for a company's new shares depends *inter alia* on its dividend rate in comparison with other companies', while its supply too depends, among other things, on the same variables. When a company wants to raise funds by issuing new shares, its dividend rate is decided such that the new shares are all accepted by the new shareholders; or, in other words, the company can only issue the new shares which correspond to its dividend rate. For those other companies which do not issue new shares the equilibrium is established with supply and demand both being 0.

Then, in equation (6.8) of the previous chapter, stating in mathematical symbols that:

savings = investment + the sum of the excess demand for shares, new shares, bonds, time deposits + the excess demand for money,

the excess demands for shares, new shares and time deposits all vanish. The above equation is simplified such that it includes, apart from the investment term, the excess demands for bonds and money only. However, it should be remembered that it does not take the central bank into consideration explicitly. Bearing (7.1), (7.2) and:

$$\sum \bar{B}_h + \sum \bar{B}_f + \sum \bar{B}_b + \sum \bar{B}_c = 0$$

in mind, we may put (6.8) or the previous equation in the form:

$$(I-S)+(B+B_c)+(M-(\bar{M}+\delta M_c))=0, \qquad (7.4)$$

where $B=\Sigma B_h+\Sigma B_f+\Sigma B_b$, that is the total demand for bonds of the private sectors and $M=\Sigma M_h+\Sigma M_f$, i.e., the total demand for money in the non-banking private sectors, $\bar{M}=\Sigma\bar{M}_h+\Sigma\bar{M}_f+\Sigma(\bar{M}_b-M_b)$, i.e., the total amount of money circulating through the non-banking private sectors and δM_c being, of course, the new money created by the central bank.

It has already been seen in chapter 6 that the real subsystem has one degree of freedom or indeterminacy. It will determine the rate of profits which is equalized throughout all production processes, in addition to the activity levels of the processes and relative prices. However, the absolute level of prices p remains undetermined but will be determined by the monetary subsystem which satisfies (7.4) above. In this subsystem it is assumed that the central bank behaves such that it clears the bond market and keeps the interest rate r' at r'^0. Then the quantity of money must be flexible. This is the world examined by Wicksell.[7] He has observed that if the r'^0 referred to by him as the money rate of interest is lower than the 'natural rate of interest' to be defined below, inflation will be generated, i.e., p increases from period to period. On the contrary where r'^0 is higher than the natural rate, deflation will emerge.

4 Let us first derive the natural-rate-of-interest curve which is very similar to Hicks' IS curve. We assume Say's law, despite, as has been seen before, Wicksell is generally against the law. I consider that it is taken for granted by him in the analysis of the cumulative process. As has also already been seen, a full employment equilibrium is established under the law. The activity levels X, the relative prices, P/p and W/p, and the rate of profits are all determined. Then this rate of profits of the industry is converted to the rate of interest of bonds r' because the former is equal to the rate of profits of the banks, which depends on the interest rate of bonds. (Note that $Q=0$ and p/w is determined under Say's law.) Inverting this correspondence we obtain $r'=f(r)$. We call this interest rate, denoted by r'^n, the natural rate which is the interested rate corresponding to the industry's rate of profits and obviously establishes $S=I$. The equilibrium rate of profits and,

---

[7] K. Wicksell, *Über Wert*. For a critical view of Wicksell see F. H. von Hayek, *Prices and Production*, Routledge and Kegan Paul, London, 1931, pp. 22–31, and G. Myrdal, *Monetary Equilibrium*, William Hodge, London, 1939. There are a number of interpretations of the Wicksell theory which intend to correct its imperfections; Hicks, as has been said, presented three different versions in his *Value and Capital, Trade Cycle*, and *Capital and Growth*, respectively. The following is, as I have said, an adaptation to the system in this volume of my interpretation of the Wicksellian theory in my *Walras' Economics*.

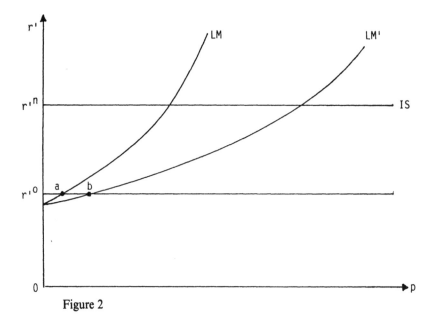

Figure 2

therefore, the natural rate of interest are both independent of the price level p. Thus the pair of r'^n and p fulfilling $S = I$ traces out a horizontal line as is shown in figure 2 above.[8] In Hicks' terminology it is the IS curve.

In the monetary subsystem, on the other hand, share prices, dividends and the interest rate of time deposits, q's, d's and r''''s, are all determined in the markets of shares, new shares and time deposits, respectively. Accordingly, (7.4) contains, apart from δM_c, only two variables, price level p and the rate of interest of the bonds r'. We may now derive the two curves, each giving r' as a function of p, from $B + B_c = 0$ and from $\bar{M} + \delta M_c = M$, respectively. We may call them the bond curve and the LM curve. Taking into consideration the equation $S = I$ that is obtained wherever forces to establish temporary equilibrium work in the real subsystem, it follows from

[8] In his *Trade Cycle*, Hicks interprets Wicksell's case as the case of the IS curve being horizontal, as we have in figure 1. See J. R. Hicks, *A Contribution to the Theory of the Trade Cycle*, Clarendon Press, Oxford, 1950, pp. 139n–40n. But this is not essential for the cumulative process. As I have already pointed out, the process may be generated regardless of the slope of the IS curve (see figure 2 of my *Walras' Economics*, p. 166 where the slope is positive). What is crucial for the cumulative process thesis is the property that the rate of interest determined by either the IS, the bond, or the LM curve remains constant when the quantity of money and the price level change proportionately. Hence the three curves shift rightwards in proportion to the change in the price level.

(7.4) that whenever $B + B_c = 0$, $\bar{M} + \delta M_c = M$, and *vice versa*. Therefore, the bond curve and the LM curve are identical. We then have figure 2.

Let p_0 be the initial price level and r'^0 be the corresponding money rate of interest at which the bond market is cleared, so $B + B_c = 0$. The initial point $a = (p_0, r'^0)$ is on the LM curve. Where the money rate is lower than the natural rate r'^n the firms would raise the funds for investment from the bond market, rather than issuing new shares. Thus $\Delta\bar{\theta}_f$ would be zero or a negligible negative number implying that B_f would take on a substantial negative number. Therefore $\Sigma B_h + \Sigma B_f$ would exceed the limit that commercial banks can afford. In order to keep the bond market in equilibrium, the central bank must buy bonds to eliminate its excess supply. Thus we have $B_c > 0$, so that $\delta M_c > 0$.

Following Wicksell, let us assume that net demand for bonds, $B_i - \bar{B}_i(1 + \bar{r}')$, $i = h, f, b$, net demand for time deposits, $T_i - \bar{T}_i(1 + \bar{r}'')$, $i = h, f$, b, cash holding M_i, $i = h, f, b$, net supply of shares $\Delta\bar{\theta}_i - \bar{\theta}_i d_i$, $i = f, b$, and acquisition of new shares $\Delta\bar{\theta}_{ih}$, $i = f, b$, are all homogeneous of degree one in all of the following variables: prices of commodities P, prices of factors of production W, prices of shares q and the quantity of money, $\bar{M} + \delta M_c$. Secondly, holdings of shares θ_{ih} are homogeneous of degree zero in the same variables.

Then we can easily show that P, W, q will increase at the same rate as the quantity of money will do, but rates of interest r' and r'' remain unchanged. Thus, under the homogeneity assumptions, the price level p increases or decreases in proportion to the quantity of money. Thus the quantity theory of money holds true. By accepting this theory, Wicksell has implicitly taken for granted the supply and demand functions having the homogeneity property as the basis of the theory. We have, consequently:

$$\frac{\delta M_c}{\bar{M}} = \frac{\delta p}{p_0}$$

so that $p_1 = p_0 + \delta p$. Then it can be shown that the LM curve shifts rightwards and goes through the point $b = (r'_0, p_1)$.

Therefore there is no need to change the money rate of interest which remains at r'^0. We now still have the same gap between the natural and money rates as we had in the previous period. It yields an imbalance between industries and banks in favour of the former. The industries issue a great amount of bonds but commercial banks do not want to (and are not able to) buy them as much as that. The bond market is left in a state of excess supply. As the central bank adopts the neutral monetary policy, it buys at the given rate of interest all the excess amount of bonds to keep the market in equilibrium. Thus the rate of interest is kept constant whilst the price level increases as a result of the creation of money. In this way inflation continues. At a critical moment when the bank c feels that it can no longer afford a further increase of money, the excess supply in the bond market has to resolve itself by raising the rate of interest.

A rise in the interest rate, if it is a significant one, may give rise to a converse state of affairs in which the money rate exceeds the natural rate of interest. Then the economy will begin to move in the opposite direction. At such a high rate of interest, industries will raise funds by issuing new shares rather than bonds. Accordingly the bond market will be left in a state of excess demand. Then the central bank will decrease the bonds it holds, so that $B_c < 0$. This means that δM_c is negative. Then the price level will fall proportionately, and the same state of excess demand for bonds is reproduced by virtue of the homogeneity assumptions. The same process will be repeated; the quantity of money diminishes and the price level falls. The central bank will eventually restore a position so that it can expand the quantity of money. Finally the rate of interest will be reduced and may be set at a level lower than the natural rate.

5 We have so far assumed that Say's law prevails. In addition, it is implicitly assumed that the equilibrium to be established in the real subsystem is stationary; the endowment of factors of production $\bar{N}$, as well as that of physical commodities $\bar{X}$, does not change from period to period. This implies $\bar{X} = X$.[9] Otherwise, the full employment equilibrium p^e, W^e, X^e, r^e would have fluctuated during the process of inflation or deflation. It is worth emphasizing that the constancy of the natural rate of interest, that is r'^n such that $r^e = \pi(r'^n)$, is the most important premise of the Wicksellian theory of the cumulative process, otherwise the gap between r'^n and r'^0 would have reduced or expanded, rather than remained unchanged. This means that the monetary equilibrium, where $r'^n = r'^0$ and the price level is kept constant, may be stable or unstable, rather than neutral. This conclusion, however, follows, even though the money rate of interest is kept constant, from the fact that the natural rate of interest is revised due to the changes in the real side of the economy. The Wicksellian thesis of monetary neutrality may not be the correct conclusion if the real economy is not assumed to be stationary.

There is, nevertheless, another special case of the economy being neutral

9 As Hicks correctly points out, Wicksell has implicitly assumed that the real economy is in the state of stationary equilibrium. See his *Capital and Growth*, p. 59. Wicksell also assumes that a rise in the price level does not affect the temporary equilibrium of the real subsystem. This is true only if the elasticities of expectation of all prices are unity. In our case too, unless this expectation condition is fulfilled, the natural rate of interest cannot be independent of the price level, that is to say, we do not have the horizontal IS curve.

with respect to the creation of money. That is the case dealt with by von Neumann. As has already been seen, he examined the state of affairs where the levels of activities grow in balance. That is to say, $X^e = aX$. This state is not generally realized for the $\bar{X}$, historically given. It only occurs for a very special $\bar{X}$, but once it is established, it will be preserved forever as long as there is no obstacle in the factor markets. To make supply and demand relations for factors of production smooth, von Neumann has assumed that excess demand for factors are fulfilled by importing necessary amounts from foreign countries at the prevailing prices, while excess supplies are exported without any difficulty. Under these conditions, the temporary equilibrium to be established is repeatable, albeit the levels of production are expanded at a common rate g; we write $1 + g = a$. It is moreover seen that relative prices of commodities and factors remain constant through time, in spite of the economy expanding in terms of the commodities produced. Of course this constancy of relative prices assures the rate of profits of industries being constant, and, hence, the natural rate of interest being so too. Consequently, we have the same conclusion that the Wicksellian monetary process is cumulative in this von Neumann case.

Since money should be created in this case to cover not only that part of excess demand for money loans which is due to the fact that the money rate of interest is lower than that natural rate r^* which would obtain where the real economy were in the von Neumann equilibrium, but also the part resulting from the fact that production activities expand at rate g, we have $\delta p/p_0 = v + g$, where v stands for the ratio of the former part to these total existing amounts of money $\bar{M}$. Even though the money rate is set at r^*, so that $v = 0$, we have inflation, $\delta p/p_0 = g$, where the real economy expands, while we have Wicksell's pure cumulative process in the case of $g = 0$.

It is clear that the von Neumann state is merely imaginary but has no real basis at all. It is nevertheless useful as a reference state of affairs in economic analysis. Let r^v be the von Neumann rate of profits and r'^v the corresponding natural interest rate, $r'^v = f(r^v)$. Let r_t^e be the actual equilibrium rate of profits in period t. If either the initial configuration $\bar{X}$ is not set on the von Neumann path or the factors of production are not freely importable or exportable, then r_0^e is not equal to r^v. We may focus our attention on the following two possibilities. The first is the case in which r_t^e approaches the von Neumann rate r^v from above as t tends to infinity. The second is the opposite case of r_t^e approaching r^v from below. There are many other possibilities; first of all, r_t^e may trace out an irregular course, and secondly, there is no reason why the von Neumann state should be stable.

Nevertheless, we may derive the following conclusion regarding these cases which is depicted in figure 3, where $r_t'^n$ is the natural state of interest corresponding to the equilibrium profit rate r_t^e; we have $r_t'^n = f(r_t^e)$ of course.

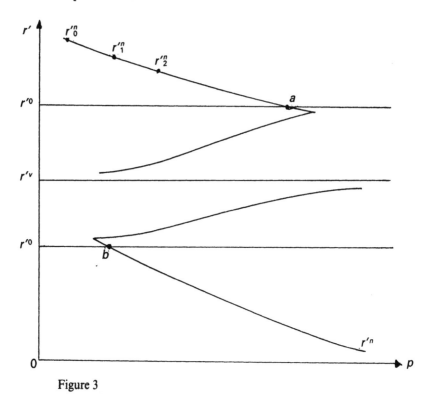

Figure 3

If the money rate of interest r'^0 is set at a point below the natural rate r_0''' but above the von Neumann rate r'^v, inflation starts in the same manner as we explained above.[10] In the next period $t = 1$, the gap between the natural rate and the money rate diminishes because the former declines while the latter is kept constant. In this way, the gap becomes smaller and smaller and in the end the economy may settle at an equilibrium point where the natural rate curve crosses the money rate line; then inflation ceases to exist. In this case the point of intersection a (of figure 3) is stable. However, after that point in time we would have a natural rate of interest which is nearer to the von Neumann rate, so that it is lower than the fixed money rate. On the other

---

[10] As the money rate is lower than the natural rate, the bond market is in excess supply, so that the quantity of money is increased. Then by the quantity theory of money, we have a proportional increase in the price level. This gives rise to a rightwards shift of the LM (or bond) curve, and there is no change in the money (or bond) market, provided the same money rate of interest prevails as it did in period 0. Since the Wicksellian assumption of stationary real equilibrium is not made (i.e., $\bar{X} \neq X$), the real equilibrium in period 1 would be different from the one in 0. Thus $r_1' \neq r_0'$.

hand, where the sequence of the natural rate $r_0'^n$ jumps over the money rate r'^0, that is to say, there is some u such that:

$$r_u'^n < r'^0 < r_{u-1}'^n,$$

then the relative position of the natural rate and the money rate is reversed in period u. The money rate then becomes higher than the natural rate, so that the price level will begin to decline. The natural rate $r_t'^n$ will continue to converge to the von Neumann rate r'^v while the price level will be lower and lower (see figure 3).

On the other hand, where the natural rate converges to the von Neumann rate from below, the economy will follow a path in the opposite direction. Suppose the initial point may be located in the region where the natural rate is lower than the money rate. Starting with any initial price level p_0, we shall have deflation. As $r_0'^n$ is lower than the money rate r'^0, that is lower than r'^v, and $r_t'^n$ is approaching the von Neumann rate, r'^v, it is possible that $r_t'^n$ reaches r'^0 at some point of time. If this happens, the deflation ceases to exist; we have a monetary equilibrium temporarily and then afterwards an inflation will be brought forth. In the case of the natural rate jumping over the point of monetary equilibrium (b in figure 3), the phase of monetary adjustment is switched over to the opposite one. The natural rate will now be higher than the money rate, and, therefore, inflation will emerge. The gap between the two rates becomes larger in the next period. We have further inflation at an accelerated speed.

It is obvious that the usual analysis of the Wicksellian process which assumes the real economy being stationary has to be extended to the case of moving real economic equilibria. It is then seen that there is a possibility of stable monetary equilibrium a or b,[11] provided that the real economy is stationary at that point. Wicksell's thesis that the monetary equilibrium defined as a state of equal natural and money rates of interest is unstable with respect to a change in the money rate is valid without any reservation only in the case that the real economy is stationary. In fact, as the above example of the stable von Neumann equilibrium illustrates, we cannot rule

[11] By using approaches which are different from ours, Lindahl and Myrdal have been concerned with the problem of how to overcome Wicksell's assumption of stationary equilibrium. See E. Lindahl, *Studies in the Theory of Money and Capital*, George Allen and Unwin, London, 1939, and G. Myrdal, *Monetary Equilibrium*, William Hodge, London, 1939. As we may remove our assumption that the von Neumann path is stable, there is no assurance that a sequence of temporary equilibria X_t, $t = 0, 1, 2, \ldots$ generated from the initial point X should smoothly approach a von Neumann balanced growth path. The natural rate of interest $r_t'^n$, $t = 0, 1, \ldots$ then may wander around on the $r' - p$ plane. There may exist no monetary equilibrium point (hence, no stable equilibrium point) as long as the money rate is fixed at a certain level.

out the possibility that, in keeping the money rate of interest constant at a level which is lower or higher than the original natural rate, we may eventually be able to conquer inflation or deflation, provided that the natural rate changes during the process and coincides with the constant money rate at some point of time and remains constant afterwards.

6 Now we turn to the problem of Say's law. We find, in the previous chapter, a duality property between the real economy and the money economy. It has also been seen that the coupling of these two subsystems is unilateral, namely a one-way coupling connecting the monetary economy to the real economy but not *vice versa*, if (and only if) Say's law holds true. Where this law is removed as we deny the law, the situation is completely changed. Not only the real economy influences the monetary economy, but also the latter influences the former and, therefore, it becomes impossible to analyse the real economy independently from the monetary world. Moreover, because Say's law is very far from reality the actual world should not be examined by applying the law to it. Thus the method of analysis dichotomizing economics into two specialized departments, real and monetary, is harmful and defective. We must deal with the economy as a whole uniting and interlinking the two subsystems. Mutual interactions between the two are most important subjects which we have not yet seriously been concerned with, by virtue of economists' implicit (and unconscious) acceptance of Say's law.

Under anti-Say's law, the levels of investment activities X_i^0 are decided by the bankers according to whether they have enough money to support the firms' investment plans or not. When the economy is in shortage of money, a severe choice is made on X_i^0s. Some of them will not be supported by banks at all, while others are given approval only at a low level of X_i^0. Of course, banks may borrow the amounts they need to realize the investment plans proposed by firms, from the central bank. If it takes the policy of the neutral creation of money, it will pour the amount it is requested into the market. Otherwise the bond market is left in a state of excess supply, that is to say, borrowing exceeds lending, so that the money rate of interest r'^0 has to be raised. If the central bank adopts a less severe policy, then investment would be realized at higher levels and the rate of interest would not rise so high as it would do when the quantity of money is strictly controlled. There would be, however, a trade-off between the rate of interest and the rate of inflation. A less severe control of money would create a larger increase in the price level. On the other hand, it should not be overlooked that there are repercussions of X_i^0s, fixed low, upon other activity levels of X_i's. Low levels of all X_i's including X_i^0s imply the holding of money by transaction motives as being low. In addition, the rise in the interest rate diminishes the amount of money held by households and firms. Hence, the quantity of money remaining within commercial banks is increased, so that the lending ability of banks will be improved. There will then be further adjustments of X_i^0's, the levels of which will be raised. In this way, it is evident that mutual repercussions are made between the real and monetary subsystems.

This is the state of affairs which has been examined by Keynes in connection with anti-Say's law. The X_i^0's will finally stay at levels lower than X_i^e. This will result in underemployment as has already been seen. On the contrary, in more favourable circumstances, banks prepare for lending of larger amounts. Where there are a considerable number of promising investment programmes proposed, commercial banks will support many of them, notwithstanding that banks have to borrow from the central bank to do so. In this case, X_i^0's would be set high – as high as or even higher than X_i^e. Where promising innovations are being carried out, the rate of profits would be high. This means a high natural rate of interest being realized. Where the central bank creates money as much as it is requested, δM_c is positive and large. High X_i^0's will generate high X_i's in general; so all the factor markets are tight. As Schumpeter said, the creation of money made in this way is 'creation of purchasing power for the purpose of transferring it to the [would-be] entrepreneur'.[12] Then it is obvious that inflation follows inevitably. In these circumstances, in which Schumpeter was mainly interested, sooner or later the neutral creation of money would become impossible.

As Schumpeter himself recognized, the central bank will set a limit to δM_c, so as to keep the rate of inflation reasonable. As X_i^0's will change from period to period, the rate of profits, hence the natural rate of interest, will also fluctuate correspondingly. Then there is a possibility, though it is a slim one, as has been seen above, that inflation will die out eventually, and a stable monetary equilibrium will be established. However, during the period when δM_c is put under a severe constraint, the rationing has to be implemented in the money market. The allocation of new money will directly influence investment activities X_i^0's and, indirectly through repercussions, general production activities, X_i's too. The central bank works in this way in these circumstances, as if it is the general headquarters of the whole economy, i.e., the control tower of both the financial world and all other businesses including industry. Indeed, the future of the economy depends on the choice of investment projects, X_i^0's.

To make rationing more effective, governmental or semi-governmental banks for special purposes may be founded. Banks for small businesses, banks for farmers, or the housing loan corporation are already familiar. All

---

[12] Schumpeter, *The Theory*, p. 107.

these investment banks have their own *raison d'être* in the actual world because Say's law is not valid there. As I have sufficiently emphasized, the real sector and the monetary sector are bilaterally coupled under anti-Say's law, and the bridging of these two is crucially important, in order for the economy to work smoothly and efficiently. The efficient use of money for the sake of development of the economy, nevertheless, has been almost entirely neglected by economic theorists, because the neoclassical general equilibrium theorists who support Say's law have been accustomed to the traditional method of dichotomizing the economy into two separate sectors, real and monetary. The linkage has been left for a long time in a state of being almost unexamined.

7 Throughout this chapter, I have assumed the quantity theory of money, together with the homogeneity properties to the effect that net demand for bonds, net demand for time deposits, demand for cash holdings and net supply of new shares are homogeneous of degree one in all prices and the initial holdings of money, as long as the rates of interest are kept constant. In addition to these I have also assumed that demands for shareholdings are homogeneous of degree zero, while those for new shares are homogeneous of degree one, in the same variables. These homogeneity assumptions are complementary to the quantity theory; without them it is rather difficult to envisage the latter.

I have then generated a process of cumulative inflation or deflation of prices in the system of general equilibrium without asking whether the system is compatible with the homogeneity properties. I shall examine this below and shall at once find that the assumption *cannot* be true for aggregate demand and supply functions in the general equilibrium system. Let us write, for example, the cash holdings of agent i as:

$$H_i(P, W, \ldots, r', r'', \bar{m}_i),$$

where $P, W, \ldots$ are price variables, r', r'' interest rates, and $\bar{m}_i$ the initial holdings of money of agent i. Of course, the aggregate demand for cash holdings is given by the total sum of H_i's over all agents.

We may then assume that each H_i is homogeneous of degree one in $P, W, \ldots$ and $\bar{m}_i$, with r' and r'' being kept constant. There is no incompatibility between this and the rational behaviour of the agents in the system; under some reasonable assumptions of their portfolio selections we can derive H_i functions which are homogeneous in $P, W, \ldots, \bar{m}_i$. However, what we require in our argument of the cumulative process is the homogeneity of the aggregate demand for cash holdings, $H = \Sigma H_i$, in terms of prices $P, W, \ldots$ and the aggregate initial amount of cash holdings $\bar{M} = \Sigma \bar{m}_i$. It is true that, where each $\bar{m}_i$ increases proportionally when the total $\bar{M}$ increases, the homogeneity of the aggregate demand for cash holdings follows from the assumed homogeneity of individual H_i. But otherwise it does not follow unless an excessive change in H_i's whose $\bar{m}_i$ changes more than proportionately compensates a deficient change in H_i's with $\bar{m}_i$'s changing less than proportionately. Hence we have to conclude that the aggregate demand H is not homogeneous unless (i) the condition that all $\bar{m}_i$'s fluctuate proportionately is fulfilled or (ii) the effect of $\bar{m}_i$ on H_i is the same for all i so that the compensation mentioned above is correctly carried out.

To establish the impossibility of H being homogeneous, let us first show that the provisory condition (i) is never met. Suppose a certain amount of money, say δM_c, is created in a period by the central bank. It is made in terms of lending to some commercial banks which in turn buy the bonds issued by some firms for investment. Then the created money goes into the account of these firms. Further, it would be transferred to the pockets of workers or other firms if the original firms spend in the same period a certain portion of the loans they have been granted. These workers and firms in the secondary position in the chain of money circulation may also spend some portion of money received in the same period. In this way how far the money δM_c is distributed depends on the velocity of circulation of money. But the distribution will be different, depending on to which firms the money is originally loaned. When the loan is made to a firm producing consumption goods, the money, at least some, will go directly to firms producing machines and materials, while when it is loaned to a firm producing producers' goods, it will go into the pockets of entrepreneurs of the consumers' goods industry, only via the channel through employees of the firm. Some of the workers and the firms, depending on the circulation of money, will hardly receive any new money within a period of the creation of money δM_c being made. Therefore, δM_c is not distributed proportionately among households and firms, so that we conclude that H is not homogeneous.

As for the proviso (ii) above, we must say that it is a very stringent condition. First of all, agents i include households, firms and commercial banks, and their motives for cash holding are very different. Moreover, $\bar{m}_i$ is high for some i and low for other i; this would mean that the marginal effects of $\bar{m}_i$'s upon H_i's would not be the same. Even if $\bar{m}_i$'s are the same, H_i's would not be equal to each other because the agents propensities to hold cash may be diverse between individuals and business institutions. Hence (ii) can hardly be regarded as the base of the homogeneity of H.

Once the homogeneity is rejected, it is evident that the quantity theory of money does not hold. We cannot take for granted that the price level rises or declines in proportion to the creation or reduction of money. Therefore, from the point of view of general equilibrium theory, we have to conclude that our proof of the cumulative process developed in the previous sections is unsatisfactory. The theory must be reformulated in a modified, more accurate form.

In the following, nevertheless, we consider that the proviso (ii) is approximately true, and assume that what has been said above about homogeneity is valid as a first approximation. Then the theory of the cumulative process is more or less true; it is almost certain that the monetary equilibrium is unstable, though a possibility of stable equilibrium, as has been discussed above, cannot be ruled out. Moreover, even if inflation or deflation may autonomously come to an end, the temporary equilibrium rate of profits always shifts upwards due to technological or managerial improvements, or fluctuates upwards or downwards due to favourable or unfavourable weather, or shifts downwards due to obsolescence of machines or damages by accidents owing to various causes. Therefore, the natural rate of interest, even though it coincides with the money rate at an equilibrium point, would easily deviate from the latter for the reasons just mentioned. The inflation or deflation will start. If it would be likely that the natural rate shifts more frequently upwards than downwards, because of conscious efforts for efficiency and improvement, then inflation is more frequently generated than deflation.

We have already seen that the historical motion of the real economy is unstable, especially with respect to innovations under anti-Say's law. Even though the same menu of techniques is given to the economy, the choice of investment activities would be different, depending on the attitudes of the entrepreneurs and bankers. An obvious example is: when Japan was concerned with the problem of construction of their railway system in 1881, she chose the narrow gauge rather than the standard one. Since then it has been the major obstacle to the development of transportation in Japan. In view of the significance of railways in general economic development in the first half of this century, the choice may be said to have been a fatal one. In the same way, a big gap in physical culture (civilization) between the South and the West would be attributable, at least partly, to the difference in their choice of investment activities. There would be no doubt that the difference in physical culture results in diversifying moral culture. Thus, in the modern history of human beings anti-Say's law and the efficient linkage or collaboration between entrepreneurs and bankers are found to have played a most important role. This view, that results from Schumpeter's development theory, is not mere historical materialism. It emphasizes the importance of the superstructure (such as collaboration between firms and banks or the spirit of entrepreneurs) as well as the structure of the economy.

8 In this section let me summarize our analysis in this volume. Stability is one of the main themes, on which three theses have been discussed. First, we

have shown that under Say's law, that is, where there is no financial constraint on investment activities, the temporary equilibrium in each period is stable. Although our system is different from the conventional one discussed by Samuelson, Arrow–Hurvicz, Hahn, Negishi, and others,[13] because our model is a model for the mixed economy consisting of both flexprice and fixprice sectors, rather than a pure flexprice model discussed by them, or a pure fixprice model by Leontief, there is no substantial difference in the analysis between us and them. All of these are some kind of theory of stability to a point. Nevertheless it may be worth noting that in our analysis the activity levels of the fixprice sectors are assumed to be all flexible, so that the investment activity levels too are regarded as being adjusted.

Secondly, we have pointed out that the real economy of the present day does not satisfy Say's law, and we have seen that under anti-Say's law the sequence of temporary equilibria is unstable with respect to the investment activities X_i^0's chosen by entrepreneurs and bankers. If in the initial period a completely different set of X_i^0's were chosen, the production possibility set of the economy would be very different in the second period; so the choice of X_i^0's in the second period would also be different. In this way in the remote future the economy would obtain an entirely new frontier of economic activities. Neither price adjustment nor quantity adjustment plays a significant role in this respect. Crucial factors are the choice of techniques and their financial support. The choice brings forth trigger effects which work dynamically, and eventually produce a decisive diversion from the original path of motion. It is, of course, Schumpeter who first pointed out this kind of instability of the economy in connection with various kinds of innovations.

These stability and instability properties are concerned with the working of the real economy. As for the monetary aspect, we have also observed the instability of the price level. Thus the modern economy is always exposed to two kinds of instability, one on the real side that is Schumpeterian and the other on the monetary side that is Wicksellian. In order to deal with the former successfully, we must have a far-reaching and reliable perspective of the economic and technological future. The firms' decisions on choice of techniques must be consistent with each other. A nation-wide or industry-wide investment planning council would greatly contribute to promoting the efficiency of choice. In order to conquer inflation or deflation, on the other side, the rate of interest has to be carefully controlled and adjusted. Moreover, public finance must be put under strict discipline. It is too naive

---

[13] See F. H. Hahn, 'Stability', in K. J. Arrow and M. D. Intriligator (eds.), *Handbook of Mathematical Economics*, vol. II, North-Holland Publishing, Amsterdam, 1982, pp. 745–93.

to believe in the free enterprise system and leave the economy to free competition and an automatic price mechanism. In order to minimize damages due to inconsistent, chaotic and anarchistic choices of techniques, as well as those due to unnecessary inflation or deflation, a certain kind of planning and control on the developments of scientific knowledge as well as on the choice of investment activities has to be accepted. Of course, monetary policy is always carefully implemented.

Furthermore, to complete a large investment project it usually takes a very long time, during which prospects of the future may change, even drastically. At a number of points of time, the bank has to decide whether it should continue to support or give up the project. What is required of the banker in order for him to tide over these critical junctures is not just an ability for profit calculation; he also must have plenty of guts and deep devotion to the cause of the project. This is true for entrepreneurs too, so that the economy is more than a world of 'economic man'. All these are the most important implications of the instability theses.

The second main theme of the volume is Say's law. Where the law prevails the general equilibrium theory would produce a sequence of temporary equilibria bringing forth full employment of all natural and human resources. This path of permanent full employment would obviously be inadequate for explaining the working of the actual economy. Once Say's law is removed, as has been seen, the model should be modified so as to accommodate the material dealt with by Schumpeter and Keynes. Their real economic systems are the systems of overdeterminacy because investment activities X_i^0's are determined, under the anti-Say's law, by the banks' consent to the programmes proposed by the firms. It is then obvious that some of the general equilibrium conditions have to be violated in the actual economy, as the Keynesian theory of underemployment equilibrium illustrates.

This is a state of 'defective' equilibrium which is most difficult to deal with, because we have not enough knowledge of how a state of defective equilibrium will work and change because economists have become accustomed to the neglect of this problem and have concentrated their efforts on developing the full employment equilibrium analysis. We may, however, propose, as a tentative solution, to use the temporary equilibrium under Say's law as a reference state and assume that the economy minimizes the deviation of X from X^e, subject to the feasibility conditions and the investment activities that are fixed at X_i^0's. We may make a hypothesis that the economy settles at a state of defective equilibrium determined in this way. The prices of commodities and factors may be obtained at the shadow prices of this minimization problem.

Alternatively, we may adopt the fixprice method, as we have in fact used in some parts of the present volume. Fixing P, W, r at P^e, W^e, r^e (the equilibrium prices and the rate of profits under Say's law), we find out the repercussions upon X caused by fixing investment activities at X_i^0's. It is possible that the X thus obtained do not satisfy the feasibility conditions with strict equality. For some commodities or factors the supply may exceed the demand. The state established in this way would sustain itself as long as the assumption of downwards rigidity of the price is valid for any commodity or factor i. That is to say, we assume that P_i or W_i remains unchanged in spite of the supply of i exceeding its demand. This means that we implicitly assume that it takes a long time for the rule of free goods to work. This is the method we used in this volume which is very similar to the one Keynes used in the *General Theory*.

9 This final section is devoted to three concluding remarks. First, at what level of W_i will the wage rate lose its downwards flexibility? As Takata insisted, and as Marx discussed concerning the level of subsistence wages, the level of wages at which workers severely resist against further cuts depends on historical circumstances under which power is allocated among social classes. Where the working class has a greater social power relative to employers, and as long as this distribution of power is supported by the public, the wage rate would become rigid downwards at a high level. Thus the rigidity of investment activities X_i^0's caused by the financial constraint imposed by bankers against firms may be accompanied by rigid factor prices. Furthermore, these inflexibilities of X_i^0's and W have repercussions upon other X_i's and P, respectively, so that the whole economy would turn out to be considerably rigid under anti-Say's law. We may then say that the neoclassical rule of free goods is unacceptable, especially for labour and other factors of production, in the actual world.

It is this downwards rigidity of factor prices which sustains the state of underemployment created by anti-Say's law as a state of equilibrium. Then we have to deal with the problem of how to support those unemployed during the period they have no income. Either the trade unions should be able to help their unemployed members, or the state must arrange a social security system of such an ability for the general public. In any case it is clear that the economic system consisting of workers, landowners, capitalists, entrepreneurs and bankers only is incomplete; it should be extended so as to include the trade unions and the state (or the government).[14] Then the model becomes a more 'mixed' one with more heterogeneous sectors but provides room for the fiscal and tax policies. It goes without saying that the model would be more influenced by political and social elements.

Secondly, on the significance of the bankers' role in the modern economy

---

[14] It is not difficult to introduce the state sector into our model. It would be accomplished in the same way as I did in my *Economics of Industrial Society*, pp. 125–76.

under anti-Say's law the following findings have been obtained. Even where great technological opportunities are found out by engineers and accepted by entrepreneurs, innovations would not be carried out and remain abortive if bankers did not support their ideas. On the other hand, we may say that the civilization in the future is swayed by the innovations which are carried out and meet with success; we should not underestimate the bankers' role even from the point of view of the history of culture or civilization. We have to make this conclusion because the actual economy does not satisfy Say's law. In the actual world the dichotomy is impossible. Equilibrium investment could not be determined in the subsystem of the real economy, solely by entrepreneurs, independently from the bankers' behaviour. Bankers would play a role that is much more than mere agents of transmitting money.

Thirdly, whereas dynamic theory was a popular subject in economics in the prewar period, it has not been the focus of the largest magnitude which attracted the most talented theorists' interest in the postwar period. In the field of general equilibrium theory too, dynamization no longer remains an item on the top agenda; it seems to have lost that position to the problem of efficiency and optimality of the system. For this change in academic interest the following idea, due to G. Debreu, would seem to be responsible.

Debreu introduced uncertainty into general equilibrium theory. Those alternatives which may happen at time t are called events at t. He defines a commodity (or a factor) not only by its physical characteristics, but also by its location and its event.[15] We may then assume that activities in an economy extend over a sufficiently large number of period T. Each commodity has a market which is spot or futures; prices of all these commodities are determined in the current period 0 either by Walras' tatonnement procedure, or Scarf's algorithm, or any other method.[16] We may then make T very large, say 100 or even 1,000 years. Because all uncertainties have been taken into account, agents only carry out through these years the contracts already made in period 0; thus perfect foresight will be widespread. As Hicks has quoted from *Faust*, it is the world that may be described as 'ihre vorgeschriebene Reise vollendet sie mit Donnergang'.

Of course, it is true that there is a lease contract for land (or a building) of over ninety-nine years or even 1,000 years. But the reader would agree to my saying that I would be regarded as a madman if I refer to Arrow's, Debreu's and Hahn's authorities to make the following order to a shoe shop on the high street: 'For a price to be paid now, deliver a pair of shoes to my grandson if he exists and is twenty years old in forty years' time, and if not,

[15] G. Debreu, *The Theory of Value*, John Wiley, New York, 1959, pp. 98 ff.
[16] H. Scarf, 'On the Computation of Equilibrium Prices', in W. Fellner *et al.*, *Ten Economic Studies in the Tradition of Irving Fisher*, New York, John Wiley, 1967.

deliver nothing.'[17] The reason is simple: I am mad because I assume the infinite capacity of utility calculation (or finding out rational behaviour solutions) for ordinary persons, in spite of the fact that they are actually much happier by being released from worrying about trifles which might happen in the far future. Then for most commodities, long-term future markets do not exist, and to make up for this imperfection, the economy adjusts itself dynamically. The dynamics is a practical and efficient way of tackling the problem of long-run optimality. This is common sense, and economics is a science concerning the world of common sense.

[17] K. J. Arrow and F. H. Hahn, *General Competitive Analysis*, p. 34.

8   Perspectives into the future

1 As I wrote at the very beginning of this volume, I began my study of economics with reading Hicks' *Value and Capital* (*VC*). My first research results produced my first book, *DKR*, in Japanese. It was fourteen years after its appearance, that my first book in English was published in 1964, when I was privileged to be invited by Hicks to work with him at All Souls College. I was not entirely happy with my books; I had already started to query the appropriateness of the *VC* paradigm of general equilibrium (GE) to which my book belonged.

The work assigned to me at Oxford was to read the manuscript of *Capital and Growth* (*CG*), 1965, which Hicks was then writing and to comment on it. I soon realized that he too was no longer satisfied with his previous book that had long been regarded as a living classic of economics. He was groping for a new paradigm. If I am allowed to point out one title from his bibliography which he would consider as the one which would be closest to his new paradigm, I would say that he himself would single out his *Capital and Time*, 1973, but even this does not fully represent his new paradigm. I consider that he devoted his entire life after 1965 to the work of searching for a new paradigm (*CT* is one of the products of such efforts), and he would have been more satisfied from constructing a new GE model on the basis of the observations obtained in his *A Market Theory of Money*, 1989, published after his death. In any case *CG*, which I read carefully and repeatedly during the course of his writing it, is no more than a work written in a period of transition from an old to a new paradigm.

While I was in Oxford I also started to write, in parallel with Hicks, a GE book, which was later published with the title, *Theory of Economic Growth*, 1969. However, I then found this too unsatisfactory, so I too continued to search after my own new paradigm. It was when an International Economic Association conference was held in Bologna, in 1989, celebrating the fiftieth anniversary of the publication of *VC*, that most of the basic ideas of this book was formed. I did not attend the conference but was talking at home about *VC* to my wife. My dissatisfaction with the *VC* type of economics burst out, and I realized that I had at last got what I had been searching for since 1964. Soon after this Hicks died; I regret that I had no chance to talk to him on any part of this book.

Nevertheless, I have to admit that the model is still incomplete and unsatisfactory at various points. For its improvements we need empirical studies of our economy and society. We have already enough experience to know that axiomatization for axiomatization's sake does not progress the theory much. How should the theory be developed in the future? In order to make my view regarding this question clear, a paper which I wrote recently for the *Economic Journal* in response to the invitations of the editors is reproduced in the following sections with some adaptations and additions.[1] I hope, it will serve to explain my standpoint in this book, as well as to make a bridge between our current academic activities and the general equilibrium theory in the twenty-first century.

2 In trying to predict what the shape of economic theory will be in the twenty-first century, I am going to take as my time period the latter half of the century, and to limit my consideration to the field of General Equilibrium Theory (GET), the area within which I have up to now been conducting research. The purpose of GET is to try to clarify how the social economy works. Models are constructed, and these are then strictly and rigorously subjected to theoretical analysis. In order to do this, it is necessary to start off with a broad vision of the movement of the economy, such as is portrayed, for example, in macroeconomics. GET then elaborates on this at the microeconomic level, with the aim of supplying a microeconomic foundation to the macroeconomic vision. GET owes a great deal to developments in macroeconomic theory; in the latter part of the last century theorists such as Marx and Walras refined Ricardo's economics (I regard the theories of Marx and Walras as old GET). In the second half of this century Hicks, Patinkin and Malinvaud were inspired by the theories of Keynes, and Arrow–Debreu and Arrow–Hahn have axiomatized Hicks' theory to form new GET. In the period of transition from the old to the new GET there was a post-Walrasian period when such neoclassical economists as Böhm-Bawerk, Wicksell, Marshall and Hayek played dominant roles.

Given the complexity of society, GET has tended hitherto to deal with a model constructed on the basis of an exaggerated and deformed view of economic society, shedding light on only a few facets of that society. Ricardo and Walras looked at the question of how population and capital must adapt within a given area of land; Marx looked at the exploitation of

---

[1] M. Morishima, 'General Equilibrium Theory in the Twenty-First Century', *The Economic Journal*, January 1991, pp. 69–74.

one class by another, while the focal point of the models conceived by Walras, Hicks and Leontief was the repercussion of prices and outputs from one sector of the economy to another. Böhm-Bawerk's, Wicksell's, Hayek's and Hicks' analyses concerned the time structure of the modern production system – for example what length of roundabout production is the most appropriate, and when machines and capital equipment should be discarded and replaced. All of these views are entirely pertinent, but each by itself is essentially a distortion, seeking out no more than a single facet of reality. We need a comprehensive multiple-facet model; the various theories must not just be advocated by separate schools, but must be brought into synthesis.

In reaching such a synthesis, however, conflicting views will have to be harmonized. We are only too aware how scholars are divided between approval and disapproval of exploitation theory, and there are doubtless a host of other views which are mutually contradictory if we examine them in more detail, and which will need to be rationalized. Unlike physics, economics has unfortunately developed in a direction far removed from its empirical source, and GET in particular, as the core of economic theory, has become a mathematical social philosophy, or a theology for modern bourgeoisie if not an instrument of logics training. In spite of its scientific presentation, the Arrow–Hahn book[2] may remind us of Baruch Spinoza's *Ethica Ordine Geometrico Demonstrata*.

I have discussed myself in a separate essay[3] how Japanese mathematics (or *wasan*) in the Tokugawa period, though it had attained a high level of sophistication, came to a wretched end due to its total absence of interaction with natural science. It turned into a technique for the setting of puzzles, and the *wasan* scholars were reduced to being the playmates of culture-loving samurai and members of the newly risen merchant class, just like the masters of the tea ceremony, of flower arrangement and of the *haiku*. At the same time, the mathematics itself regressed. The following words by John von Neumann can be read as a warning against decadence of this kind: 'At a great distance from its empirical source, or after much "abstract" inbreeding, a mathematical subject is in danger of degeneration.'[4] In fact, GET economists, along with the specialists in von Neumann economics who are just one element of them, have sunk into

[2] K. J. Arrow and F. H. Hahn, *General Competitive Analysis*, North-Holland, Amsterdam, 1971.

[3] M. Morishima, 'The Good and Bad Use of Mathematics', in P. Wiles and G. Routh (eds.), *Economics in Disarray*, Basil Blackwell, Oxford, 1984.

[4] M. Dore, S. Chakravarty and R. Goodwin, *John von Neumann and Modern Economics*, Clarendon Press, Oxford, 1989, p. xiv. Notwithstanding a citation of this kind at the start of this volume, the empirical content of the various pieces contained in it is surprisingly thin and meagre.

excessive mental aestheticism. If this bad habit is not corrected, and if what von Neumann said is right, then the twenty-first century will see the degeneration of their subject.

3 In the models of theorists such as Hicks, Arrow, Debreu and Hahn which are the focal influences in GET, not just households but firms as well are assumed to act as price-takers. These models are exactly applicable only to agriculture, forestry, fishing and part of the mining sector, industries whose outputs account at the very most for 20% of GDP in most modern industrial economies. In most remaining industries, individual enterprises make decisions on the price of their respective outputs, according to the mark-up theory, either of the version called the full-cost principle or of the version known as the marginal-cost principle. Competition is carried on through devising methods of production or methods of selling which will permit a lower mark-up rate.

Within these industries there used to be a fair number of industries where prices were determined by haggling of the GET type. In the case of taxi fares, for example, negotiation over the price on the street actually disappeared as meters were installed in all the taxicabs. This means that methods of determining prices differ according to the stage of technological development. With technological development, communication of a kind hitherto impossible is available at a low price, and hence becomes accessible to a large number of people. This in turn means that the price of many commodities – such as equities and foreign currency – is determined by methods very different from those postulated under GET. For example, under GET price determination is carried on in a situation of universal knowledge in a perfectly open market which can be entered by anyone, while the banks' foreign exchange dealers conduct price negotiations over the telephone without the intervention of a third party.[5] However, this kind of chain of activity, where prices are determined in isolation, ultimately causes the price to converge on an equilibrium price. To obtain this effect each dealer may not negotiate in a selfish fashion over the price, but must keep to the established rules, and it is essential for GET to clarify the nature of the rules which will bring about price stability. Thus the institutional elements of the economy are important. It is not surprising to see that the theory of stability, that mountain of empty theorizing accumulated between the mid 1940s and the late 1960s, was a total failure.

And that is not all. As methods of preserving goods are developed, the

---

[5] For how the foreign exchange markets actually work, and what sort of rules the dealers have to adhere to, see, for example, M. Morishima, *The Economics of Industrial Society*, Cambridge University Press, 1984, pp. 99–132. For the structure of other markets, there is a splendid account in Hicks' *A Market Theory of Money*, Clarendon Press, Oxford, 1989.

ways of determining their prices also change. The cut-price sale of strawberries on the street in the evenings, for example, is likely to disappear once we reach the stage where strawberries can be perfectly preserved, and the price of strawberries will be determined, like those of manufactured products, according to the full-cost principle. The rule of free goods, which is most fundamental among the neoclassical rules of pricing, is thus greatly affected by whether convenient methods of storage and maintenance are available or not. In so far as these sorts of method of determining prices are dependent on technology, price theory too must inevitably change in accordance with the stage of technological development. It is strange to see that all those who might be referred to as neoclassical economists have not up to now made any positive attempt to come to terms with the full-cost principle, and it will become abundantly clear in the twenty-first century that such a conservative attitude is out of tune with the times.[6] The eyes with which we look at an economy differ depending on the theory that we use, and in the case of economics a theory is never totally self-sufficient and autonomous, but dependent on material conditions (especially on technology).

4 It is also the case that the world of GET is in fact a dream world, a world which is not totally workable in the context of actual society. The number of actors on the stage in this GET world are far too few. The old general equilibrium theorists were strongly aware of this. Walras, for example, in his *Elements of Pure Economics*, emphasized the existence not only of capitalists, landlords and workers, but of a fourth group as well, namely entrepreneurs, who acted as independent agents. Moreover, in Schumpeter's *Theorie der Wirtschaftlichen Entwicklung* (1911), not only did the author stress the importance of entrepreneurs, but bankers were brought on to the scene for the first time. Entrepreneurs without bankers are like soldiers without weapons; without bankers it is extremely hard for entrepreneurs to discharge their own functions.

This kind of trend showed that GET was progressing in the right direction. With the new GET, however, both entrepreneurs and bankers have virtually ceased to exist. There are no innovations nor founding of new enterprises, and the head of each enterprise earns his profits by operating production possibility sets given to him, i.e., bequeathed to him by his ancestors or some unexplainable entity, say God, in the past. This is a reversion to a truly medieval, hereditary economy if ever there was one. I will grant that such a retrogressive approach is an easy path if one wants to

<hr>

[6] My criticism is directed at neoclassical economists, but the Sraffians are far worse in their disregard of empirical content.

construct a model axiomatically, and it may also be of some use as a
temporary means of facilitating the dichotomizing method, whereby
entrepreneurs and bankers are put to sleep for a while. (I also give due credit
to the fact that GET now has monetary theory as one of its elements, even if
it is a monetary theory whose entrepreneurs and bankers are either absent
or asleep.) Nevertheless, once the existence of equilibrium in this fictional
world has been proved, GET theorists go crazy. They pursue their model
too far, under the illusion that by clarifying its optimum properties they
have also clarified the optimality of the modern capitalist economy, in
which entrepreneurs and bankers play such an important role, whereas all
they have in fact done is to clarify the optimality of a hereditary economy.
GE economists have neither compared, as I have pointed out before, the
GE economy with Anglo-American financial markets to the one with
German–Japanese banking system, nor examined them for finding out
which of them is more efficient and more stable, if judgement is made from
the long-run point of view. In this area we observe many untouched and
unresolved problems of great practical and theoretical significance.

5 GET, moreover, following the fundamental premise of seventeenth- and
eighteenth-century English rationalism, makes the assumption that each
agent acts in accordance with the principles of utility maximization and
profit maximization. As long as the economies with which we are dealing
are those of Western countries (especially those of North Europe and North
America), there was no particular objection to this in the twentieth century,
but during the course of the twenty-first century the countries of Asia,
starting with Japan, and of South America, are likely to become the objects
of GET analysis. When that happens, if we continue to act upon the same
assumptions as we do now, GET will in these countries no longer be able to
play the role of an instrument of economic analysis and a theoretical system
capable of cultivating a vision of the economy. It will be too far removed
from their own reality. It will come, therefore, to be regarded merely as an
instrument for training students' power of logic. Peoples possessing a
philosophy (or a set of guiding principles) very different from Western
European rationalism, have already acquired the skills needed to operate
capitalism or highly productive economies which can compete effectively
with capitalist ones. In the context of this development it is essential for
GET to throw off its adherence to eighteenth-century Western rationalism,
to attempt to become more universal, and to consider of its own volition the
kind of ethos appropriate to an economic system with a high degree of
productivity.

It goes without saying that as long as people's work ethics are different,
the industrial organization constructed upon them will be different as well.

GET needs to maintain a relationship of close cooperation with both sociology and social psychology, and we need to look very deeply into the sociological aspects of the GET system. The bureaucratic operation of enterprises and industries should be paid more attention in GET analysis, because the middle management's behaviour, or even the top one, of large businesses, would be better understood and explained by applying the sociology of bureaucracy and meritocracy, rather than the economic theory of utility maximization or profit maximization; in fact, big firms are operated quite differently from what we may conjecture by relying upon the present standard theory of economics. It may also be expected that at the same time even research into family relationships is likely to become a research topic within GET, as the twenty-first century will see the flourishing of small, family-based enterprises in the wake of robotization. It would be difficult to find anything differing more between North and South Europe, and between Oriental and Occidental countries, than family relationships. Here, too, is something that cannot be easily determined by principles of utility maximization and profit maximization.

The question of convergence between the economies of Western Europe and those of Eastern Europe has been much discussed, and in the twenty-first century the issue of convergence between the Eastern and Western hemispheres is likely to become a research topic as well. That means, in essence, a convergence of cultures. Should the various disciplines which concern themselves with trends in society come in this way to be more aware of the differences between cultures and to look at the issue of convergence of different cultures, then GET, too, must go along with this trend, overcome the limitations of Western European rationalism, and look closely at the differing kinds of ethos which may be compatible with capitalism or with the operation of a modern social economy.

The issue of the appropriateness of various kinds of ethos to modern technology was one which deeply concerned Max Weber. It was at the beginning of this century that he first posed this question, at a time, perhaps, when the issue was somewhat premature. It was a time when the Christian cultural area, in particular the countries with a strong protestant tradition, had almost total command over modern technology, and of the countries outside this area only Japan had entered into this privileged company. Even in the case of Japan, it was not clear whether or not the country was well-established as a group member.

For that reason the issue was discussed in the context of inadequate empirical materials. It was extremely difficult, therefore, to reach any sort of scientific verdict on the argument, and the result was inevitably that the debate advanced in a very ideological fashion. Now in the twenty-first century we will have at our disposal the results of substantial empirical observations, and be able to discuss objectively how economic systems change according to the different ethos. Not just that, we shall be able to discuss on the basis of empirical evidence the reverse relationship, namely how technology influences an ethos, whether it brings about convergence of ethos, and stimulates a degree of uniformity. If it is to be able to examine this sort of range of questions, then GET must become truly multidisciplinary by being more closely tied to sociology and other disciplines.

6 I have mentioned before that, in the general meetings of shareholders of a firm, each shareholder has a right to exercise votes whose number is in proportion to the number of shares he holds; the firm makes its decisions according to the majority rule of this type of weighted voting. In the case of financing an investment project with money which is acquired by issuing new shares, therefore, the composition of shareholders may be affected by the issue; moreover, shares, old and new, can be sold in the market. The new shareholders may elect new top executives, who are not current board members. In an extreme case it is possible that a new team of executives who are elected after new shares have been issued for accomplishing an investment programme are not anxious at all to carry out the programme. In order to have consistent programmes over a considerable length of time, it is very important to stabilize the composition of shareholders; at least most of the main shareholders must remain to be as influential as before in terms of the number of voting rights they have, throughout the period concerned. However, this is extremely difficult to realize, wherever shares of the firm are publicly sold and bought in the market. The firm always exposes itself to the danger of being taken over by some other persons, or being merged into a certain other firm. Whenever a hostile take-over is made against an important firm, the whole economy will suffer from it considerably.

In order to keep away from this danger, the firm should not look too attractive. This consideration would discourage entrepreneurs from making management and production efficient; the top executives of the firm tend to suppose that there is an optimum degree of efficiency which should be neither too high nor too low to stabilize the composition of shareholders. Thus lukewarm management would be taken as optimum management. Moreover, in a difficult situation the entrepreneur of a firm may prefer his firm to be taken over by someone else, rather than he himself should find a way out of the difficulty for his firm; such an entrepreneur naturally gets to be feeble and gutless. To tackle these the sociology of entrepreneurs is much needed.

There is another unsatisfactory aspect of the joint-stock company system. Whereas any person becomes one of the joint owners of the firm even if he has never visited it, any employee, who has worked for the firm for even more than ten years, has no right to join in its decision-making. This asymmetry in the treatment of shareholders and employees could easily make the latter unhappy and unsatisfied, and this could be another source of inefficiency.

On the other hand, in the case of financing an investment project by borrowing money from a bank (the German–Japanese type of financing), the firm can expand its scale of activities without disturbing its composition of shareholders. The firm's decisions are kept steady, viable and consistent over a considerable span of time. As far as this aspect of the effects of investment finance is concerned, the German–Japanese system is preferred to the Anglo-American one. In any case, in order to make joint-stock companies more efficient and their employees more motivated, we have to introduce more elements of community spirit into them and transform them into community-type working places, so as to remove the 'us and them' feeling from both of the owners of the companies and their employees and establish a unity feeling between them.[7] It is clear that sociological or institutional analysis is needed to deal with this sort of problem.[8]

Like Modigliani and Miller's initial conclusion on the invariance of the firm's capital structure,[9] the above argument or conjecture is based on a number of stringent and unrealistic assumptions; for example, the corporation tax advantage of debt which is usually made in the real world is completely ignored. The problem of the optimal capital structure should be discussed by taking account of all policy measures, such as taxes on dividends or capital gains, the corporate tax advantage of debt, subsidies to new investment projects, and others, which may actually be carried out. In any case, examination of the economy for the optimality of capital structure is much more economically meaningful and significant than the usual examination of the GE system of production for Pareto optimality.

7 Of the two pillars of economics – mathematical analysis and social scientific analysis – it is the latter which will become relatively more important in the twenty-first century, and it must become so, at least as far as GET is concerned. What must be emphasized, however, is that there is no question of my making this prediction on the basis of any 'anti-

---

[7] A similar view is found in H. Okumura, *Kigyo Baishu* (Acquisition and Takeover of Enterprises), in Japanese, Iwanami, 1990. The German–Japanese method of finance too cannot avoid a danger that the firm may be occupied by the bank. A number of executives of the former may be appointed or decided by the latter when the firm's borrowing from the bank reaches to some critical level and its business prospects are very gloomy, so that the bank feels it is necessary to participate or intervene in the firm's decision making.

[8] See, for example, J. G. Gurley and E. S. Shaw, 'Financial Aspects of Economic Development', *American Economic Review*, Vol. 14, 1955.

[9] F. Modigliani and M. H. Miller, 'The Cost of Capital'.

mathematics' sentiment. In June 1900 Walras wrote: 'The twentieth century, which is not far off, will feel the need . . . of entrusting the social sciences to men of general culture who are accustomed to thinking *both* inductively and deductively and who are familiar with reason *as well as experience*'[10] (my italics). What I am saying here is very much the same thing. However, whereas in his time mathematics lagged behind in becoming widely used, and he was urging mathematicalization, in the contemporary world it has gone too far, leading theorists to have an inadequate concern for actuality. I, therefore, am arguing for rather the opposite. The pillars can serve together to support a building, but should one become too big and too strong the other will become correspondingly weak, and the building will collapse. Clearly, a strong and healthy construction cannot be founded upon such a basis.

Whether or not my prediction comes true will depend upon the good sense of all GET theorists in the future, but various encouraging things have occurred which make me feel optimistic. One such factor is the appearance during the 1980s of works such as A. M. Okun's *Prices and Quantities*[11] and Hicks' *Market Theory*, mentioned above, works which could well serve as starting points for the kind of GET which I have in mind. I know of course that one section of GET scholars may regard with hostility those who make statements such as I have made above, on the grounds of their loyalty to mathematics. Scholars of this group expend their energies on competing with each other in demonstrations of intellectual and mathematical ability, and regard as their inferiors those who contend the need to observe the real world. This phenomenon is a palpable symptom of scientific degeneration.

However, should there by any chance appear a group of brave souls who are prepared to forgo the easy pleasure of demonstrating their mathematical abilities and to hone the skill of building a model on the basis of empirical observation, the history of theory will move off in a completely different direction. GET would become a multi-disciplinary systems analysis of the economy in which relevant disciplines such as economic theory, history, sociology, psychology, and others are all used for constructing a satisfactory empirical model of the system. Although mathematics too is used and will serve as the most powerful weapon of analysis, the new empirical model itself must come first; its axiomatization and mathematical refinement must be the second stage.

---

[10] Leon Walras, *Elements of Pure Economics*, George Allen and Unwin, London, 1954, p. 48.
[11] A. M. Okun, *Prices and Quantities*, Oxford, Basil Blackwell, 1981. My own *Industrial Society*, referred to previously, also describes this kind of schema. A recent addition to this stream is R. M. Solow, *The Labour Market as a Social Institution*, Oxford, Basil Blackwell, 1990.

APPENDIX I   Existence of temporary equilibrium

1 We use the same notation as in chapter 4 and show that there is a non-negative, non-zero set of solutions (X, P, W, r) where r is $\frac{1}{z} - 1$, to the following system of inequalities:

$$E = AX + D(P, W, X) - B\bar{X} \leqslant 0, \tag{1}$$

$$F = LX - \bar{N} \leqslant 0, \tag{2}$$

$$G = z\psi B - PA - WL \leqslant 0, \tag{3}$$

$$H = W\bar{N} - PD(P, W, X) - [z\psi BX - PB\bar{X}] \leqslant 0, \tag{4}$$

$$PE + WF + GX + H \equiv 0, \tag{5}$$

$$\psi_{-1}B\bar{X} = PB\bar{X}, \tag{6}$$

where $\psi = \psi(P, W)$ and P_{-1}, W_{-1}, z_{-1}, ψ_{-1} are all given. It is assumed that

$$(*) \quad W\bar{N} \geqslant PD(P, W, X).$$

We assume Say's law, so that Q is assumed to be 0 in the price–cost inequality (3).

2 To establish the existence of equilibrium we use Brouwer's fixed point theorem. Let the price of good i (or factor i) be adjusted according to its excess demand; we have:

$$\begin{aligned} P_i(\tau + 1) - P_i(\tau) &= aE_i(\tau) \\ W_i(\tau + 1) - W_i(\tau) &= aF_i(\tau), \end{aligned} \tag{7}$$

where a is named the adjustment coefficient which is positive, and τ does not refer to the period to which prices or excess demands belong, but to the round of adjustment within a particular period. The adjustment coefficients may differ from one good (or factor) to another; but for the sake of simplicity we assume that all goods and factors have the coefficient of an equal value. Equation (7) shows that where E_i (or F_i) is positive (or negative), the price increases (or decreases). This type of adjustment, however, may create a negative price, where E_i or F_i is negative and sufficiently large in absolute value. To prevent this nonsense, prices are assumed rigid downwards, that is, (7) is modified such that the price is set at the same value wherever $E_i(\tau)$ takes on a negative value, while it is flexible upwards. Similarly, for $W_i(\tau + 1)$. This revised version of (7) may be written as:

204

$$P_i(\tau+1)=P_i(\tau)+a \max (E_i(\tau).0),$$
$$W_i(\tau+1)=W_i(\tau)+a \max (F_i(\tau).0). \tag{8}$$

Let us next fix, through the process of adjustment, the level of prices such that the sum of all the prices is equal to Π, a constant arbitrarily taken, then:

$$\sum_i P_i(\tau)+\sum_i W_i(\tau)=\Pi \quad \text{for all } \tau. \tag{9}$$

Π may be any positive number throughout the following argument but will be finally determined at the end in such a way that the condition of macroscopic correctness of expectations (6) is fulfilled. From the point of view of the stationaryness of the level of prices, the formulas (8) are found unsatisfactory. That is to say, even though $P_i(\tau)$ and $W_i(\tau)$ satisfy (9), $P_i(\tau+1)$ and $W_i(\tau+1)$ obtained by the formulas (8) may not necessarily satisfy it. Therefore, we must normalize $P_i(\tau+1)$ and $W_i(\tau+1)$ such that their sum becomes equal to Π. For this purpose we multiply both sides of (8) by Π and divide them by $\Pi + S$, where:

$$S=a\left[\sum_i \max (E_i(\tau),0)+\sum_i \max (F_i(\tau),0)\right]. \tag{10}$$

On the left-hand sides of (8) after this operation we rewrite the normalized prices $P_i(\tau+1) \, \Pi/(\Pi+S)$ and $W_i(\tau+1) \, \Pi/(\Pi+S)$ simply as $P_i(\tau+1)$ and $W_i(\tau+1)$; we then obtain:

$$P_i(\tau+1)=\frac{[P_i(\tau)+a \max (E_i(\tau),0)]\Pi}{\Pi+S} \qquad i=1,\dots,n, \tag{11}$$

$$W_i(\tau+1)=\frac{[W_i(\tau)+a \max (F_i(\tau),0)]\Pi}{\Pi+S} \qquad i=1,\dots,l. \tag{12}$$

In view of (10) it is at once seen that $P_i(\tau+1)$ and $W_i(\tau+1)$ determined in this way satisfy the condition that the sum of them is equal to Π.

3 Let us next imagine that the activity level of process j, X_j, is adjusted according to its profitability, that is by the formula:

$$X_j(\tau+1)-X_j(\tau)=b \max (G_j,0), \tag{13}$$

where G_j is the discounted excess profit of process j, and b positive. The formula implies that X_j is flexible upwards but rigid downwards. That is to say, where G_j is positive, X_j increases, while there is no changes in X_j whenever G_j takes on a negative value. However, such an adjustment may be explavsive, that is, X_j may eventually become infinitive. To avoid this perversity, let us define $\bar{\bar{X}}_j$ as a number which satisfies:

$$\bar{\bar{X}}_j > \min\left[\frac{(B\check{X})_1}{a_{j1}}, \frac{(B\check{X})_2}{a_{j2}}, \dots, \frac{(B\check{X})_n}{a_{jn}}, \frac{N_1}{L_{j1}}, \dots \frac{N_l}{L_{jl}}\right],$$

where $(B\check{X})_i$ denotes the i-th component of the column vector $B\check{X}$, L_{ji} denotes the (j, i) element of the matrix L. Then production at $\bar{\bar{X}}_j$ thus defined is infeasible because at least one of the feasibility conditions,

$$(B\check{X})_i \geqslant (AX)_i \qquad i=1, \dots, n,$$

$$(N)_k \geqslant (LX)_k \qquad k=1, \dots, l,$$

is not fulfilled, when the j-th component of X is set at $\bar{\bar{X}}_j$, regardless of the values of other components, which are non-negative. We modify (13) into the form:

$$X_j(\tau+1)=\bar{\bar{X}}_j\frac{X_j(\tau)+b\max{(G_j,0)}}{\bar{\bar{X}}_j+b\max{(G_j,0)}+S}\,.\tag{14}$$

Where $X_j(\tau)\leqslant\bar{\bar{X}}_j$, it follows from (14) that $X_j(\tau+1)\leqslant\bar{\bar{X}}_j$.

In a similar way, we assume that the variable $z(\tau)$, which is the reciprocal of 1 plus the maximum rate of profits $r(\tau)$, is adjusted by the following formula:

$$z(\tau+1)=\bar{\bar{z}}\frac{z(\tau)+c\max{(H,0)}}{\bar{\bar{z}}+c\max{(H,0)}+S}\,,\tag{15}$$

where c is a positive constant and $\bar{\bar{z}}$ is a large enough number to bring about that the inequality:

$$\bar{\bar{z}}(\psi B)_j>(PA+WL)_j,\tag{16}$$

is satisfied for at least one process j, no matter how the prices are set such that (9) is satisfied. (This implies at least one component of ψ being positive even if all P_i are zero.)

4 Let us now define a closed convex set,

$$\Gamma=[P,\,W,\,X,\,z\,|\,P\geqslant0,\,W\geqslant0,\,\textstyle\sum P_i+\sum W_i=\Pi,\,\bar{\bar{X}}\geqslant X\geqslant0,\,\bar{\bar{z}}\geqslant z\geqslant0\}$$

which is non-empty and bounded. Then (11), (12), (13), (14), (15) give a continuous mapping of $(P,\,W,\,X,\,z)$ from Γ into itself,[1] so that by Brouwer's fixed point theorem there is a fixed point $(P,\,W,\,X,\,z)$ such that:

$$P_i=\frac{[P_i+a\max{(E_i,0)}]\Pi}{\Pi+S}\qquad i=1,\ldots,n\tag{17}$$

$$W_i=\frac{[W_i+a\max{(F_i,0)}]\Pi}{\Pi+S}\qquad i=1,\ldots,l\tag{18}$$

$$X_j=\bar{\bar{X}}_j\frac{X_j+b\max{(G_j,0)}}{\bar{\bar{X}}_j+b\max{(G_j,0)}+S}\qquad j=1,\ldots,m,\tag{19}$$

$$z=\bar{\bar{z}}\frac{z+c\max{(H,0)}}{\bar{\bar{z}}+c\max{(H,0)}+S}\,.\tag{20}$$

---

[1] Note that the denominators of (11), (12), (13), (14) and (15) are always positive and E_i, F_i, G_j and H are all continuous.

We can now show $S = 0$ at the fixed point.[2] Then (17) and (18) are reduced to:

$$E_i \leqslant 0, i = 1, \ldots, n, \text{ and } F_i \leqslant 0, i = 1, \ldots, l, \tag{21}$$

respectively. If $G_j > 0$, while $S = 0$, then we have $X_j = \bar{\bar{X}}_j$ from (19), but by the definition of $\bar{\bar{X}}_j$, production at the level of $\bar{\bar{X}}_j$ is infeasible and contradicts (21); therefore:

$$G_j \leqslant 0 \qquad j = i, \ldots, m. \tag{22}$$

In the same way, where $H > 0$ while $S = 0$, we obtain $z = \bar{z}$. Then (16) holds for at least one j, which is a contradiction of (22). Hence,

$$H \leqslant 0. \tag{23}$$

We thus obtain (21)–(23) at the fixed point; that is to say, the fixed point is a temporary equilibrium point.

If (16) holds with $\bar{z} < 1$, we have $r > 0$. This specification of $\bar{z}$ plays the same role in our system as the agio thesis that present goods are valued higher than those in the future does in Böhm-Bawerk's theory. Of course they are different but result in a positive equilibrium rate of interest.

Finally Π which has so far been regarded as given is determined by the condition for macroscopic correct expectations (6). Of this equation, the left-hand side is constant, while P on the right-hand side depends upon Π. An adjustment is made of Π so as to satisfy (6).

---

[2] Suppose the contrary, that is $S > 0$. We have at the fixed point:

$$P_i S = a \max (E_i, 0)\Pi$$
$$W_i S = a \max (E_i, 0)\Pi$$

These mean that $P_i > 0$ if and only if $E_i > 0$, and $W_i > 0$ if and only if $F_i > 0$. As the fact that $S > 0$ implies that at least one of E_i's or F_i's is positive. Hence $PE + WE > 0$.
We also have from (19)

$$X_j[b \max (G_j, 0) + S] = \bar{\bar{X}}_j \, b \max (G_j, 0)$$

from which we find that $X_j > 0$ if and only if $G_j > 0$ as S is assumed to be positive. Hence $GX \geqslant 0$. Similarly we obtain from (20) that $z > 0$ if and only if $H > 0$.
Thus we have $PE + WF + GX > 0$ where $S > 0$, which means $H < 0$ by virtue of the extended Walras identity. Hence $z = 0$. Then we have from the definition of H

$$H = W\bar{N} - PD(P, W, X) + PB\bar{X}.$$

In view of (*) and $PB\bar{X} \geqslant 0$ we now find that $H \geqslant 0$, which contradicts $H < 0$ obtained above from $S > 0$. Hence $S = 0$.

APPENDIX II   Increasing returns

1 Matrices A and B in appendix I are now replaced by $A(X)$ and $B(X)$ which are defined as (4.29) and (4.30) of chapter 4 wherever $X_i < 1$. Let X of $A(X)$ and $B(X)$ be fixed at some point, say $\hat{X}$, in the equilibrium system (26)–(30). The definition of $\overline{\overline{X}}_j$ in appendix I is revised. Let it be:

$$\overline{\overline{X}}_j > \min\left[\frac{N_1}{L_{j1}}, \ldots, \frac{N_l}{L_{jl}}\right].$$

Similarly, we define $\overline{\overline{Y}}_j$ as:

$$\overline{\overline{Y}}_j > \min\left[\frac{N_1}{L'_{j1}}, \ldots, \frac{N_l}{L'_{jl}}\right].$$

On the other hand, $\overline{\overline{z}}$ is defined in the same way as (16) in appendix I defines it.[1] It is noted that these $\overline{\overline{X}}_j$, $j = 1, \ldots, m$, and $\overline{\overline{z}}$ are independent of $\hat{X}$.

Let us now consider a mapping of (P, W, X, Y, z) from $\Gamma = \{P, W, X, Y, z \mid P \geq 0, W \geq 0, \Sigma P_i + \Sigma W_i = \Pi, \overline{\overline{X}} \geq X \geq 0, \overline{\overline{Y}} \geq Y \geq 0, \overline{\overline{z}} \geq z \geq 0\}$ into itself, which is similar to the one having been used to establish a temporary equilibrium point in the previous system. The only changes which have to be made are the replacement of A and B by $A(\bar{X})$ and $B(\bar{X})$ or $A(\hat{X})$ and $B(\hat{X})$. Then we at once see that the mapping is continuous and, therefore, yield a fixed point.[2] We can show that temporary equilibrium conditions:

$$E_i \leq 0, i = 1, \ldots, n; \qquad F_i \leq 0, i = 1, \ldots, l;$$
$$G_j \leq 0, j = 1, \ldots, m; \qquad G'_j \leq 0, j = 1, \ldots, k; \qquad H \leq 0$$

are all satisfied at the fixed point, provided that A and B of E_i, G_i and H are replaced by $A(\bar{X})$ and $B(\bar{X})$ or $A(\hat{X})$ and $B(\hat{X})$. Let this point be denoted by $\{\tilde{P}, \tilde{W}, \tilde{X}, \tilde{Y}, \tilde{z}\}$, which is in Γ.

2 Let $\Lambda(\hat{X})$ be the set of temporary equilibrium points obtained when X is set at $\hat{X}$ in $A(X)$ and $B(X)$. Let us suppose that, in association with the same $\tilde{Y}, \tilde{P}, \tilde{W}, \tilde{z}$, there

---

[1] Dividing the both sides of (16) by $\hat{X}_j$, we have, in view of $A(\hat{X})_j = A_j/\hat{X}_j$ and $B(\hat{X})_j = B_j/\hat{X}_j$:

$$\overline{\overline{z}}\psi B(\hat{X})_j > (PA(\hat{X}) + WL)_j + W(L_j/\hat{X}_j - L_j).$$

As $\hat{X}_j \leq 1$, the last term is non-negative. Hence:

$$\overline{\overline{z}}\psi B(\hat{X}) > PA(\hat{X}) + WL$$

with no change in $\overline{\overline{z}}$. Note that Q is set at 0 as in appendix I.

[2] Evidently, five sets of conditions, similar to (4.24)–(4.28), hold at the fixed point.

are finitely and infinitely many temporary equilibria such as $\tilde{X}^{(1)}$ or $\tilde{X}^{(2)}$, that is to say, both $(\tilde{X}^{(1)}, \tilde{Y}, \tilde{P}, \tilde{W}, \tilde{z})$ and $(\tilde{X}^{(2)}, \tilde{Y}, \tilde{P}, \tilde{W}, \tilde{z})$ belong to $\Lambda(\hat{X})$. Let T be the set of all such $\tilde{X}^{(i)}$'s. It is clear that T depends on $\hat{X}$. We can show first that it is a convex set. To see this we assume that $D(P, W, X, Y)$ is linear-homogeneous in X and Y, that is:

$$D(P,W,X,Y) = D_x(P,W)X + D_y(P,W)Y.$$

As we have, for $i = 1,2$:

$$E(\tilde{X}^{(i)},\tilde{P},\tilde{W},\tilde{z}) = A(\hat{X})\tilde{X}^{(i)} + A'\tilde{Y} + D_x(\tilde{P},\tilde{W})\tilde{X}^{(i)} + D_y(\tilde{P},\tilde{W})\tilde{Y} - B(\hat{X})\tilde{X} - B'\tilde{Y} \lessgtr 0,$$

it can be clearly be shown that the same inequality holds for:

$$\tilde{X}(t) = t\tilde{X}^{(1)} + (1-t)\tilde{X}^{(2)},$$

provided that $P = \tilde{P}$, $W = \tilde{W}$ and $z = \tilde{z}$. That is to say, $E(\tilde{X}(t), \tilde{P}, \tilde{W}, \tilde{z}) \leq 0$. It can easily be seen that this holds true for all values of t between 0 and 1. Similarly, for $F_i \leq 0, i = 1, \ldots, l$ and $H \leq 0$. Therefore, in view of $G \leq 0$ and $G' \leq 0$, which hold at $\tilde{P}$, $\tilde{W}$, $\tilde{z}$, we find that $(\hat{X}(t), \tilde{P}, \tilde{W}, \tilde{z})$ is an equilibrium point for all t between 0 and 1. This proves that T is a convex set.

Furthermore, we can show that the correspondence $\hat{X} \to T(\hat{X})$ is an upper semi-continuous mapping of the set $U = \{X \mid \bar{X} \geq X \geq 0\}$ into itself.[3] Then, by Kakutani's fixed point theorem, there is a point such that $X \in T(X)$, which of course depends on the prescribed value of Π. We finally adjust it so that the condition of macroscopically correct expectations is fulfilled.

[3] Let $\{x^i\}$ and $\{y^i\}$ be any sequences with limits $\bar{x}$ and $\bar{y}$ respectively. A multi-valued mapping $x \to F(x)$ is said to be upper semi-continuous at x if $y^i \in F(x^i)$ for all i implies $\bar{y} \in F(\bar{x})$. To show the upper semi-continuity, let $\{\hat{X}^i\}$ and $\{\tilde{X}^i\}$ be sequences such that $\tilde{X}^i \in T(\hat{X}^i)$ for every i, with the limits $\hat{X}$ and $\tilde{X}$.

Also let $\{\tilde{Y}^i, \tilde{P}^i, \tilde{W}^i, \tilde{z}^i\}$ be temporary equilibrium values of $\{Y, P, W, z\}$ which are in association with $\tilde{X}^i$, and let their limits $(\tilde{Y}, \tilde{P}, \tilde{W}, \tilde{z})$ be those in association with $T(\hat{X})$. As:

$$B(\tilde{X})\tilde{X} + B\tilde{Y}^i \geq A(\hat{X}^i)\tilde{X}^i + A'\tilde{Y}^i + D_x(\tilde{P}^i, \tilde{W}^i)\tilde{X}^i + D_y(\tilde{P}^i, \tilde{W}^i)\tilde{Y}^i$$

for every i, we have in the limit:

$$B(\tilde{X})\tilde{X} + B\tilde{Y} \geq A(\hat{X})\tilde{X} + A'\tilde{Y} + D_x(\tilde{P}, \tilde{W})\tilde{X} + D_y(\tilde{P}, \tilde{W})\tilde{Y}.$$

This means that $\tilde{X}$, together with $\{\tilde{Y}, \tilde{P}, \tilde{W}, \tilde{z}\}$, satisfies equilibrium conditions $E_i \leq 0$ with $A(X)$ set at $A(\hat{X})$. Similarly for the other conditions. Therefore, $\tilde{X} \in T(\hat{X})$ which means that $X \to T(X)$ is upper semi-continuous at $\hat{X}$.

Index

Åkerman, G. 6, 7
Aoyama, H. 1
Arrow, K. J. 1, 5, 10, 21, 25, 28, 33–41, 76, 86, 93, 113, 130, 150, 189, 193–7

Bamford, Julia 136
bank
   lending constraint for 161
banker 3, 42
bankruptcy 40
Block, H. D. 131
von Böhm-Bawerk, E. 6, 7, 103–7, 195–6
Brouwer's fixed point theorem 204, 206
budget equation for
   bank 144
   firm 143
   household 142
Buchardt, F. 53
Burmeister, E. 7

capital 4
capital goods
   as joint output 56
   economic lifetime 53
   indivisibility of 79
   physical lifetime 53
capital intensity condition 158–9
capitalist
   as a holder of real stocks of commodities 30–2
   as a shareholder 34–7
Catephores, G. 22, 157
Cockaigne
   no land of 50
consumption multiplier 137
credit 41
cumulative process 169, 171

Dasgupta, P. 45
Debreu, G. 2, 5, 10, 21, 28, 33, 37, 86, 93, 113, 192–7
dichotomy 67
   of production from finance 4, 150–2

dominant diagonal matrix 130
Dore, M. 196

elementary period 54
Eliasson, G. 45
entrepreneur 3, 6
entrepreneurial resources 27
equal rate of profit between banks and firms 146
event 192
ex ante financial arrangement between firms and banks 22
ex post equality between savings and investment 22, 148

financier 3
fixprice
   model 10, 13
flexprice
   activities 101
   model 10, 12
   sector 2, 112, 122
full-cost principle 14

Gale, D. 86
Georgescu-Roegen, N. 50
GND Lemma 87, 151
Goodwin, R. 196
Grandmont, Jean-Michel 26

Hahn, F. H. 2, 5, 10, 21, 28, 33–41, 76, 86, 93, 113, 115, 186, 193–7
Harrod, R. 174
von Hayek, F. A. 6, 103, 105, 177, 195–6
Hicks, J. R. 1–21, 25–6, 37, 46–54, 89, 105, 113, 155, 173–80, 195–7, 203
Hilferding, R. 24
Hurwicz, L. 131, 189

income effect 3
increasing returns 107–9, 208–9
inflation 177ff.
instability

210

Schumpeterian 189
Wicksellian 189
innovation 6, 40, 110, 139, 162–3
  credit 163
  inflation 164
  instability 189
  issue of new shares 40
  Japanese type 110–11
  trigger-effect 133–4, 137, 140
invention 132–3
  Harrod neutral or biased 139
  Hicks neutral or biased 139
investment planning council 189
IS curve 177–80

Kakutani's fixed point theorem 209
Keynes, J. M. 10, 16, 17, 20–3, 48, 68–76,
  82, 96, 103, 137, 152–8, 160–5, 169,
  172, 185, 190–5
Keynesian
  ex post savings-investment equality 22,
  148
  involuntary unemployment 154, 156
  liquidity preference theory of interest 169
Koopmans, T. C. 76

La Volpe, G. 20, 38
L-economy 76, 107
Leontief, W. 8, 52, 114, 189, 196
Liapounoff function 130
Lindahl, E. 174, 183
liquidity function 48–9
LM condition 169, 178
long-run equilibrium point 115–17

McKenzie, L. 33
Malinvaud, E. 2, 4, 10, 12–15, 28, 41, 105,
  195
Malthus, T. R. 56
marginal-cost principle 14
Marshall, A. 195
Marx, K. 2, 27–30, 54–6, 77, 95, 136, 191,
  195
mixed flexprice–fixprice model 10, 19,
  114
Modigliani–Miller irrelevance theorem 63,
  69, 202
Morishima, M. 2, 7, 12, 27, 34, 56, 62, 77,
  84, 86, 89, 104, 121, 133, 196
multiple equilibria 114
Myrdal, G. 177, 183

Negishi, T. 189
neoclassical growth theory 139, 140
von Neumann, J. 7, 9, 11, 50, 56, 83–4, 86,
  172, 196

von Neumann equilibrium 180, 181
  factor markets 11–12
  inflation and deflation 180–3
Nikaido, F. 33
numeraire 68

Okumura, H. 110–11, 202
Okun, A. M. 203

Pareto-efficiency 4, 93, 97, 98, 103, 109, 202
Patinkin, D. 2, 174, 195
perfect equilibrium 104–5
perfect forsight 104–5
plan
  demand–supply 46, 47
  input–output 46, 47
  stock 46, 47
prices
  internal 7
  market 7
primitive accumulation 30
production
  facility, lifetime 8
  financial cost 62–3
  genealogy 56–8
  indivisibility 79
  instantaneous 63
  interuptable 8
  multiplicity 78
  separable 8
  stoppable 8
  synchronization 55, 104–5
  truncatable 8
production function
  separability 52
production lag 29
production period
  construction 8, 53
  final stage 8
  pipeline-filling 8
production possibility set
  given 2
  production of 3

quantity theory of money 68, 169, 173, 179,
  186
  homogeneity assumption 186, 187
Quirk, J. 28

rate of interest
  money 170, 171, 177–9
  natural 170, 171, 177–81
rationing 166, 167
  in the money market 185, 186
  in the saving-investment market 166

Recardo, D. 2, 20, 30, 43, 44, 55, 77, 86, 97, 115–17, 137, 195
robotization 134
  and Labour Standards Law 135
  in small firms 135
rule of free goods 11–12, 87, 89, 91, 155
rule of profitability 65, 91

Samuelson, P. A. 20, 25, 76, 77, 84–6, 113–15, 127, 189
Saposnik, R. 28
saving
  actual 166
  notional 165, 166
Say's law 10, 15–16, 72–82, 86–93, 95–8, 101–9, 137, 156–72, 177, 189–91
  Anti- 10, 20–2, 72–80, 108–9, 137, 157, 165, 172, 185, 189–92
  extended 92
  in Keynes' sense 17, 75, 82
  in Lange–Patinkin sense 17
Scarf, H. 192
Schumpeter, J. A. 3, 10, 20–2, 40–4, 71, 110, 137–40, 162–4, 185, 189–90
Schumpeterian 41–4
shares
  acquisition and merger 40
  Arrow–Hahn's treatment 38, 39
Simon, H. 7, 133
simple commodity production model 27, 28, 136
Slutsky–Hicks properties 3, 12, 25
Smith, A. 56–7
social elements (or power) 191
  fair wages 18
  in factor market 154–5
  relativity 154
Solow, R. 18, 20, 84, 115, 155, 163, 172, 203
Spinoza, B. 196
Sraffa, P. 55
Sraffian 114
stability

and non-negative solution 121
of equilibrium motion 116
of equilibrium point 116
Stiglitz, J. 45
substitution (or non-substitution) theorem 76

Takata, Y. 18, 155–8, 191
tatonnement 115, 116, 126–31
  case I 118
  case II 118, 119
time 116, 117
time lag 4
Torrence, R. 55–6
trigger effect 7, 189
  direct 133
  indirect 133
  self-generated endogenous 134
truncated production function 52

unemployment
  involuntary 154–6
  Keynesian 13
  Marxian 13
Uzawa, H. 121

Vagliasindi, P. A. 12
Varian, H. R. 28, 41

Walras, L. 2, 16, 17, 20, 44, 138, 139, 152, 192–6, 202, 203
Walras'
  continuous market 139
  identity 88, 90
Weber, M. 200
Wicksell, K. 1, 6–7, 23, 103, 105, 169–74, 177–80, 195–6
Wicksellian cumulative process 169ff.
  and quantity theory of money 169, 173, 179, 186
  and Say's law 184
Wiles, P. J. D. 95
work regulation 154

For EU product safety concerns, contact us at Calle de José Abascal, 56–1°,
28003 Madrid, Spain or eugpsr@cambridge.org.

www.ingramcontent.com/pod-product-compliance
Ingram Content Group UK Ltd.
Pitfield, Milton Keynes, MK11 3LW, UK
UKHW042316180425
457623UK00005B/29